The 1930s concern with recording the speaking voice is virtually unrivaled in American cultural history. In that decade, scores of writers traveled into the field to record the voices of African Americans, American Indians, migrant workers, tenant farmers, and immigrants.

In this innovative study, Michael E. Staub recasts 1930s cultural history by analyzing those genres so characteristic of the Depression era: genres that relied on a presumed relationship to real experience for their effect and that sought to persuade their audiences of urgent political truths. Demonstrating the seldom-discussed multicultural diversity of Depression-era literature, and paying special attention to narrative strategies for representing the speech of disinherited and minority peoples, Staub shows how several writers from the thirties anticipated dilemmas and perspectives currently engaging cultural studies critics. New interpretations of such canonized authors as James Agee, John Dos Passos, Zora Neale Hurston, John G. Neihardt, and Tillie Olsen are coupled with critical discussions of previously little-known works of ethnography, journalism, oral history, and polemical fiction.

Voices of Persuasion sheds new light on the relationship between art and politics in the 1930s. It will interest all who are concerned with the problematic relationship between representation and social reality and their mutual inextricability.

T0381935

CAMBRIDGE STUDIES IN AMERICAN LITERATURE AND CULTURE

Voices of Persuasion

Continued on pages following the Index

Voices of Persuasion

Politics of Representation in 1930s America

Michael E. Staub
Michigan State University

CAMBRIDGE
UNIVERSITY PRESS

CAMBRIDGE UNIVERSITY PRESS
Cambridge, New York, Melbourne, Madrid, Cape Town, Singapore, São Paulo, Delhi

Cambridge University Press
The Edinburgh Building, Cambridge CB2 8RU, UK

Published in the United States of America by Cambridge University Press, New York

www.cambridge.org
Information on this title: www.cambridge.org/9780521111942

First published 1994
This digitally printed version 2009

A catalogue record for this publication is available from the British Library

Library of Congress Cataloguing in Publication data
Staub, Michael E.
Voices of persuasion : politics of representation in 1930s
America / Michael E. Staub.
p.   cm. – (Cambridge studies in American literature and
culture; 78)
Includes bibliographical references (p.   ) and index.
ISBN 0-521-45390-9 (hc)
1. American literature – 20th century – History and criticism.
2. Politics and literature – United States – History – 20th century.
3. Literature and society – United States – History – 20th century.
4. Representative government and representation in literature.
5. Ethnic groups in literature.   6. Minorities in literature.
7. Persuasion (Rhetoric)   I. Title.   II. Series.
PS228.P6S73   1994
813'.5209358 – dc20   93–30372
CIP

ISBN 978-0-521-45390-5 hardback
ISBN 978-0-521-11194-2 paperback

A different version of Chapter 3 appeared in *American Quarterly* 43 (September
1991).

Contents

Acknowledgments

I HAVE received support from numerous people as I researched and wrote this book. I am particularly indebted to my many students, beginning with those in my first seminar at Brown University who asked why I was making them read *Let Us Now Praise Famous Men;* in my halting reply, the idea for *Voices of Persuasion* was born. I am also grateful to Sabrina Cherry for a timely invitation to conduct an oral history project among Appalachian community activists; my ensuing immersion in daily Kentucky life taught me volumes about the predicaments inherent in fieldwork. For critical comments and insights on various portions of the evolving manuscript, and for intellectual encouragement, I owe thanks to Mari Jo Buhle, Aníbal González, the late Roger Henkle, Victor Jew, Gary Kulik, Tillie Olsen, Alessandro Portelli, Kathleen Sands, Geneva Smitherman, Werner Sollors, William Stott, Eric Sundquist, and the late Edward Thompson. I am also indebted to Peter Berg at the Michigan State University Library and Linda Green at Rhode Island College's Adams Library for helping me locate crucial source materials.

For providing models of political and personal integrity within the academy, I am deeply grateful to the three best teachers I have ever had: John Dittmer, Jill Lewis, and Barry O'Connell. For their supportive friendship during the time it took to complete this book, I owe special thanks to Arno Armgort, Logie Barrow, Jim Henle, Amy McKenzie, Paul Podolsky, and Michael Topp. For her intelligence, goodness, and editorial assistance, and for her love (and much more), I thank Dagmar Herzog.

Preface

THIS BOOK is about representation and its discontents. It rewrites 1930s cultural history by analyzing Depression-era writings from a wide range of genres – documentary, ethnography, oral history, folklore, journalism, and social fiction – in light of the decade's unprecedented concern with recording the speech of disinherited and marginalized Americans for persuasive purposes: to encourage social change and foster political and cultural awareness. The first objective of the book, then, is simply to bring the crucial subject of voice back to the cultural history of the thirties, where it once belonged. One need only glance at the standard cultural histories of that period – such as those by Aaron, Susman, Stott, Pells, and Wald – to see that this central subject has been omitted or moved to the margins of discussion.

The subtitle announces another objective of this study: to explore the politics, and hence the partiality, of all representations that refer to real experience as the legitimating source for their narrative authority. Only recently, these sorts of writings have come under increasingly heavy fire from poststructuralist critics who find such texts' inherent assumptions concerning truth, reality, history, identity, and objectivity highly suspect. And yet – and despite *and* because of these critiques – nothing could be more crucial than to reintroduce historical context, however contingent our access to it may be, as an important explanatory factor in the evaluation of literary narratives, most especially in the evaluation of texts that explicitly struggled to refer themselves to the real. For it is my argument that a number of thirties writers, precisely because of their encounters with disinherited peoples, anticipated

dilemmas that poststructuralist theory would identify: an awareness of the contestedness of historical truth, and the impossibility
of representing reality without being complicitous in its dis-
tortion.

This book therefore also works to recast the terms of debate
now characterizing the scholarly and popular consensus about the
reality-based writings of the Depression era. Previously, it was
held that the dilemma of these kinds of writings resided in the
conflicting demands of art and politics, and thus that the reality-
based narratives of the 1930s largely failed as literature because of
their political didacticism. This conceptual framework, however,
misses the point because no text (aesthetic *or* didactic – as if these
qualities could be distinguished!) can adequately represent lived
reality. Given this circumstance, the more pertinent dilemma of
these writings was how to persuade readers of their version of
reality. This dilemma was particularly pressing in the 1930s because of the horrific aspects of American history – both remembered and immediate – with which writers of that period were
confronted: the enslavement of African Americans, the slaughter
and disinheritance of Native Americans, the executions of Nicola
Sacco and Bartolomeo Vanzetti, and the astonishingly indecent
living and working conditions of millions of sharecroppers, tenant farmers, and migrant workers. Speaking out on these (and
other) topics, the writers discussed in this study developed a
panoply of diverse narrative strategies in their attempts to represent persuasively their subjects' perspectives, while attending constantly to the complex power relations between authors, subjects,
and readers.

This book, then, is written for historians, literary critics, and
ethnographers, indeed, for all who are interested in the always
problematic relationship between representation and social reality
and their mutual inextricability. It seeks to avoid both the pitfall
of seeing American history purely as an intellectual puzzle with
no real consequences and the equally dangerous possibility of
neglecting the poststructuralist critique and simplistically assuming that there is a unified reality out there that texts can objec-
tively reflect and represent. In negotiating between these two
critical directions, my textual analyses continually engage such
(still unresolved) issues as the embattled authority of concepts like

"evidence" and "experience," the romanticization of fieldwork and exoticization of its subjects, the power imbalance between oral and written sources, and most especially, the dilemmas of representing a reality lived by others in the face of a readership that cannot possibly care enough.

1

Spoken Testimony,
Unwritten History

MY FRIEND, I am going to tell you the story of my life, as you wish; and if it were only the story of my life I think I would not tell it; for what is one man that he should make much of his winters, even when they bend him like a heavy snow?"[1] So begins John G. Neihardt's 1932 account of a Sioux Indian's oral remembrances, *Black Elk Speaks*. It is one of many cross-cultural ventures from the 1930s that sought to transform the speech of the disinherited into a more lasting written form.

Although it has never been examined as such, *Black Elk Speaks* is fully representative of what Alfred Kazin called "the preponderance of descriptive nonfiction" that typified 1930s writing.[2] The (overlapping) genres of documentary, ethnography, oral history, folklore, journalism – as well as reality-based fiction – became the Depression era's characteristic avenues for representing a widespread societal preoccupation with the plight of the disempowered. The 1930s were a time when not only writers sponsored by the Works Progress Administration, but also scores of other ethnographers, documentarians, and journalists sought to preserve oral perspectives they perceived as rapidly vanishing. They thus traveled into the field and recorded black, American Indian, migrant worker, tenant farmer, and immigrant voices. Citing the real voices of living subjects as their authoritative sources, thirties writers often produced timely social commentary designed to shock a middle-class readership into greater awareness of widespread suffering.

During the thirties, insightful cultural critics recognized that, for countless American writers, documenting society had supplanted the project of creating fiction. For example, Kazin believed that the thirties saw "a literature of Fact – one of those

1

periods in which, despite the emergence of so many brilliant individual sensibilities, the chief effort of many writers seemed bent only on reporting."[3] Kazin's overstated phrasing suggests an ambivalence about the proliferation of this documentary-style expression. Similarly, William Phillips and Philip Rahv used an odd past tense in 1937, as if to distance themselves from the culture of the time: "The mood of the thirties required objectivity, realism, and an interest in the social manifestations of individual life."[4] Yet neither Kazin nor Phillips and Rahv stressed that the central value of these proliferating reality-based writings lay in their records of American speech.

In many field reports, there was a special emphasis on the ways Americans spoke. Representations of "the people's voice" were enormously popular subjects during the thirties. For example, the Federal Writers' Project's *Lay My Burden Down,* an oral history of slavery, began this way: "From the memories and the lips of former slaves have come the answers which only they can give to questions which Americans still ask: What does it mean to be a slave? What does it mean to be free? And, even more, how does it *feel?*"[5] In a related vein, the Southern Tenant Farmers' Union published letters from sharecroppers in a collection whose cover photograph strategically showed a torn scrap from a tenant's letter lamenting that "we have no voice"; the collection was entitled *The Disinherited Speak.*[6] Thirties documentarians and ethnographers believed that only by listening to and recording actual voices could they hope to realize the goal of authenticating history in its fullest sense.

The 1930s concern with recording the speaking voice is virtually unrivaled in American cultural history. In that decade, writers especially sought the speech of the dispossessed and the marginal. Concurrently, there was suddenly enormous interest in the folkways of ordinary Americans: in music, in theater, in film, in sociology, in fiction, and in journalism. "Folks" were perceived as the very backbone of the American heritage, and as the cultural consensus affirmed, their voices needed to be preserved in textual form. As in the case of the ex-slave oral histories already cited, writers believed that time was short and that before too long these spoken memories would be lost forever. There was a widespread sense of historical urgency to their projects. In his introduction to *These Are Our Lives,* a collection of oral histories of American southerners, for example, W. T. Couch insisted that "the people, all the people, must be known, they must be heard. Somehow they must be given representation, somehow they must be given voice and allowed to speak, in their essential character."[7] Couch's rhetorical flourishes were more typical than not. Letting the people speak was one basic aim of thirties documentary-style literature.

Yet most scholars now consider the reality-based writings produced in the thirties as "failures." In the "Instructions to Writers" provided to fieldworkers by the Federal Writers' Project, for example, one of "the criteria to be observed" was "literary excellence."[8] But many of the documentary efforts from the thirties do not survive as literature. As William Stott noted, "The timely being timely for a little while only, it no longer is: thirties social documentary in general is now as dead as the sermons of the Social Gospel."[9] Stott asserted that the documentaries' failure to last as literature was largely due to their didacticism and their lack of aesthetic sophistication, as well as their tendency to oversimplify and sentimentalize their subjects.

During the past decade, further criticisms of 1930s documentaries and ethnographies (and other more recent efforts like them) have come from within anthropological circles. There is a growing insistence that the ethnographic narrative is inherently and necessarily fictional or, at best, a "partial truth."[10] Heated critical debates concerning the methods of anthropological fieldwork have spilled over into nonanthropological books and journals as well.[11] These debates make clear just how crucial investigations of the ethnographic narrative are for American studies, American history, and literary critical audiences. For scholars of both culture and history, studying the difficulties involved in producing ethnography sheds light on all dilemmas surrounding reality's representation in narrative form. At the same time, the direction and intensity of these recent debates have put forth the false impression that nearly all previous documentary and ethnographic writing could not possibly have grappled in a theoretically sophisticated manner with questions of power, ethnic bias, and representation. According to this school, documentarians and ethnographers only infrequently examined their own presumed authority to narrate the speech of others and rarely questioned (what Renato Rosaldo called) the "mythic tale" that reality-based writing "resembled a mirror that reflected other cultures as they 're-ally' were."[12] Partially as a result of these debates, recent literary scholars have (with rare exception) leveled increasingly harsh criticism at documentaries and ethnographies from the thirties as inauthentic, inaccurate, and unreliable. For example, as evidenced by recent developments in scholarship on ethnographic narrative, it has become commonplace to criticize the "traditional" ethnographic model of fieldwork and writing.[13] One scholar has even gone so far as to state, with respect to this ethnographic model, that "until the 1960s, its legitimacy went virtually unquestioned."[14]

These various low estimations of 1930s documentary and ethnographic writing, however, leave unattended a crucial area of study, that is, how these writings sought to represent the voices of oppressed people. Representing the oral within writing, especially when the encounter being documented brings together someone from a primarily oral culture with someone from a primarily literate culture, raises significant questions about the social relations of power that inevitably shape a text derived from real encounters with living subjects. Written cultures have often inscribed the terms of what counts as rational expression into their self-understanding and then transcribed a spoken heritage's words with forms that fit those terms. A people, to prove that it had a culture, had to document that culture in writing. As Henry Louis Gates, Jr., put it in another context:

> Writing, especially after the printing press became so widespread, was taken to be the *visible* sign of reason . . . So, while the Enlightenment is characterized by its foundation on man's ability to reason, it simultaneously used the absence and presence of reason to delimit and circumscribe the very humanity of the cultures and people of color which Europeans had been "discovering" since the Renaissance.[15]

To examine and analyze how the resulting power imbalance between oral and written cultures was handled in some thirties documentary and ethnographic narratives reveals that, in the Depression era, there were important (though partial) precursors to current efforts at self-conscious, sophisticated, politically engaged documentary and ethnography.

By way of entry into this study, let me begin with a brief

discussion of *Unwritten History of Slavery: Autobiographical Account of Negro Ex-Slaves;* the dilemmas inherent in representing the perspectives of ex-slaves anticipated the problems all writers on the dispossessed were to encounter. *Unwritten History* was published in 1945 by the Social Science Institute at Fisk University, though it was based on interviews conducted in 1929–30. It remains an almost entirely neglected work that emerged out of the aforementioned thirties preoccupation with representing the "folk" and their speech, and in many respects, it is a pathbreaking document – a great unacknowledged oral narrative of the decade. More than sixty years after the end of the Civil War, *Unwritten History* may be credited with being one of the first large-scale attempts to document the spoken memories of former slaves.[16] These interviews with thirty-seven ex-slaves in and around Nashville, Tennessee, represent a crucial precursor to the twenty thousand pages of interviews with thirty-five hundred former slaves from twenty-six different states collected under the supervision of the Federal Writers' Project of the Works Progress Administration principally during the years 1936–38.[17] But unlike the Federal Writers' Project's collection of ex-slave narratives that they anticipated, the Fisk University interviews bear the personal imprint of one interviewer, Ophelia Settle Egypt, and her two coeditors, J. Masuoka and Charles S. Johnson. Egypt was trained in sociology and was also the granddaughter of ex-slaves who had communicated the African-American oral tradition to her.[18] The Fisk narratives can therefore be analyzed collectively as the result of one internally coherent project's evolving methodology toward representing its subjects' oral remembrances.

This project faced some immediate dilemmas. In particular, the editors of *Unwritten History* confronted a scholarly community that was extremely hesitant about using ex-slave testimonies as historical evidence, a hesitancy that would go unchallenged (with rare exception) even for a generation after them.[19] For example, as late as 1963, Charles H. Nichols would eloquently open his defense of the slave narratives' validity with these sentiments: "Nearly everyone concerned with American slavery has had his say, but in our time we have forgotten the testimony of its victims."[20] To this day, the ex-slaves' testimonies in the Fisk narratives, as well as in the Federal Writers' Project, while no longer "forgotten," are still contested as authoritative sources for historical inquiry.[21] Certainly these testimonies have not been used as inspirations for how to rethink and reshape the very way history gets told – although I propose they should be.

Due mainly to this utterly contested authority of ex-slaves' testimony, Egypt and her coeditors had to deal with a peculiar paradox. Since historians of slavery discredited the credibility of both oral and written testimonies of ex-slaves during this period, if the editors of *Unwritten History* were to minimize editorial interventions, they risked perpetuating this devaluation.[22] But if they intervened in obvious, visible ways, that would also call into question the authority of their subjects. The contradictory methods employed by the editors reflect the almost impossible situation they confronted.

On the surface, there is little that is unusual in *Unwritten History*'s structure or presentation, and that is precisely the point. The thirty-seven interviews are headed by either straightforward titles (such as "I Was a Boy Slave") or quotations (such as " 'Blacks Have No More Chance Than Slaves Had' "). The interviews are not subdivided or grouped in any way. They include no framing narratives, no attempts to introduce their informants with brief explanatory or biographical passages, and little or no commentary. There are no concluding statements or summaries. Only occasionally the interviewer's question will be reproduced parenthetically in the body of the narrative or a word will be clarified parenthetically if the reference is unclear. More often than not, however, obscure references are not explained, and informants respond to questions that are not included. Typeset on a typewriter and mimeographed on typewriter paper, even the physical appearance of the document is drab. In large part, then, *Unwritten History* makes no attempt to render "literary" what is "actual" through artful strategies, stylized techniques, or colorful packaging.

Aware that it was the subjectivity of ex-slaves' perspectives that caused them to be discredited, the editors (in a four-page introduction) countered by stating that subjectivity itself was a worthy object of scholarly inquiry. Documenting the very processes by which slaves accommodated themselves to slavery and made sense of their lot was a necessary supplement, the editors proposed, to the extant studies of "the slavery system as an aspect of the economic order."[23] (Though the editors do not say this, that "economic" focus had led to such statements as this one on slave children by Ulrich B. Phillips, perhaps the best-known and most influential scholar on American slavery of his generation: "The new-born pickaninny had a value purely because at some day his labor would presumably yield more than the cost of his keep. If he died early his owner was out of purse to an amount somewhat greater than his maintenance had cost. If he proved an idiot, or blind or crippled, the case would be worse, for he must prove a 'dead' expense until in fact he died.")[24] Given the prevalence of such an interpretive approach, the editors of *Unwritten History* — all the while cautiously couching their remarks in sociological language — insisted that slavery needed to be understood as "a moral order" as well (i). Anticipating that their documents would be discounted as "personal stories," as "not always accurate and not always true to the objective facts," the editors suggested that "the merit" of their sources lay "not so much in the accurate recording of the historical events" but in "the individual's subjective evaluation of them" (iii).

In establishing sets of oppositions — slave and master, "subjective evaluation" and "accurate recording," spoken memory and written text — the editors at once engaged and evaded the dilemmas of representing speech in writing. If the editors' goal had been to authorize and authenticate their speakers' testimony, as it is clear they also wished to do, then they did so in a curious fashion. By casting doubt on the historical accuracy of their oral sources, they seemed to suggest the opposite of what they intended, even while pressing the idea of these sources' historical uniqueness. Ironically, then, it was left to the speaking subjects themselves to suggest how and why the methods of history needed to be recast and reconceived. The ways in which the editors sought to validate their informants' perspectives emerge from a close examination of the book's structure, as well as from an analysis of the ex-slaves' own reflections on the power imbalance between whites and blacks and between written and oral cultures.

As I have mentioned, the thirty-seven interviews are not subdivided or grouped, but their organization is clearly not entirely random either. The opening few interviews, for example, establish the enormous range of responses existing among ex-slaves when they remember their early years in bondage — from vague nostalgia to absolute fury. The very first interview, entitled "One of Dr. Gale's 'Free Niggers,' " begins with the informant saying: "Just the other day we were talking about white people when they had slaves" (1). The elderly ex-slave continues that she recalls how her owners "were saving me for a breeding woman" and observes that "all of the colored women didn't have to have white men, some did it because they wanted to and some were forced" (1–2). Yet despite that this might have been her own fate if slavery had not been abolished, the woman adds: "Of course, . . . you couldn't expect much from them" – referring to the children of white masters and slave women (2). In short, this first witness to slavery repeatedly indicates its horror but does not express malice; her testimony is remarkably evenhanded. For example, she notes that "the meanest thing they did was selling babies from the mother's breast," but quickly adds, "but all of them didn't do that" (2). Or again, indicating the character of slaves, she comments that "it is just natural for Negroes to steal," and remarks that "of course [the whites] whipped [the slaves] but some of them need it, and when I look around and see [African Americans] doing some of the things they do now, I think it would be a good thing if some of them could be whipped now" (9). Finally, with a small anecdote about how idioms changed before and after the Civil War, this former slave summarizes her feelings about the directions of history:

> You notice most white people [today] in the South say "daddy" and "mother." In slavery time colored couldn't say papa; they had to say "daddy" and "mammy" and when they got free they started saying "papa" and then the white people started saying "daddy." Now the colored are right back at "daddy" again; they will copy after them. (5)

Once more, in the aptly titled " 'White Folks' Pet" (*sic*), the second interview, there is further evidence for the view that slaves were treated equitably by their masters and that race relations were not especially strained during the years before the Civil War. "I knows 'em, I knows white folks from their birth," this ex-slave comments. "Only difference is I ain't birthed one, that's the only difference" (22). She remembers that "all the white folks was so nice to me" (26), and (somewhat ironically, given the special treatment she received) she summarily condemns the slave community: "You know, our folks just won't hang together" (23). In her concluding remarks, she repeats herself for emphasis: "Yes, my white folks was good to me" (29). That *Unwritten History* opens with two accounts that register mainly positive memories of masters and negative impressions of slaves establishes a counterpoint for much of what follows.

The next two narratives, for example, break sharply with these initial characterizations of slavery, and in the third interview, "When It's Right To Steal from Your Master," there is explicit commentary (as there is from several others) on the extent of masters' savage abuse of their slaves: "I heard the old people say that some of them would take the niggers and strip their clothes down and lash them till they put blisters on their backs, and then mix salt and pepper and put it on their backs to make them more miserable" (40). And the fourth interview opens with a suspicious question – "For what intent have you come here?" – and continues with an unforgiving bitterness and anger: "Now you talk about hard times, I have had hard times" (43). This informant brings up an especially painful memory by addressing himself directly at the Fisk University representatives listening to his words:

> You as teachers used to whip the children with a paddle or something, but my whip was a raw cowhide. I didn't see it but I used to hear my mother tell it at the time how they would whip them with a cowhide and then put salt and pepper in your skin until it burn. The most barbarous thing I saw with these eyes – I lay on my bed and study about it now – I had a sister, my oldest sister, she was fooling with the clock and broke it, and my old marster taken her and tied a rope around her neck – just enough to keep it from choking her – and tied her up in the back yard and whipped her I don't know how long. There stood mother, there stood father, and there stood all the children and none could come to her rescue. (43–4)

Because the prior written records downplayed such abuses and agonies, all this man had was his memory, a memory so resilient that many years later "I lay on my bed and study about it now." The inclusion of this subjective memory challenges all "objective" writings that exclude perspectives like this one.

The interactive process of the interview itself leads the infor-

mant to further reflections about the imbalance of power between
oral and written sources:

> In slavery they used to teach the Negro that they had no soul.
> They said all they needed to do was to obey their mistress. One
> old sister was shouting in the back of the church and her mistress
> was up in the front and she looked back and said, "Shout on old
> 'nig' there is a kitchen in heaven for you to shout in too." The
> people used to say "dis," "dat," and "tother," now they say
> "this," "that" and "the other." In all the books that you have
> studied you never have studied . . . Negro history, have you? (45)

The seeming ramble of these words represents one man's open-
ended reflections on how social relations of power have con-
structed African-American identity, speech, history, and writing.
Far from being confused, this man is strikingly alert to the whole
obfuscating process by which blacks' own relationship to God
was denied and by which the hierarchical order of life on earth
was presented as divinely ordained. Furthermore, he is intensely
aware that white scholars did not acknowledge the significance of
an ex-slave's testimony as a means of understanding the social
experience of slavery and its consequences. This ex-slave is not
insensible of these historical constructions; he speaks with a self-
awareness that his firsthand experiences will not be considered
persuasive testimony precisely because it is the firsthand experience of a former slave and is therefore classified as unreliable
or prejudicial.

The narrative strategies of *Unwritten History* are all the more
remarkable for representing the prescience of these ex-slaves, their
awareness that their "truth," their "reality," and their experience
are in competition with more empowered "white" versions of the
past and would face enormous difficulties in achieving legitimacy.
Unwritten History addresses this problem in part by representing
the ex-slaves as active collaborators in the process of making
known through writing what their lives have taught them.

Several of the ex-slaves interviewed by Egypt in 1929 and 1930
knew that theirs would be an unpopular version of history, one
that might result in a backlash. "Yes, I was a slave and knows
plenty about it but I don't care to talk about it," says one informant. "Nope, I don't care to give out nothing I know about it;
just don't think it would do any good" (141). The same informant

continues: "You see the reason I say I don't care to have anything to say is because they disbelieve it anyway . . . I don't want a bit o' scratch made on any book about me" (142). Another informant, eighty-five years old, remembers that he had not realized "I was a slave until once they cut darkies heads off in a riot. They put their faces up like a sign board. They said they was going to burn niggers up by the hundreds. I have heard a heap of people say they wouldn't take the treatment what the slaves took, but they woulda took it or death. If they had been there they woulda took the very same treatment" (296). Immediately, however, this former slave breaks his own reflections on the past to comment on the present: "Say, is there any danger in this talk? If so, I want to take back everything I said" (296). For these men and women, remembering their bondage is a reminder that times have not changed so terribly much: "They had a right to whip you just like the police now" (239). And another informant summarizes the times this way: "We ain't got a bit more show now than we had then" (192). Informants in *Unwritten History* are themselves persuaded that those who write histories will discount and dismiss their words. How, then, to change how people read in order to persuade them to accept what the ex-slaves remembered?

A partial answer lies in how and why it matters that these interviews are conducted by an African American (with another black woman acting as stenographer), a fact that is self-reflexively represented throughout *Unwritten History*. Its textual strategies highlight how centrally important the subjective relationship between the interviewer and her informants can be. Thus, rather than obscuring Egypt's role in shaping what is said by these former slaves, which might have strengthened their case as "objective" evidence in contemporary terms, the narratives postulate the opposite: They state that a white interviewer would never have been told the same stories in the same way by these former slaves. "A white man can't give the history of the Negro," one eighty-eight-year-old informant tells Egypt bluntly, and other informants reinforce this position (87). For example, an informant complains that "these white folks here don't like to hear about how they fathers and mothers done these colored folks" and "would tell me it was all a damn lie," but in recognition of who his two listeners are, he adds that "of course you knowed" since "your mothers and fathers told you" (142). Another informant, describing whippings the slaves received, says, "I tell you, daughter, it was mighty hard," adding that "girls like you two, they might take you up and sell you for $1000" (229–30). And a fourth ex-slave acknowledges Egypt's subjective position toward her own childhood memories this way: "You never were in bondage, but you know about it" (244). Repeatedly, then, the representations of these oral memories implicitly call into question analyses of African-American history that do not acknowledge the inevitable subjectivity of *all* writings.

Unwritten History also represents how the activity of having their words recorded by two African-American women reminds these informants how forbidden literacy skills had been under slavery. "White folks wouldn't learn you how to read and spell," says one informant. "You had to slip and learn it" (249). Another former slave remembers: "Then, a Negro wasn't allowed a book in his hand. What little they got they would steal it" (45). Another adds: "Niggers couldn't have no book then . . . They wasn't 'lowed to touch a book. If you did you got a good whipping" (129). And a fourth speaks of the crippling punishment for writing: "Back there if they'd catch you writing they would break you if they had to cut off your finger" (259–60). That reading and writing emerge as subjects of discussion for elderly former slaves while two black women interview and take notes concerning their childhood represents another aspect of the dialogic process of *Unwritten History*. Reflecting on the fact that no previous scholars had ever bothered to use the testimony of former slaves in their books, another informant adds: "These young people don't know nothing about [slavery] days. They think they got something but it is only a book knowledge . . . just got ideas and no sense" (148). And witnessing her memories written down for the first time, one ex-slave comments, "I tell you if it was so fixed that these generations could dwell in what I heard my mammy talk about, it would learn them something" (192). The documents self-reflexively identify how aware of the transcription process these former slaves are and how momentous they (generally, but not always) believe this attempt to record their spoken words could be for them and future generations. In sum, then, there existed an unresolved tension within much of the spoken testimony in *Unwritten History*: between a hope that their version of history, once written, would be persuasive, and a fear that this version would not be believed after all.

Denied the skills of reading and writing for so long, and denied a historical community interested in their testimony for almost as long, the narrators in *Unwritten History* finally reflect on their own inability to be finished and done with the past through any retelling. Thus, informants speak recurrently of their interviews as open-ended and express how much has been left unexpressed. "Now ladies," one ex-slave says, aware of the dialogic dimension embedded in all interviews. "I can't think of everything, but if you want to ask me any questions I will answer them for you" (50). And another states, "I can just keep on talking now if you is got time to listen; yes I can just keep on going" (153). A third concludes her interview this way: "Now, children, I'se tired, and I ain't gonna fool with yo'all no longer, yo'all go on home now. I tell you one thing, I done forgot more'n you young folks will ever know" (168). And another former slave opens with this remark: "Oh *zam!* it's too much of my life to tell it all today" (220). Such meditative and self-conscious references to the passage of time, the inevitability of physical exhaustion, and the limits of anyone's (and everyone's) memory serve to comment on how what counts as history is completely dependent upon whose stories get told, when they get recorded and by whom, and how they get recorded. In other words, in *Unwritten History* it was the subjects who pinpointed the insufficiencies of all documentary efforts, whether initially derived from oral or from written sources.

I open with an analysis of *Unwritten History* because it points to an overarching need to reconceptualize cultural productions of the thirties. This documentary narrative calls attention to the way any and all perspectives are partial, both in the sense of being incomplete and in the sense of taking a stand. It foregrounds how the relationship between interviewer/transcriber and informant/ speaker shapes what gets told. Furthermore, quite a number of the informants' statements in *Unwritten History* reveal extraordinary alertness to the politics of representation and the way power relations structure all aspects of (hi)story telling. The ex-slaves themselves identify what would be called in contemporary debates aspects of the postmodern condition, that is, the difficulty of adjudicating truth from falsehood, and of rendering faithful representations of reality. Their testimony suggests that a text about their lives should reflect upon power relations in society, especially between slave and freeborn and between the oral and the literate. Finally, perhaps, both the ex-slaves and the editors of *Unwritten History* (as the title suggests) were also stressing the impossibility of any adequate representations for lived experience. In their introduction to *The Slave's Narrative,* Charles T. Davis and Henry Louis Gates, Jr., state: "No written text is a transparent rendering of 'historical reality,' be that text composed by master or slave. The slave's narrative has *precisely* the identical 'documentary' status as does any other written account of slavery."[25] It is striking how many of *Unwritten History*'s subjects articulated an understanding of the subtleties of this position more than sixty years ago, and it is no less remarkable that their editors, to their considerable credit, struggled hard to honor their perspectives and to highlight their critical significance.

I AM NOT alone in suggesting the need to revise our stock assumptions about the thirties, for in recent years cultural historians have begun some of this work. Perhaps the process of revising the decade's cultural history began with Warren Susman, when he concluded in his essay "The Culture of the Thirties" that although the decade has been criticized "for its commitment to 'ideologies,' " he found "little evidence that such a commitment existed."[26] Similarly, Lawrence Levine has challenged "the mistaken urge of a number of scholars to impose symmetry and order" on the thirties, rather than acknowledging the era as "a complex, ambivalent, disorderly period which gave witness to the force of cultural continuity even as it manifested signs of deep cultural change."[27] Furthermore, in our reading of literature and viewing of documentary photography from the thirties, Levine criticized scholars' condescending tendency, "whether conscious or not, to deprive people without power of any determination over their destiny, of any pleasure in their lives, of any dignity in their existence." Among the faces of the disinherited, he contended, we search "for the perfect victims" and thus "crowd out truths" that do not fit our preconceptions.[28] More recently, drawing on the work of both Susman and Levine, Michael Denning recommended a reconsideration of what he called the "distorted" harsh evaluations of thirties popular culture. In particular, Denning's work moved to reclaim "the overlooked richness and vitality of popular front culture" through an examination of Orson Welles's Mercury Theatre, whose productions "may be read as allegories of their contradictory populism."[29] Finally, Paula Rabinowitz and others have worked to "provide access to a gendered history of 1930s literary radicalism that revises many of the accounts already written about this period and explains why women have been occluded in most of them."[30] Rabinowitz's work in particular reestablished the enormous breadth of leftist women novelists' contributions to thirties culture.

In concert with these recent lines of inquiry, I also believe that we need to rethink our (distorted) consensus that the thirties' characteristic genres of "descriptive nonfiction" were continually short-circuited by sentimentalism, condescension toward their subjects, or didacticism. While any number of thirties efforts were indeed problematic in these ways, the authors I discuss in this book were much more self-conscious about the ambiguities of their own roles as interrogators and interpreters.

While no one has denied the greatness of a select few nonfiction books from the thirties and no single documentary has received more admiration than James Agee and Walker Evans's *Let Us Now Praise Famous Men,* scholars always treat it as the exception that proves the rule. For example, a typical view is that this book surpassed the "limitations, the tragic superficiality, of a way of seeing and speaking, of a perspective on life, and – in some measure, perhaps – of a time."[31] Reexamining a broader range of documentary, ethnographic, journalistic, folkloristic, and polemical fictional writings from the thirties fundamentally calls into question both the general consensus about the failure of Depression-era reality-based writings and the notion of *Famous Men*'s uniqueness.

Accordingly, Chapters 2 through 5 evaluate a variety of narratives from these reality-based genres, all of which engaged with (what I call) the politics of representation and focused on strategies for writing the speech of the American "folk." Each in their own way defied generic boundaries, and simultaneously, each became a statement on the intensely problematic process of representing voices in writing. Throughout, my analyses acknowledge the legitimate and important recent critiques (usually bundled together under the heading of poststructuralism) of assumptions about history, reality, identity, truth, and objectivity that have underpinned traditional scholarship, critiques that have led some scholars to abandon claims to some or even all of these assumptions. My argument is that far from abandoning their belief in truth, my subjects nonetheless were painfully aware of its contestedness. An awareness of the power relations that construct what counts as history, reality, identity, and objectivity thus lay at the heart of all their projects.

Chapter 2 stakes out the temporal parameters of the period under discussion and explores the peculiar dilemmas of documentary expression by engaging with John Dos Passos's *Facing the Chair* (1927) and Agee and Evans's *Famous Men* (1941). Both texts are transitional: *Facing the Chair* was one beginning of the modern documentary form, while *Famous Men* marked the onset of yet another beginning, one whose movement into New Journalism and postmodern documentary film is still evolving today.[32] *Facing the Chair* represented a desperate (and vain) attempt to overturn the death sentences of Sacco and Vanzetti; a discussion of Dos Passos's textual strategies highlights documentarians' difficulty in asserting their version of historical truth against competing discourses. *Facing the Chair* thus signaled a shift from the assumptions of Progressive Era muckraking (in which simply "telling the truth" often seemed enough to effect social change) to a more agonized self-understanding on the part of documentarians. A decade later, *Famous Men* self-consciously made such agony part of the documentary form itself, torturously wrestling with the power relations between informants, authors, and readers, centering the text around the impossibility of conveying the suffering and dignity of others without exploiting one's subjects.

In Chapters 3 and 4, I explore ethnographic and folkloristic efforts to represent Native American and African-American culture during the thirties. The three Indian texts I discuss are John G. Neihardt's *Black Elk Speaks* (1932), William Ralganal Benson's "The Stone and Kelsey 'Massacre' " (1932), and Ruth M. Underhill's *The Autobiography of a Papago Woman* (1936), works that share the common task of reconstructing nineteenth-century Native American realities through a documentation of spoken memories. Attention to the narrative forms chosen and close readings of the texts reveal the documenters' highly self-reflexive writing processes. Making the dilemmas inherent in the inevitably imprecise transformation of spoken word to written text a central aspect of their projects, the documenters' strategies for representing Indian speech resist a white culture's erasure of Indian oral remembrances through (often fallacious) textbook accounts and – in a manner not unlike *Unwritten History* – question the authority of literate over supposedly nonliterate cultures.

In Chapter 4, I examine Zora Neale Hurston's *Mules and Men* (1935), placing Hurston's efforts in the context of black folklore studies of the time, studies that were often limited due to a condescending sentimentalization of their subjects or to the constraints of "scientific" fieldwork practices. My argument is that Hurston's text not only documents African-American performative story-telling styles, but also appropriates them in ways that meditate on and mock the very process and purpose of ethnographic writing. Thus, I show how *Mules and Men* repeatedly calls attention to the impossibility of impartiality, analyzes the power imbalance between blacks and whites, highlights the performative aspects of the ethnographer's role, and plays on reader expectations of romanticized exotic "others."

Finally, in Chapter 5, I look at the relationships between Tillie Olsen's Depression-era writings and the Communist press of that time, concentrating on previously unexamined journalistic pieces as well as her unfinished novel, *Yonnondio: From the Thirties.* Focusing particularly on the functions of "voice" and the tension within the Communist Party between letting people speak and speaking for "the people," I analyze the complex mix of narrative strategies and modes of address Olsen uses in her fervent effort to persuade readers to care more about desperately impoverished and disempowered workers. Throughout, I explore how Olsen wrestled with problems of authenticity, authority, and the difficulty of adjudicating among proliferating versions of reality, issues quite similar to those confronting self-conscious ethnographers and documentarians.

The narratives I analyze in this book together exemplify that cluster of interconnected genres that relies on a presumed relationship to real experiences for its effect and that seeks to persuade its audiences of urgent political truths. Currently, cultural critics in a wide range of fields are raising compelling questions about such genres. Stuart Hall, for example, criticizes the "ideology of objectivity" still evident in contemporary journalism. Hall comments that "the absolute distinction between fact and value, the distinction which appears as a common-sense 'rule' in newspaper practice as 'the distinction between facts and interpretation,' " is something that "derives from one of the most profound myths in the liberal ideology: . . . the empiricist illusion, the utopia of naturalism."[33] In turn, Edward Said, in analyzing current anthropological practices, directs attention to "the problematic of the observer," that is, "how someone, an authoritative, explorative, elegant, learned voice, speaks and analyzes, amasses evidence, theorizes, speculates about everything – except itself. Who speaks? For what and to whom?"[34] And finally, Michel de Certeau, expounding on the writing of history, charges that a self-identified nonfictional text "gives itself credibility in the name of the reality which it is supposed to represent, but this authorized appearance of the 'real' serves to camouflage the practice which in fact determines it." "Representation," he thus concludes, "disguises the praxis that organizes it."[35] My contention throughout this book is that the thirties writers whose works I analyze, specifically because of their engagement with disinherited and/or persecuted peoples, anticipated critical perspectives such as these.

In sum, my aim in this book is to challenge the consensus that the reality-based writings of the thirties were largely literary – and even political – failures. To the contrary, it is my argument that many of the thirties narratives discussed in the pages that follow self-reflexively grasped the problems of representation and, through a variety of shifting discursive strategies, sought to provide persuasive readings of social conditions. Furthermore, with a critical attitude toward literacy's assumed power over orality as one starting point, many of the documents I address also acknowledged the significance of spoken testimony, even as they recognized the necessary incompleteness of any written history. Despite these similarities, however, the texts also make clear that there can and should be no universalizing theories about the relationship between orality and literacy; for as I will show, voices function differently in each and every historical and cultural context. Last, I must simply confess that these narratives move me greatly for the integrity of their struggles and the largesse of their social visions. So let me close by quoting the jazz poet Charles O. Hartman who puts it far better than I could: "My aim has been not to cover the ground, but to interrogate landmarks; less to build a wall than weave a net."[36]

2

John Dos Passos and James Agee: You Won't Hear It Nicely

"DOCUMENTARY" was a new word in the 1930s, coined by the film critic John Grierson in 1926.[1] The strongest intentions of Depression-era documentary expression were simply to dramatize immediate political agendas, to heighten awareness and intensify discussion of social ills. Most documentary writers assumed that their writing might bring readers a direct experience of persecution, poverty, or oppression. Much of this outpouring thus promoted the position that documentary provided a transparent lens onto the real, rather than opaque representations. This claim was crucial to the documentary's immediate political effectiveness, and yet it masked deeper problems. But there were other documentarians, among them John Dos Passos and James Agee, who suspected or realized that this assumption was false.

Dos Passos's *Facing the Chair* (1927) and Agee and Walker Evans's *Let Us Now Praise Famous Men* (1941) roughly mark the historical parameters of this study. Examining these two documentary narratives that bracketed the thirties can elucidate the dilemmas of the genre while reconceptualizing the cultural-historical importance of those dilemmas. *Facing the Chair,* written on behalf of the Defense Committee for Nicola Sacco and Bartolomeo Vanzetti in an effort to stave off their executions, was a documentary that emerged out of a Progressive Era tradition in which journalists advocated improved social conditions by dramatizing how a political failure to act would eventually disrupt the security of their middle-class readership. A well-known example is provided by the activist writings of Jacob Riis, which succeeded in catalyzing a range of Progressive Era legislation. *Facing the Chair* differed from Riis's writings in two respects: It sought to persuade its readership not to fear the poor, but rather to identify with them. And, through a desperately chaotic structure – though not in its explicit message – it strongly suggested its probable failure to save Sacco's and Vanzetti's lives. Thus, while it was partially enmeshed in Progressive Era strategies, *Facing the Chair* also represented a partial break with that tradition.

Let Us Now Praise Famous Men, by contrast, was a documentary that emerged after the genre had risen to unprecedented nationwide popularity, and it operated as reaction against and assault on the genre's social realist conventions. Faced with the immense proliferation and popularity of the genre, Agee struggled to convey the grueling reality of rural poverty – and the dignity of the lives lived within it – while challenging the sentimentalizing and distorting tendencies of the genre.[2] As Agee sardonically proclaimed, his book was "written for all those who have a soft place in their hearts for the laughter and tears inherent in poverty viewed at a distance, and especially for those who can afford the retail price."[3] As this remark suggests, Agee was especially preoccupied with the power relations between his subjects and his readers – and between his subjects and himself. Above all, Agee believed that the process of listening to the dispossessed was not and should not be easy or comfortable. As he put it, "You won't hear it nicely" (16). The dilemmas of documentary, only suggested by the tensions within *Facing the Chair,* had fourteen years later become *the* problem around which *Famous Men* organized itself.

Furthermore, a comparison of Dos Passos's and Agee's efforts suggests that it was the triple processes of speaking, listening, and writing that resulted in the experimental narrative strategies and structures of *Facing the Chair* and *Famous Men.* More conventional documentarians did, of course, also speak with, listen to, and write about the dispossessed American. But what Dos Passos initiated and Agee carried far further was a *foregrounding* of the difficulties inherent in those processes. Since the thirties, and most especially in the past three decades, the ambiguous consequences of literacy, the dilemmas inherent in oral history, and the questionable authority of nonfiction authors to portray a reality lived by others have increasingly been scrutinized by scholars, though these have remain unresolved theoretical debates.[4] Though in different ways, Dos Passos and Agee each anticipated this height-

ened theoretical and self-critical awareness. Their engagement
with these questions resulted in part from their dialogues with
living persons situated within political and social struggles for survival.

How to represent their subjects' speech and the false discourses
drowning out that speech, how to avoid the dangers of speaking
for their subjects, and how to cope with the frustration of speaking a truth that no one heard – these questions were central to
Dos Passos's and Agee's work. How speech got represented was
intimately connected to the power relationships between speaker,
listener, and reader. Recognizing this, literary experimentation
became neither gratuitous nor playful. Rather, it was deeply earnest, highly political, and in the case of Agee, angrily ironical.
Agee's text embodied the torment of a documentary narrative
that wore its own failure boldly on its sleeve as proof that the
genre could never make real the actual lives and – most importantly, in terms of this study's focus – the actual speech of its
living subjects in a written form.

These texts were transitional: *Facing the Chair* was one beginning of the modern documentary form, as I hope this chapter will
demonstrate. *Famous Men* signaled the emergence of an even more
hybrid genre, one that, as I have said, constituted a precursor to
such important new approaches as New Journalism and postmodern documentary film. But Agee's break with social realist conventions and his move into fiction also prefigured such contemporary phenomena as docudramas and television programs that
employ dramatized reenactments. Yet this particular brand of
genre blurring camouflages the complexity of the relationship
between reality and representation, rather than highlighting it,
and was not what Dos Passos and Agee anticipated as the likely
legacy of their experimentations into form and language. It is thus
crucial to rehistoricize their cultural contributions. The nonfiction
writings of Dos Passos and Agee moved into fiction precisely
because of their serious concern with the actual. They aimed to
persuade readers that historical reality was an arena of struggle
and that the written word and its representations of speech played
a powerful role in shaping that reality.

TRIALS, like theater, are full of speech.[5] Both are performances of oral testimony – either prepared in advance and

rehearsed or improvised along predetermined structures – and both are, to a degree, ritualized activities, scripted according to certain cultural and social criteria and intended to create out of an enclosed space a version (and vision) of the world outside. Yet theater is art, while trials – and especially political trials – concern social power and historical truth. Speech in a trial has real-life consequences. Courtroom trials are decided after two competing discourses, the defense and the prosecution, perform the oral interrogation and cross-examination of witnesses who swear to tell the truth. As the trial proceeds, there is the interplay of voices competing for their version of historical truth. Yet once the final verdict is reached, these oral performances are assimilated into the written documentation, and the hierarchy of sources – with the written sources ranking above the oral ones – is reestablished.[6] Guilty or innocent: Once a final text has been decided and the memories of what was spoken become practically irrelevant, what remains are the court transcripts and the verdict. The political space that had been opened through speech is now closed again by writing. If the trial has been a success, then it does, like theater, leave the audience satisfied by the experience. That satisfaction is called justice.

On May 5, 1920, the story of one of America's most angrily contested political trials began. On that day, Nicola Sacco and Bartolomeo Vanzetti were arrested in Brockton, Massachusetts, for the robbery and murder of a shoe-factory paymaster and his guard. After their trial a year later, they were sentenced to death in the electric chair. On August 22, 1927, when a series of legal appeals and massive outpourings of support had failed, the two men were executed. In many respects, the beginnings of the radical literature most usually associated with the thirties can really be dated to the martyrdom of Sacco and Vanzetti.[7] And no American writer became more deeply involved in the campaign to save the two men than John Dos Passos. The famous passages Dos Passos wrote in *The Big Money* (1936) remain the most lyrical and passionate pronouncements on the case and the executions:

> they have clubbed us off the streets   they are stronger
> they are rich   they hire and fire the politicians the newspa-
> pereditors the old judges the small men with reputations the col-
> legepresidents   the   wardheelers   (listen   businessmen
> collegepresidents judges   America will not forget her betrayers)

they hire the men with guns   the uniforms the policecars the
patrolwagons
    all right you have won   you will kill the brave men our
friends tonight. . .
    they have built the electricchair and hired the executioner to
throw the switch
    all right we are two nations[8]

Dos Passos's involvement with the Sacco–Vanzetti case began
in 1926 when he traveled to Boston to interview the imprisoned
men and witness a motion for a retrial. He first published an
article on the case in *New Masses* in August 1926 and then agreed
to prepare a full-length pamphlet for the Defense Committee.
*Facing the Chair: Sacco and Vanzetti – The Story of the Americaniza-
tion of Two Foreign Born Workmen* appeared in the spring of 1927
after Dos Passos had made a second trip to Boston to gather
more information. By this time, there were few if any remaining
options for appeal, and there appeared little hope that the men
could be saved.

In the case of Sacco and Vanzetti, the struggle for historical
truth was played out against the backdrop of powerful social and
political forces that assumed a significant role in the trial's outcome. Given this situation, *Facing the Chair* needed to speak persuasively against what it determined were the falsehoods of legal
authorities and the governing powers. The *legal* truth of the case
had already been long settled by 1927: Sacco and Vanzetti were
guilty men. What Dos Passos thus worked to address in his
narrative were the political and historical necessities of challenging
the legitimacy, authority, and power of what he called "law-
words" and "death-words," and he did so almost entirely
through the representation of actual voices. The goal was to write
a text that would reopen a closed case; its purpose was to wrest
the truth back from the self-serving and obfuscating rhetoric of a
powerful elite who had laid claim to its own version of truth and
sentenced two innocent men to death.[9]

The crucial point is that *Facing the Chair* did not simply report
the historical truth; indeed, it could not do only that if it hoped to
achieve its ends, for the discourses declaring innocence had much
less power than the discourses intoning guilt. The *written* record
had closure, had shut down debate and a sense of possibility, had
already determined guilt. Redirecting attention to *speech* was one

method for reopening the political space in which a different verdict might be possible.

Facing the Chair used speech in a number of strategic ways. To evoke emotional involvement in the reader, the text made use of contrasting, powerfully allegorical, popular traditions of speaking about the United States. In order to discredit the prosecution's case, *Facing the Chair* also presented transcripts of multiple and contradictory oral testimony from the prosecution's witnesses. To dramatize the moral bankruptcy of the U.S. justice system, the text repetitively invoked the judge's rhetorical questions concerning the government's role in framing the two men. To persuade readers that Sacco and Vanzetti could not have committed violent crimes under any circumstances, *Facing the Chair* highlighted how they spoke about their families, the immigrant's plight in America, and their anarchist ideals. Yet the strategies of *Facing the Chair,* as I will explain, became internally inconsistent as the text both worked within and partially broke out of a Progressive Era muckraking tradition. The result was a chaotic and cacophonous narrative, arguably the first modern American documentary.

Allegorical strategies in *Facing the Chair* highlighted contrasting ways of speaking about the United States and provided the text with its most lyrical moments. In a populist fashion that evoked resonant vernacular traditions, Dos Passos's text anticipated the rebirth of folk nationalism that would characterize later thirties documentary narrative. At one point, for example, Dos Passos wrote:

> Circumstances sometimes force men into situations so dramatic, thrust their puny frames so far into the burning bright searchlights of history that they or their shadows on men's minds become enormous symbols. Sacco and Vanzetti are all the immigrants who have built this nation's industries with their sweat and their blood and have gotten for it nothing but the smallest wage it was possible to give them and a helot's position under the bootheels of the Arrow Collar social order. They are all the wops, hunkies, bohunks, factory fodder that hunger drives into the American mills through the painful sieve of Ellis Island. They are the dreams of a saner social order of those who can't stand the law of dawg eat dawg. This tiny courtroom is a focus of the turmoil of an age of tradition, the center of eyes all over the world.

Sacco and Vanzetti throw enormous shadows on the courthouse walls.[10]

The vernacular phrasings (such as the ethnic slurs and "the law of dawg eat dawg") called attention to how Americans spoke about America; it represented one (unsympathetic) version of the United States that the text argued was gaining in authority and legitimacy. By contrast, Dos Passos also referred to the story of U.S. democracy with its "smouldering tradition of freedom" since "after all everyone learnt the Declaration of Independence and *Give me Liberty or Give me Death* in school, and however perfunctory the words have become they have left a faint infantile impression on the minds of most of us" (55). Here the memories of another vernacular heritage familiar to every schoolchild (Thomas Jefferson's declaration and Patrick Henry's final speech) indicated a contrasting version of how to speak about America, though this (ennobled) position had been increasingly battered by a legal system "more and more the instrument of the governing orders" (56).

Indeed, versions of history, both spoken and written, beget more versions of history in *Facing the Chair,* and the question is how to determine which ones are truthful. Ultimately, the reader must choose; the text links that decision to an ethical dilemma through its presentations of proliferating "truths." For example, in its later sections, the narrative recounts events that occur early in the story's chronology: the initial Sacco–Vanzetti trials. Numerous eyewitnesses are here quoted verbatim from the court transcripts. *Facing the Chair* thus tries to persuade readers by implication that the justice system has gone awry: eyewitnesses openly and repeatedly contradict one another and (at times) even themselves. The question "What is the truth?" transforms into another question: "Which of the several truths represent the real truth?" What gets told at the trial is not *the* truth; rather, it is a truth in a state of constant revision in order to satisfy the immediate needs of whichever party is asking the questions:

> In an affidavit sworn to by Mrs. Andrews nine months after the trial she declared that her original statement before trial was true, and that her trial testimony was untrue and had been given under the coercion and intimidation of the District Attorney's office . . .
> Six months later Mrs. Andrews, in a statement to the District

Attorney's office, said that her first statement to the defense lawyer was false, her trial testimony true, her subsequent affidavit to the defense counsel untrue and her last statement true. (119)

In other oral testimony reproduced in *Facing the Chair,* a four-teen-year-old high school student explains how he identified Van-zetti at the crime scene:

> "I could tell he was a foreigner by the way he ran," young Shaw testified at the trial.
> "What sort of a foreigner?" asked the defense.
> "Either Italian or Russian."
> "Does an Italian or a Russian run differently from a Swede or a Norwegian?"
> "Yes."
> "What is the difference?"
> "Unsteady." (77)

In short, Dos Passos's narrative dramatizes the absurdity of the prosecution's case, even as it painfully documents the underlying nativism it argues had motivated that case. Because *Facing the Chair* must discredit the oral testimony that has condemned men that the documentarian believes to be innocent, it works hard to illustrate how easily "truth" can get deliberately manipulated within the U.S. justice system.

The symbol of justice in any trial is the judge, and *Facing the Chair* devotes special attention to Judge Webster Thayer. It is especially significant that a portion of the judge's decision to deny a final motion for a retrial is repeated no less than four times in the text. It is a question that Judge Thayer asks rhetorically and that *Facing the Chair* turns into the choral refrain of this particular American tragedy. It articulates the judicial fatalism against which *Facing the Chair* must pit itself:

> Have Attorney General Sargent and his subordinates . . . stooped so low and are they so degraded that they are willing by the concealment of evidence to enter into a fraudulent conspiracy with the government of Massachusetts to send two men to the electric chair, not because they were murderers but because they were radicals? (33–4)

In counterpoint to this question, the accumulating evidence in *Facing the Chair* dramatizes the cold ethical infirmity of Judge

Thayer, while it argues that the government did conspire to kill Sacco and Vanzetti.

Against the "death-words" of the empowered, *Facing the Chair* sets the vibrant voices of the dispossessed. The entire structure of *Facing the Chair* juxtaposes two ways of speech against one another: the feelingful warmth of immigrant voices against the dehumanized, mechanistic legalese of native-born Americans like Judge Thayer. It is the most elaborately developed device used throughout the text, so much so that it is not truth per se that gets debated, but opposing "sets of words," rhetorical discourses whose struggles for primacy determine life or death.

In order to reinforce this dichotomy further, Dos Passos includes passages in which Sacco and Vanzetti speak for themselves. Thus, for example, Nicola Sacco tells Dos Passos that "he can't understand" the people "who cooly want him to die in the electric chair," because when he (Sacco) "was cool he's never wanted anyone to die. Judge Thayer and the prosecution he thinks of as instruments of a machine" (66). Similarly, consider this excerpt from Bartolomeo Vanzetti's *Story of a Proletarian Life,* a portion of which is reprinted in *Facing the Chair:*

> On July 9, 1908, I left my dear ones [for the United States]. My sorrow was so great at the parting that I kissed my relatives and strained them to my bosom without being able to speak. My father, too, was speechless in his profound sorrow, and my sisters wept as they did when my mother died . . . The steerage passengers [were] handled by the officials like so many animals. Not a word of kindness, of encouragement, to lighten the burden of fears that rests heavily upon the newly arrived on American shores . . . How well I remember standing at the Battery, in lower New York, upon my arrival, alone, with a few poor belongings in the way of clothes, and very little money. Until yesterday I was among folks who understood me. This morning I seemed to have awakened in a land where my language meant little more to the native (so far as meaning is concerned) than the pitiful noises of a dumb animal. Where was I to go? What was I to do? Here was the promised land. The elevated rattled by and did not answer. The automobiles and the trolleys speed by, heedless of me. (60–1)

Here are remarkable reflections on speech, speechlessness, and their relationship to "Americanization," and their inclusion in

Facing the Chair calls attention to that which has been lost, or perceived as lost, in the United States. Vanzetti's story, like Dos Passos's subsequent text, has interwoven elemental immigrant narrative formulas: the nostalgia of origins and the romanticization of a "vanished" kinship network, the quest for acceptance in an adopted land and language, and the destructive impact of a "cold" and mechanized new society on the "warmth" of an ethnic in America.

Extending and developing Sacco and Vanzetti's own metaphors, Dos Passos explains how, in their six years of imprisonment, they "feel themselves being inexorably pushed towards the Chair by the blind hatred of thousands of wellmeaning citizens, by the superhuman, involved, stealthy, soulless mechanism of the law" (71). In the Massachusetts courtroom, human feelings have been banished in favor of "quiet, dignity; almost like a class in a lawschool. The case has been abstracted into a sort of mathematics" (23). The courtroom is "a world of phrases, *prosecution, defence, evidence, motion, irrelevant, incompetent and immaterial*" (69). Sacco and Vanzetti have been trapped in a system that is killing them by degrees, tying them "tighter and tighter in the sticky filaments of law-words like a fly in a spiderweb. And the wrong set of words means the Chair" (69).

However, this division along ethnic–native-born lines is not a consistently held perspective in the text – Dos Passos could not sustain it without injuring the narrative's overall persuasive message – and the ways it breaks down are worthy of examination. First, there are laudatory stories of "native" Americans, notably Defense Attorney William G. Thompson who feels "that as a citizen it is his duty to protect the laws and liberties of his state and as a man to try to save two innocent men from being murdered by a machine set going in a moment of hatred and panic" (45). The lesson implicit here is that native-born Americans do not always work for the governing forces. Similarly, there are also ethnic stories that differ sharply from those of Sacco and Vanzetti, especially "the story of the life of Celestino Madeiros, a poor Portuguese boy brought up in New Bedford," who confesses to the crimes for which the two Italians have been convicted (24). At one and the same time, the narrative describes Madeiros as a criminal and as an oppressed ethnic:

> He learned Americanism all right, he suffered from no encumbering ideas of social progress; the law of dawg eat dawg was morbidly vivid in his mind from the first. Hardly out of school he was up in court for "breaking and entering." No protests from him about the war . . . By the spring of 1920 he was deep in the criminal world that is such an apt cartoon of the world of legitimate business . . . For three years the leaders of society had been proclaiming the worthlessness of human life. Is it surprising that criminals should begin to take them at their word? (24)

This passage provides a cutting analysis of the insidious influence of "Americanism" and "Americanization" on an immigrant's life, and it insults the values communicated by the word and deed of U.S. leaders. At the same time, however, there is an inescapable implication that not all ethnics were as incorruptible as Sacco and Vanzetti. This passage, like the one about a "wellmeaning" "nativeborn" American like Defense Attorney Thompson, acknowledges that there can be no racially essentializing categories (e.g., "ethnics are decent" or "native-borns are amoral"). In order to persuade its readers – most of whom were presumably "nativeborn" – to participate in defending the falsely accused immigrants, *Facing the Chair* could not afford to sustain absolute dichotomies.

When compared with earlier efforts in this and other respects, the transitional character of Dos Passos's text becomes particularly evident. A generation before Dos Passos, in the 1890s, one of America's most representative muckrakers had been Jacob Riis, the Danish immigrant whose *How the Other Half Lives* shocked middle-class New Yorkers into confessing that a horrid poverty existed all around them. A partly sociological, partly evangelical tract, *How the Other Half Lives* succeeded in mobilizing support for a series of tenement housing laws.[11] Yet rarely did Riis portray the urban and impoverished ethnics as anything other than objects of pity and fear. According to *How the Other Half Lives*, middle-class readers were to assist the poor in order to protect their own interests. This is a brief scene from Riis:

> A man stood at the corner of Fifth Avenue and Fourteenth Street the other day, looking gloomily at the carriages that rolled by, carrying the wealth and fashion of the avenues to and from the big stores down town. He was poor, and hungry, and ragged. This thought was in his mind: "They behind their well-fed teams have

no thought for the morrow; they know hunger only by name, and ride down to spend in an hour's shopping what would keep me and my little ones from want a whole year." There rose up before him the picture of those little ones crying for bread around the cold and cheerless hearth – then he sprang into the throng and slashed around him with a knife, blindly seeking to kill, to revenge.[12]

Riis's text presumed a poor man's thoughts and motivations and used this strategy to induce anxiety in the minds of its readers. The consequences of poverty were dramatized to extremes. In Riis's text, the poor were exotics: irrational and capable of anything. The reader was asked to heed these cautionary words not for the sake of the other, but for his or her own sake.

In *Facing the Chair,* Dos Passos comments that it was precisely such a social climate (even in part perpetuated by well-intentioned reformers like Riis) that "put the average right-thinking citizen into such a state of mind that whenever he smelt garlic on a man's breath he walked past quickly for fear of being knifed" (53). Dos Passos suggested that it was exactly this atmosphere of tension, in which foreign-born workers were reduced to emblems like the smell of garlic and the threat of irrational violence, that made Sacco and Vanzetti an easy "focus for [the native-born Americans'] bitter hatred of the new, young, vigorous, unfamiliar forces" that the immigrants represented. Consequently, by attempting to create identification with the ethnic underclass *rather than* with the privileged middle class, *Facing the Chair* deliberately broke with the muckraking convention of the Progressive Era. Dos Passos stated his alternative strategy explicitly, directing himself at the reader:

> Put yourself in their place. Haven't there been times when you who are reading this would have been pretty embarrassed to explain your actions if suddenly arrested . . . It's time that you realized fully, you who are reading this, man or woman, laborer or whitecollar worker, that if Sacco and Vanzetti die in the Chair as the result of a frameup based on an unlucky accident, your chance of life will be that much slimmer. (81–2)

Another way *Facing the Chair* broke with the Progressive Era's muckraking tradition was in its recognition that just conveying "the facts" was not enough to ensure social change. Instead,

Facing the Chair is a book that shouts into the ears of a justice system it perceives as not blind, but partially deaf, a justice system that reproduces its own "reality," one that has little to do with justice or truth. In order to dramatize his anger at such deafness, Dos Passos's narrative exhibited wildly inventive strategies that nearly self-destructed. The use of a demanding proliferation of multiple perspectives, an achronological time line, lengthy transcriptions from court proceedings, observer-participation episodes, blunt editorializing, and so forth make it a difficult narrative to read and a text with which readers might easily lose patience. Yet what it managed to become was a hybrid text that traversed any one genre, while grabbing snatches of several at once: reportage, polemic, confession, and fiction. Most significantly, *Facing the Chair* was a documentary book divided against itself, pulling itself apart even as it attempted to persuade each reader to "demand the truth about Sacco and Vanzetti . . . if they die what little faith many millions of men have in the chance of Justice in this country will die with them" (127). This call to action stood beside simple and also truthful statements that any efforts to save the two men represented "a pretty forlorn hope" (22). Thus, the narrative's exploded structure and frantically inconsistent strategies could not reconcile within themselves the "fact" of injustice with their own "fiction" that justice could (and would) prevail. Just saying the truth over and over again would not make it so, and the lesson of *Facing the Chair* is that no one text could embody this living contradiction without doing damage to itself.

AS THE THIRTIES progressed, the New Deal arts projects were inaugurated: massive government-sponsored enterprises intent on representing American culture in accessible forms and mediums for as many people as possible. The New Deal arts programs – including the documentary efforts of the Federal Writers' Project and the Farm Security Administration's photography division – were specifically geared to supporting, promoting, and displaying what was special and good about everyday America to everyday Americans. The impulses behind such projects were self-defined as democratic; the goals included nothing short of a reconceptualization of what it meant to be an American.

This particularly meant giving fuller attention to ethnic groups, African Americans, and other minorities left out of the cultural equation in years past.[13]

Ironically, however, just as there was such an outpouring of institutional support and such a proliferation of subjects of study, new doubts crept into the journalistic profession about the very possibility of conveying reality adequately. As Michael Schudson has demonstrated, it was, perhaps paradoxically, precisely in the post–World War I and Depression-era atmosphere of insecurity and disillusionment that the twentieth-century preoccupation with "objectivity" was formulated. As the hopes of the Progressive Era faded and there grew the creeping modern suspicion that all factual accounts were little more than subjective individual testimonies, "objectivity" emerged as the new buzzword of the profession.[14] Thus, one actually sees in the thirties a widespread return to many of the social realist conventions of the Progressive Era, but not for the reasons one might have expected. As Schudson argues, the ideal of objectivity arose "not so much as an extension of naive empiricism and the belief in facts but as a reaction against skepticism . . . It was not the final expression of a belief in facts but the assertion of a method designed for a world in which even facts could not be trusted."[15] This effort to achieve objectivity was, logically, almost always closely linked with an affirmation of authorial authority. Significantly, and not coincidentally, there was enormous newfound interest in radio broadcasting as a source of news and information, while documentary photography and film excited widespread public fascination as well; for all these mediums gave the distinct impression of objective and direct perceptions of actuality, an immediacy that, William Stott observes, "cannot be achieved in print."[16] It was in this context that creative writers also turned to the genres of documentary, ethnography, and journalism to communicate the "essence" (as Stott terms it) "not of imagined things, but of real things only."[17]

This was the milieu in which James Agee came of age as a professional journalist. Just as Dos Passos had struggled within and outside of the assumptions and conventions of the Progressive Era, so Agee would have to wrestle with the conceptual frameworks and preoccupations of the decade of "objectivity." And this difference explains the divergence in their attitudes toward authorial authority. Unlike Dos Passos, who (despite the passionate frenzy of his text) did speak for his subjects and for truth at every point, and without ironic self-inquiry, Agee's text repeatedly and obsessively undermined its author's authority to write the very text we read, rejecting therefore one of his era's most-valued documentary conventions. This agonized struggle to come to terms with the relationship between subjectivity and objectivity and the power relations between himself and his subjects, along with his fury at the New Deal's self-congratulatory mode, would prove to be the hallmarks of his style and vision.

How Agee arrived at this point in his critical thinking about documentary expression is a complex question whose answer lies partly outside the scope of this study.[18] Suffice it to say that as an associate editor for *Fortune* since 1933, Agee had had ample opportunity to write more standard New Deal–type documentary narratives. For example, in May, 1935, he published a lengthy piece on the Tennessee Valley Authority – written with much of the style and many of the strategies *Famous Men* would later attack. A typical passage from this article described a worker for the TVA:

> The average workman on Norris Dam – and you may take him as the average TVA workman – is thirty-two years old. The chances are two to one he's from a town or city – by all odds most likely from a small town and a farm background. The chance that he has ever done such work before is next to nil. He has completed one year of high school; the chances are two to one he's married; if so, he has between two and three dependents; the chances are two to one, also, that he's taking one or more of the free training courses. After his five-and-one-half-hour shift he boards a truck and rides the four miles to Norris where he loafs, works in his garden, studies, eats, plays games, or sleeps, according to his disposition and the time of day.[19]

Little more than a year later, assigned "to prepare . . . an article on cotton tenantry in the United States, in the form of a photographic and verbal record of the daily living and environment of an average white family of tenant farmers" – the project that would become *Let Us Now Praise Famous Men* – Agee would assault all journalism that spoke in terms of "average" individuals (xiii). Of George Gudger, tenant farmer, Agee would write in

Famous Men: "He is not some artist's or journalist's or propagandist's invention: he is a human being: and to what degree I am able it is my business to reproduce him as the human being he is; not just to amalgamate him into some invented, literary imitation of a human being" (240). It is not surprising that *Fortune* was never to publish this radically different approach to documentary expression, and for a time, no one else was prepared to do so either.[20]

Reading *Famous Men* quickly reveals why the text faced significant difficulties finding a publisher; it is an intensely self-reflexive text, and highlighting its own failure as a documentary really becomes one of the book's central subjects. *Famous Men's* means of doing this operate in at least five ways: first, through becoming in large part a structural parody of a New Deal government report on farm tenancy; second, through highly allegorical passages that critically frame and comment on the text as a documentary entity; third, through individual passages that dramatize Agee's inadequacies as journalist and as "tour guide"; fourth, through a multiplicity of points of view and strategies of address that complicate reader identification; and fifth, through variously inconsistent representations of actual speech that encourage the reader to "re-form" his or her conventionalized notions about the relationship between representation and real experience.

An analysis of the overall structure of *Famous Men* reveals its strategy as parody and critique of a U.S. government report on farm tenancy, published during the precise period Agee researched and began writing his book on the same topic. Entitled *Farm Tenancy: Report of the President's Committee* (1937), it is a sensitive and sensible progressive document, whose goal was to persuade the U.S. government to take immediate action on "the problem of tenancy and the related problems" that had for so long been perceived as "in general, nobody's business."[21] Indeed, *Farm Tenancy* includes strong rhetorical language, citing the "unsatisfactory" and "objectionable" conditions in which many tenant farmers lived, although it balanced these harsher statements with sentences like this one: "Tenants still move with some freedom up the agricultural ladder" (4). Yet its overall assessment was that tenancy problems were worsening and change was imperative. In a section entitled "Official Documents," the report included correspondence between President Roosevelt and Henry

Wallace, chairman of the Special Committee on Farm Tenancy, stating that "the usefulness of the report will consist largely in its general educational value" (27). To this end, the report spoke in a firm and cautiously optimistic tone: "We have to deal with abuses that have been developing for two centuries. We cannot correct them overnight. But we can begin" (iv). This was certainly a modest enough claim.

It is clear from *Famous Men*'s structure and language that Agee was infuriated by *Farm Tenancy;* his writing mocks and parodies its New Deal hopes and claims. In contrast to the government report's positive tone, in *his* report on farm tenancy, Agee writes, "As a matter of fact, nothing I might write could make any difference whatever" (13). He also states: "If I could do it, I'd do no writing at all here. It would be photographs; the rest would be fragments of cloth, bits of cotton, lumps of earth, records of speech, pieces of wood and iron, phials of odors, plates of food and of excrement" (13). In addition, *Famous Men* included biting and sarcastic scenes like this one of tenant life "improved" by government-sponsored social reform:

> They were clients of Rehabilitation. They had been given a young sick steer to do their plowing with; the land was woodsclearing, but had been used as long as the house (whose wood was ragged and light as pith); no seed or fertilizer had been given them until the end of May. Nothing they had planted was up better than a few inches, and that was now withering faster than it grew. They now owed the Government on the seed and fertilizer, the land, the tools, the house, and probably before long on the steer as well, who was now so weak he could hardly stand. (35)

In short, *Famous Men* rejected the argument that writing political rhetoric whose "usefulness" will "consist largely in its general education value" was an act for which one should reap political gain or feel any sense of self-satisfaction. Instead, Agee wrote, "A piece of the body torn out by the roots might be more to the point" (13).

The unusual structure of *Famous Men* is also an important part of the text's aesthetic-political challenge to *Farm Tenancy* and all other standardized documentaries that were designed to persuade the powerful of the need for social reforms. Such calculated appeals, according to Agee's scheme of things, obscured rather than illuminated the reality of the tenants' situation. Moreover, language's relationship to the complexity of lived reality was, to borrow Agee's own phrase, "such a Rube Goldberg articulation of frauds, compromises, artful dodges and tenth removes as would fatten any other art into apoplexy if the art were not first shamed out of existence" (236). But as a foil, *Farm Tenancy* had its purposes as Agee designed his own text.

Famous Men is, in its outlines, a burlesque of the government report's structure. The main body of *Famous Men* is subdivided into three parts, with further separate sections for photographs, for a number of incidental essays and poems, and for references and notes. This form mimics and mocks the *Farm Tenancy* report, which also had three parts to it, a photographic supplement, a technical supplement, a statistical supplement, and a section for references. Agee's allusion to a Rube Goldberg contraption is telling since his book actually embodies all the basic components of the New Deal documentary, but not in any "proper" order or proportion. For example, the government report's briefest section, "Part I. Findings," a five-thousand-word survey of the tenant farm problem, becomes Agee's "Part Two: Some Findings and Comments," which devotes more than forty-five thousand words just to a description of one tenant family's house. The government's "Selected References" lists several dozen scholarly titles, beginning with W. W. Alexander, Edwin R. Embree, and Charles S. Johnson's *The Collapse of Cotton Tenancy*.[22] By contrast, Agee's "Notes and Appendices" lists one dozen "suggested" references, beginning with "detail of gesture, landscape, costume, air, action, mystery, and incident throughout the writings of William Faulkner" (449). Also suggested are films, photographs, sketches, gospel and blues music recordings, newspapers, postcards, and road maps of the South. Thus, *Famous Men*'s inversion of *Farm Tenancy* includes Agee's privileging of such cultural artifacts' ability to convey the truth of the South, rather than placing these artifacts further down on documentary's conventional hierarchy of sources. Furthermore, *Farm Tenancy*'s abstract graphs and tables are, in Agee's view, gross distortions of an intensely immediate and individual crisis. "George Gudger is a human being," Agee writes, "a man, not like any other human being so much as he is like himself" (232). Agee continues that "he is exactly, down to the last inch and instant, who, what,

where, when and why he is" and "in those terms living, right
now, in flesh and blood and breathing, in an actual part of a world
in which also, quite as irrelevant to imagination, you and I are
living" (233). As a specific condition repeated tens of thousands
of times across the country, Agee felt that Gudger's life should
not (and indeed, could not) be abstracted in the manner of *Farm
Tenancy*.

The discrepancies between the "official" text and Agee's text
also reveal the relationship between them. That things are not
where they should be in the text of *Famous Men* reinforces the
interpretation that things are not *what* they should be in the real
world of the United States. Agee's "Rube Goldberg articulation"
was not a casual gesture randomly developed, as others have
suggested, but a deliberate response to and critique of an "official" document.

The government's *Farm Tenancy* report had also been a silent
text, which neither quoted nor appeared to have been the result
of interviews or dialogues with tenants themselves. By contrast,
Famous Men reveals a consistent preoccupation with the importance of listening closely to the text's subjects. Significantly, the
text begins and ends with passages that can be read as allegories
for documentary's difficult activities of speaking, listening to real
voices of actual people, and then writing. As framing devices, the
passages comment variously on the theme of orality, its relationship to literacy, and the essential role of the reader. The first
passage concludes the text's preamble, and its direct address is
designed to engage more fully that silent reader:

> Get a radio or a phonograph capable of the most extreme loudness
> possible, and sit down to listen to a performance of Beethoven's
> Seventh Symphony or of Schubert's C-Major Symphony. But I
> don't mean just sit down and listen. I mean this: Turn it on as loud
> as you can get it. Then get down on the floor and jam your ear as
> close into the loudspeaker as you can get it and stay there, breath-
> ing as lightly as possible, and not moving, and neither eating nor
> smoking nor drinking. Concentrate everything you can into your
> hearing and into your body. You won't hear it nicely. If it hurts
> you, be glad of it. (15–16)

Perhaps no allegory could better suggest the difficulties of documentary expression in the thirties. An author travels far to hear

the speaking of Alabaman tenant farmers; yet the text he writes could only be a wretchedly crippled and inadequate reproduction of that real experience. Imperfect and failed, that text would never fully convey the presence of the real or embody a real person's entire life within it. Could readers of *Famous Men* ever know the truths the author had been assigned to document?

Sticking our heads into an incredibly loud loudspeaker and thus causing our eardrums to ring and rattle with pain becomes the narrative's troubling recommendation for readers in the divisive era its author announced had been already partially deafened by the blurring of distinctions between the real and the "real." Given the deafening roar of political rhetoric masquerading as truth in a flood of documentary expression, *Famous Men* argued the need for modern forms that might communicate alternative "readings" of actual experiences *more* aggressively than those of a prior generation. Just stating the truth, as Dos Passos had begun to realize in 1927, would not make it so. Asking readers to experience physical discomfort as preparation for a book about real hardships was the price Agee demanded of his presumably privileged readership – a price he assumed they could easily afford to pay. Reading documentary had to be more than a casual indulgence; it should make readers question what the purpose of prose writing about painful reality could be, how exactly it should be accomplished, and how complicit we are in the success or failure of that process.

The final passage of *Famous Men* complements the first. It returns several hundred pages later to the same theme and question about the role of listening in a text about the real. Lying awake late one night on the porch of a tenant family's home, the photographer Walker Evans and Agee hear "a sound that was new to us" at the onset of "(On the Porch: 3," the last of the text's several multiple endings (463). Rather than jammed up close and loud, as in the loudspeaker episode, the new sound is faint and distant; concentrated listening becomes the key toward understanding this unclassifiable and utterly new aural encounter: "We now engaged in mutual listening and in analysis of what we heard, so strongly, that in all the body and in the whole range of mind and memory, each of us became all one hollowed and listening ear" (463). A sound of nature is intricately described in unnatural terms – "It was perhaps most nearly like the noise hydrogen makes when a match flame is passed across the mouth of a slanted test-tube" – and neither Agee nor Evans can identify its source (463). Subsequently, this first sound is followed by a second, which, "identical with the first but, coming from a good deal farther away, seemed higher, hollower, and thinner: scarcely more, yet very definitely more, than a loud clear echo" (465). Agee and Evans speculate on which sound represents the seeker and which "was the thing sought by the other," although the reporters also recognize that this idea of searcher and sought-after was an "illusion," an imposed construction. Still, and despite this deeper awareness, they align themselves with the nearer sound "by nearness" and signify it as "having become the searcher with whom we had identified ourselves and taken sides and by having yet at the same time remained so entirely itself" (465).

This passage can be taken as a second allegorical comment on documentary's strategies for representing the real. First, the reporter encounters a reality that is unfamiliar; the reporter's task is to interpret its meaning in words. But the tendency of such an enterprise is to grid interpretations onto what is more complex and exists independently of such machinations. Interpreted in this way, the only side worth taking is a position against the authority of representation, against all documentation that states it has the solutions, or claims it communicates what is actual and real. It may have been well intentioned, but for Agee, identifications with "the thing sought by the other" could only result in the illusion that the subject had been comprehended, consumed, defined. Yet there is another and more hopeful way of listening implied here as well, for the documentarian's goal is to become, as closely as possible, "all one hollowed and listening ear." As the seekers, Agee and Evans *must* position themselves somehow in relation to the sought-after – in this instance, the reality of tenant farmer existence. Pragmatically speaking, a documentarian most usually will identify with the nearer subject "by nearness" yet ideally will recognize that the subject must, at all points, be understood as remaining "so entirely itself" and therefore, in an absolute sense, unknown and unknowable. Nor should the documentarian mistake who is the real artist: the subject. As Agee concluded: "At all times it was beyond even the illusion of full apprehension, and was noble, frightening and distinguished: a work of great, private and unambitious art which was irrelevant to audience" (466). These open-ended reflections about listening and identification provide a unifying theme for the entire text.

Furthermore, it is the position of *Famous Men* that documentary must "fail" as documentary in order to succeed as truth, and it can do this only by dispersing a typically coherent documentary formula to the wind. Calling into question the authoritative position of the documentary's author, as well as retraining his audience to doubt the author's authority, were necessary parts of Agee's project. Turning back, then, to the three vignettes that follow the book's preamble and are collectively entitled "July 1936," we find more of Agee's efforts at reader reeducation. The vignettes are all about the limits of journalism, and as they lead the reader through Agee's process of trial and error, they are indictments of the journalist Agee. These are ethnographic episodes that turn the frame around: Agee becomes the peculiar exotic in an environment completely familiar to all those who inhabit it. The journalist to whom we are introduced is both well meaning and inept. Thus, the text works to frustrate any "natural" respect readers may feel for the sensitive and aware journalist in conventional documentary expression. These vignettes block such responses through the imposition of the author between reader and subject; he takes up nearly the entire frame we anticipate would be filled by the subject of farm tenancy. Instead, Agee is the one who gets examined, his motives exposed and dissected for analysis. Throughout this section, the implicit question is, What gives this journalist the experience, skill, or authority to represent lives of which he has only the most incidental understanding?

An analysis of the first episode provides a good introduction to Agee's method. In this episode, "Late Sunday Morning," Agee and Evans drive with two landowners to find subjects for their report on white tenant farmers. Agee is sarcastic about the help this talkative landowner can provide him: "I was glad enough of it; nearly all his tenants were negroes and no use to me, and I needed a rest from asking questions and decided merely to establish myself as even more easygoing, casual, and friendly than he was" (25–6). They arrive at a camp where all the sharecroppers are black; there is no point to this trip. In addition, Agee quickly realizes how intrusive and unwanted their white presence is for everyone on this, the only free day in the week. Agee initially plays the casual and indifferent reporter when one landlord asserts his authority over the situation in a dialogue that is as ritualized in its form as it is racist in its content:

> They all approached softly and strangely until they stood within the shade of the grove, then stayed their ground as if floated, their eyes shifting upon us sidelong and to the ground and to the distance, speaking together very little, in quieted voices: it was as if they had been under some sort of magnetic obligation to approach just this closely and to show themselves. The landlord began to ask of them through the foreman, How's So-and-So doing, all laid by? Did he do that extra sweeping I told you? – and the foreman would answer, Yes. sir, yes sir, he do what you say to do, he doin all right; and So-and-So shifted on his feet and smiled uneasily while, uneasily, one of his companions laughed and the others held their faces in the blank safety of deafness. And you, you ben doin much coltn lately, you horny old bastard? – and the crinkled, old, almost gray-mustached negro who came up tucked his head to one side looking cute, and showed what was left of his teeth, and whined, tittering, Now Mist So-and-So, you know I'm settled down, married-man, you wouldn't – and the brutal negro of forty split his face in a villainous grin and said, He too *ole,* Mist So-and-So, he don't got no sap lef in him; and everyone laughed, and the landowner said, These yer two yere, colts yourn ain't they? – and the old man said they were, and the landowner said, Musta found *them* in the woods, strappin young niggers as that; and the old man said, No sir, he got the both of them lawful married, Mist So-and-So; and the landowner said that eldest on em looks to be ready for a piece himself, and the negroes laughed, and the two boys twisted their beautiful bald gourdlike skulls in a unison of shyness and their faces were illumined with maidenly smiles of shame, delight and fear; and meanwhile the landowner had loosened the top two buttons of his trousers, and he now reached his hand in to the middle of his forearm, and, squatting with bent knees apart, clawed, scratched and rearranged his genitals. (27–8)

Documentary reporting of this variety about farm tenancy would be of little assistance to proponents of New Deal reform. Yet it provides devastating social criticism. Silent, watchful, and listening, Agee acts the role of the decent journalist by dramatizing and satirizing the realities of the color line and its consequences. As readers we are meant to react with disgust to a lewd and provocative landowner who casually exerts his power over black men in his employment. The moment captured in this passage ends satisfactorily with the landowner shown up as the embodiment of crudity.

But what begins as critique at arm's length moves directly toward the decent journalist who has won a reader's respect for his mockery of a landowner's foibles. Journalist or not, Agee cannot jump out of his white skin, and his position at the landowners' side is not a detail gone unnoticed by the black tenant farmers. A group of men are "summoned to sing for Walker and for me, to show us what nigger music is like" (28). Agee has not wanted this to happen, but he feels that there is nothing he can do to prevent it. The men sing three songs. The vignette ends with Agee, "in a perversion of self-torture," tipping the leader of the group for the singing:

> I gave their leader fifty cents, trying at the same time, through my eyes, to communicate much more, and said I was sorry we had held them up and that I hoped they would not be late; and he thanked me for them in a dead voice, not looking me in the eye, and they went away, putting their white hats on their heads as they walked into the sunlight. (31)

These blacks cannot know who Agee is or what he believes. The journalist may wish to be understood as a most decent and concerned man who opposes white supremacist attitudes. But Agee does not, or cannot, explain himself within this context and so his "real" intentions go unspoken, unrecognized. More importantly, his intentions are rendered irrelevant, since the color of his skin determines his participation in a brutal hierarchy. In the other two vignettes as well, Agee exposes himself as ignorant, insensitive, and finally, deeply and helplessly aware of his own complicity in injustice, humiliation, and fear.[23]

Three times Agee engages the social environment of the Deep South, and three times he is shown up and confused by what he finds in it and in himself. As the listener within the text, Agee serves as our ears and eyes onto a scene we would otherwise never know. It would be most convenient (and more conventional) to trust our tour guide, and yet what is communicated with these vignettes are the failures of the well-intentioned journalist. What Agee does is not only embarrassing; it has consequences.

That *Famous Men* conveys Agee's failures creates problems of reader identification. Left in the text, Agee's self-indictments suggest that we proceed with caution, placing narrowed limits on the judgment, reliability, and authority of the author. Indeed, similar instances in which the frame is critically reversed onto Agee recur in *Famous Men*. Self-doubt pervades the book. The text obsesses over its own failures and inadequacies. For example:

> George Gudger is a man, et cetera. But obviously, in the effort to tell of him (by example) as truthfully as I can, I am limited. I know him only so far as I know him, and only in those terms in which I know him; and all of that depends as fully on who I am as on who he is. (239)

Such moments do not reconfirm the documentarian's own purposefulness and skill, nor do they stress the "knowability" of the dispossessed persons under examination. Rather, the heightened and highlighted subjectivity calls into question to what extent any documentary is capable of objectivity.

As part of this self-indicting interrogation, and as further contrast with more conventional thirties documentary expressions, *Famous Men* restlessly moves between multiple points of view. First-, second-, and third-person passages are juxtaposed throughout the book, with one perspective held for dozens of pages or less than a paragraph. These shiftings of address serve as signposts that remind the reader that what is being read is only a book, even as the text emphasizes that that same reader "should so far as possible forget that this is a book" (246). Inconsistent and contradictory? Perhaps. And yet in a fashion not dissimilar to *Facing the Chair*, *Famous Men*'s multiple versions of the "real" do not eliminate a concern for truth; rather, their inclusion foregrounds how quickly documentary's conventions can persuade readers to accept representations as real and neglect to search for the actual reality. At all points Agee's text insists on a concern for the original and actual from which these flawed and "somewhat inaccurate" words have been derived (328).

Most pervasively, the text repeatedly addresses itself to the tenants who are its subject:

> How am I to speak of you as "tenant" "farmers", as "representatives" of your "class", as social integers in a criminal economy, or

as individuals, fathers, wives, sons, daughters, and as my friends
and as I "know" you? (100)

This use of the second-person "you" and "your," which often
replace the more journalistically common third-person "them"
and "their," serves two significant purposes. First, it places the
reader outside a dialogue between author and subject. In other
words, it again highlights the problems of identification within
the documentary text, while at the same time the quotation marks
call into question any simple assumptions about generalized categories (like "tenant" or "farmer") as subjects of documentary
investigation. Second, a restlessly shifting point of view that settles into second-person plural in passages like this one immediately undermines the seeming purpose of documentary expression, which is to convey a reliably accurate "truth." But the
lesson here again is that a true objectivity must incorporate subjectivity; in fact, the boundaries between subjects and objects
must be blurred in documentary or else the perspective of the
writing will erase part of what is really there: the documentarian
who influences and participates in the reality he or she has been
assigned to document.

Less often, but significantly, the address becomes coolly de-
tached; it is a third-person voice, one that so excessively employs
the passive construction as to slow what might otherwise have
been an ordinary documentary description into a virtually mind-
numbing stasis. The lengthy section "Shelter" provides one extensive example of this strategy. The elimination of human
agency in passages such as the following is typical:

> The room is a little small for comfort, and here, as is unnecessary
> in the other rooms, everything that can be is blocked back hard
> against the wall. There are no chairs on the wall side of the table,
> but a long and quite narrow bench, close against the wall, and the
> table is brought up close against it so that the children have to
> climb to their places with a fair amount of difficulty: and in spite
> of this economizing, the table juts out beyond the hall door, the
> chairs along that side a little more, and when everyone is seated
> the room is pretty nearly blocked. The chair at the foot is crowded
> in close, too, for there is just enough room between the hall door
> and the storeroom door. (178)

Agee's language frustrates an emotional catharsis; once again, through the relentless accumulation of details, reader identification is thwarted. There is no instruction to feel pity, remorse, or guilt; there is no instruction to feel anything at all. We are abandoned by the text, which might not be so bad if we do not so casually expect documentary to attend more closely to our responses. Instead, we probably feel rather little or nothing, or only boredom; for "Shelter" is a long-drawn-out way of making a simple argument against documentary's "law of averages" strategy through an excruciating attention to the minutest aspects of one individual tenant home. In the process, an "average" reader's level of interest is summarily ignored.

Paradoxically, such a careful reaction against a reader's anticipated concerns reflects an intense awareness of audience. Indeed, *Famous Men* addresses itself directly and repeatedly at those who sit outside its margins: its readers. The desired effect is to "reform" that reading individual into an imagined and perfect reader, one who would be as serious about this text as the fallible man who wrote it. Intermittently, the text provides us with instruction on how to improve our understanding of what it is trying to tell. If we feel neglected in "Shelter," there are several other moments when the text, full of lessons to be learned, provokes us to become more immediately engaged in what it describes. For example, here Agee suggests an exercise so that we can better understand the painfully repetitive motion of picking cotton:

> I suggest that if you will try, three hundred times in succession, the following exercise: touch all five fingertips as closely as possible into one point, trying meanwhile to hold loose cotton in the palm of the hand: you will see that this can very quickly tire, cramp and deteriorate the whole instrument, and will understand how easily rheumatism can take up its strictures in just this place. (339)

As with the loudspeaker episode, Agee asks us to experience real pain if we really want to understand the subject of the book. It is an address of earnest mockery laced with traces of hostility – insisting that we should do what he has asked us to do, but also knowing that we won't. Mocking, hostile, indifferent, ironic – Agee is seldom anything but earnest, for the text never once applauds or congratulates its readers for simply reading it; there is a deeply troubling reality out there that reading alone cannot change.

Like Dos Passos's, Agee's torment in writing about the real stems from the awareness that writing only matters if it "re-forms" a reader's consciousness. But how is this to be done? It demands new ways of listening, new ways of writing, but it always remains a political question without definitive aesthetic solutions. Of one tenant woman's struggling existence, Agee states the dilemma this way:

> And how is this to be made so real to you who read of it, that it will stand and stay in you as the deepest and most iron anguish and guilt of your existence that you are what you are, and that she is what she is, and that you cannot for one moment exchange places with her, nor by any such hope make expiation for what she has suffered at your hands, and for what you have gained at hers[?] (321)

This question leads Agee not only toward the strategy of shifting points of view, but also toward efforts that represent tenant speech in the context of a complex relationship between living subject, living writer, and living reader. Sometimes tenant speech is embedded into much longer descriptive passages. Sometimes it is left outside of quotation marks or so briefly recorded that it resembles the quick jottings by the reporter in his notebook. In those few instances when tenant speech is recorded at greater length, it becomes a more highly stylized representation. Coming across three tenant children while driving his car, for example, Agee records his conversation with them this way:

> For a second I was unable to say anything, and just looked back at them. Then I said, taking care to say it to all three, Is your Daddy around? They said nawsuh he was still to meetnen so was Mama but ParlLee was yer they would git her fer me. I told them, No, thanks, I didn't want to make any bother because I couldn't stay any time today; I just wanted to ask their Daddy would he tell me where Mr. George Gudger lived. They said he didn' live fur, he lived jist a piece down over the heel I could walk it easy. Not wanting to leave the car here to have to come back for, I asked if I could be sure of the path. They told me, You go awn daown the heel twhur Tip Foster's haouse is ncut in thew his barn nfoller the foot paff awn aout thew the corn tell ye come to a woods, take the

one awn the right nanexunawn a liyuf nye come aout at the high
een un a cotton patch, cut awn thew the cotton patch, you'll see
the foot paff, ngo awn daown na heeln he's rat thur, the only
haouse. (386–7)

This spoken language is exoticized, but it is also detailed and
clear, once one has grasped the way Agee represents the idiom. It
is as extreme an attempt as *Famous Men* makes to capture empiri-
cally the speaking voice of Alabaman tenants; it is also a passage
that perhaps most fits a reader's expectations and presumptions
concerning such tenant speech.

But Agee undercuts any absolute stereotyping of tenant speech
inherent in moments like this one in various ways. First, as the
listener in the text, he writes his own responses into the text,
careful to ethnographize those responses as fully as he does the
responses of those he has been assigned to "study." The use of
dizzying prose, certain to slow even readers who thought they
could decipher the most unusual of southern dialects, also makes
a point: It reverses the convention that "educated" people can
grasp more than others can. Here it is so-called semiliterate children who understand and the Harvard graduate who gets confused. The already mentioned "July 1936" vignettes are further
examples of this strategy. Most vividly, though, the strategy of
self-ethnographizing his own voice is employed by Agee in "A
Country Letter," specifically in the section that discusses Emma,
the young woman who must leave home and live with her husband who has moved to Mississippi in search of a job. "I am fond
of Emma, and very sorry for her," Agee writes (59). We soon
learn that this feeling is at least partially mutual.

The day she leaves, there is a dialogue between Emma and
Agee that illustrates how Agee uses speech to undercut his own
legitimacy while foregrounding the superior ability of a tenant to
listen and articulate. Alone with Agee, Emma speaks first:

> She spoke in that same way, too, not wasting any roundabout time
> or waiting for an appropriate rhythm, yet not in haste, looking me
> steadily and sweetly in the eyes, and said, I want you and Mr.
> Walker to know how much we all like you, because you make us
> feel easy with you; we don't have to act any different from what it
> comes natural to act, and we don't have to worry what you're
> thinking about us, it's just like you was our own people and had

always lived here with us, you all are so kind, and nice, and quiet, and easygoing, and we wisht you wasn't never going to go away but stay on here with us, and I just want to tell you how much we all keer about you; Annie Mae says the same, and you please tell Mr. Walker, too, if I don't see him afore I go. (64)

The self-congratulatory aspect of including this speech is not permitted to linger for long. Agee is too quick to respond to Emma with a speech of his own, almost twice as long as hers, and a trifle patronizing: "I went on to say that whatever might happen to her or that she might do in all her life I wished her the best luck anyone could think of, and not ever to forget it, that nobody has a right to be unhappy, or to live in a way that makes them unhappy" (66). But it is Emma who gets the last word in, for once Agee stops speaking, she says "that she sure did wish me the same" (66). Agee places himself into the text – again, it is perhaps the strategy most frequently used in *Famous Men* – but he is not the only listener in the text. Emma listens too and, by the poignant irony of her response, actually proves herself a better listener than the professional journalist. Since listening became a privileged activity in the documentary genre, Agee's strategy reverses that privilege away from the one to whom it most typically belongs.

A second way in which Agee undercuts the potential stereotyping of tenant speech is through the use of a highly stylized and self-conscious representation, a strategy that calls attention to the deliberate artificiality of the text. For example, in a dialogue between Agee and George Gudger, a tenant farmer, the author is shown the room where he will spend the night:

All right in year hain't you? – Ah, sure, fine. Sure am. – Annie Mae told me to say, she's sorry she ain't got no clean sheet, but just have to *(oh, no!)* make out best way you can. – Oh, no. No. You tell her I certainly do thank her, but, no, I'll be fine like this, *fine* like this – She just don't got none tell she does a warshin. – Sure; sure; I wouldn't want to dirty up a clean sheet for you, one night. Thanks a lot. Door, right head a yer bed, if you want to git out. I look, and nod:
  Yeah; thanks.
  Night:
  Night:
  The door draws shut. (419–20)

In order to set the dialect of the tenant farmer against the "more proper" speaking of the New York journalist, the text's near-obsessive usage of punctuation and italics calls attention to the fact that this is a *representation,* not the real conversation. Everything but quotation marks are placed into this passage, as if quotation marks might be the one punctuation that is inappropriate. This stylization resists an easy consumption of tenant speech.

A third strategy for representing speech in *Famous Men* involves the sarcastic use of "educated" voices speaking flawless and non-idiomatic English. In one instance, the text represents the authoritative speech of reform-spirited individuals presuming to define the realities of farm tenancy. For example, when Agee quotes President Roosevelt (*"You are farmers; I am a farmer myself";* 115), Agee's ridicule is implicit. He later further mocks this self-assured identification with the poverty-stricken tenant farmers by countering with a nonassured self-identification: "Who the hell am I . . . who the hell am I, who in Jesus' name am I" (384–5).

In another instance, when the text documents a dozen voices of anonymous local townspeople, all of whom are responding to a question about the three tenant farmers Agee has chosen for his study, Agee's contempt is equally barbed. Represented in standard English so as to "sound" most like the idiom of the text's *readers* and the idiom of educated Americans everywhere, these quotes of townspeople indicate the discursive hole into which the tenants have been thrown and in which they feel themselves inextricably caught:

> George Gudger? Where'd you dig *him* up? I haven't been back out that road in twenty-five year.
>
> Fred Ricketts? Why, that dirty son-of-a-bitch, he *brags* that he hasn't bought his family a bar of soap in five year.
>
> Ricketts? They're a bad lot . . .
>
> Give them money and all they'll do with it is throw it away.
>
> Why, times when I envy them. No risk, we take all the risk; all the clothes they need to cover them; food coming up right out of their land.
>
> So you're staying out at Gudgers', are you? And how do you like the food they give you? Yeah, aheh-heh-heh-heh, how do you like that fine home cookin'; how do you like that good wholesome country food? (79–80)

The dependence of tenants on landlords and local townspeople for food, clothing, shelter, and all other essentials for living translates into an ability to speak with impunity and authoritative disrespect about the tenants as less than fully human. Rendered (falsely) in standard English, these arrogant judgments are seriously out of line with what is documented by the rest of *Famous Men;* the erroneous usage of nonidiomatic English reinforces the falsehoods these people speak so smoothly. Furthermore, this usage of nonidiomatic English doubly echoes the more subtle but equally debilitating speech by Roosevelt. Put bluntly, all the cruel liars and ignorant rhetoricians speak alike in *Famous Men* – and they all speak like "us."

Finally, there is in *Famous Men* a fourth strategy for resisting the conventionalizing and stereotyping tendencies of the documentary genre: the use of broad inconsistencies in the ways tenant speech is represented. Agee was particularly troubled by the way – though "it happens to be accurate" – "the tenants' idiom has been used ad nauseam by the more unspeakable of the northern journalists" (340). Thus, in *Famous Men,* Agee varies his approach. At one point, a tenant farmer speaks in a thick Alabaman dialect; at another point the same man speaks in a standard English voice. Likewise, a landlord's speech may or may not be represented in deep southern dialect. At times this use of dialect can highlight an individual's common sense and savvy, yet in at least one instance – it is a landlord speaking – dialect's usage heightens an appearance of ignorance and bigotry. (The quote reads: "I don't object to nigrah education, not up through foath a fift grade maybe, but not furdern dat: I'm too strong a believah in white syewpremcy") (297–8). At all points Agee speaks in a standard English, but as mentioned before, the dialect-speaking Alabamans can understand each other much better than can a more correct-sounding and educated reporter in their midst. In this fashion, dialect and speech can at various moments highlight the radical otherness of the tenants, their landlords, and the world they inhabit, or it can foreground *Agee's* otherness – due to the problematic "advantages" provided by literacy and education – in relationship to them. An inconsistent usage of dialect and standard English in the representation of speech also calls attention to the impossibility of "capturing" original speech in any absolute way. Here then, just as in *Facing the Chair,* proliferating versions of "reality" encourage readers to make an effort to reconstruct, imagine, and seek an original that exists, but has not and cannot be reproduced or fully represented in writing.

Agee considered the tenants' voices a crucial element of *Famous Men,* and the text frequently returns to the question of how to account for speech's significance and originality in a written form that conventionally negates both. Obedience to the laws of documentary writing (and all rules of writing) would be out of the question: Agee's text is ungrammatical, syntactically bizarre, and deliberately inconsistent and obscure. Against the tendency of most documentaries to direct attention away from original voices and actual lives, Agee's text argues that documenting real lives (and actual voices) in writing is like a multiply bracketed question mark –

$$(\qquad (?) \qquad) \qquad :)$$

– a central and unknowable reality imprisoned by signs (81).

In sum, each and every one of Agee's strategies and efforts are directed toward expressing and exploring the inadequacy of documentary writing in the face of the incommunicability of lived suffering, beauty, grace, and defiance. *Famous Men* contends that documentarians have to recognize this dilemma first and foremost, tormenting themselves and their readers with it and, in this way, shaking the foundations of a genre that often lies when it says it is committed to telling the truth.

WILLIAM STOTT'S seminal study, *Documentary Expression and Thirties America,* concludes that the thirties' most characteristic genre became largely a didactic tool for raising social consciousness and did not produce much of lasting literary value. However, in blaming the genre's failure on its didacticism, the central dilemma documentarians faced is skirted: that the generally apolitical modernists who opposed the methods of social realism and naturalism, and who negated language's capacity fully to represent reality, had accurately identified documentary's inherent failings. It was not political intention that caused documentary to fail, but its self-definition. Documentary, whose entire defense as a genre depended on its claim to represent the real, was, in effect, collapsing from the very first.

While it is true, as numerous critics have argued, that many thirties documentaries can be explained (and dismissed) as products of a divided age when sense, intellect, and reflection were too quickly sacrificed for short-lived ideological concerns, there is considerable evidence of an important (and neglected) middle ground. Writers like Dos Passos and Agee, as well as the others discussed in the chapters that follow, stood in a place of tension between the didacts and the aesthetes and have, largely as a consequence of their position, been misconstrued and misunderstood. In an age whose most characteristic approach to writing was documentary, here were writers that sought "to teach" (as the Latin root of "document" suggests) new ways of listening to the speech of the categorically silenced in America, even as they experimented with new ways of writing about them. By writing themselves as flawed listeners into the text, by constructing non-linear narratives that attacked documentary form in serious parody, and by devising a host of strategies for representing speech in all its variations, this group of writers struggled against conventional language and structures that did not do enough to implicate an audience, as Agee put it, "actuated toward this reading by various possible reflexes of sympathy, curiosity, idleness, et cetera, and almost certainly in a lack of consciousness, and conscience, remotely appropriate to the enormity of what they are doing" (13). Above all, both Dos Passos and Agee worked to provoke readers to listen closely and discerningly to all representations, so that they might learn to distinguish between false and true authority, and to care about the difference.

3

John Neihardt, William Benson, and Ruth Underhill: Telling Native American History

THIS CHAPTER examines how three ethnographies from the 1930s wrote Native American speech: John G. Neihardt's *Black Elk Speaks* (1932), William Ralganal Benson's "The Stone and Kelsey 'Massacre' " (1932), and Ruth M. Underhill's *The Autobiography of a Papago Woman* (1936). Each text sought to reconstruct in writing its subjects' oral remembrances of nineteenth-century Native American realities. My aim in focusing attention on thirties ethnography is threefold: to continue to re-think the much-maligned "political literature" so prevalent in the 1930s, to correct a generalized misperception about the lack of critical awareness in older ethnography, and to contribute to on-going debates about ethnographic strategy.[1]

One of the peculiarities of these three early ethnographies is that despite the critical acclaim each of the three texts has received, other critics have asserted that they are not faithful or authentic representations of Native American history, culture, and speech. *Black Elk Speaks* has received especially harsh commentary; there are suggestions that the text is more white than Indian, more fraudulent than factual account. Although commentary on Benson's account is limited, accusations focus on the ways Benson misconstrues the historical dimensions of the events he recounts. The criticism against Underhill also cites her misrepresentations of her subject's speech. According to the critics, Underhill editorializes more than she records this Papago woman's life story. In sum, these criticisms are merely a small part of more general attacks on the authenticity of thirties oral texts produced as a result of cross-cultural collaboration.[2]

I want to argue that these sweeping attacks miss the point. As I hope to show through a close reading of each of these ethnographic narratives, the fictiveness and partiality of all ethnographic writing were already a clear concern for several American writers engaged in fieldwork during the thirties. All three texts give evidence of serious engagement with precisely the questions about power relations between writer and subject and the difficulties of representing speech in text that so exercise theorists of ethnography today. Indeed, I believe it is precisely their cross-cultural process for recording oral memories and their interest in experimenting with narrative strategy that allowed these writers to defy the conventions of their era. In addition, a close analysis of these documents reveals the telling differences between Indian and white versions of history. How the three writers tried, through the structure of their texts and the narrative strategies they employed, to address the contested nature of historical truth, is a point I will return to repeatedly. Their writings may not have been considered "political" in their day, but their efforts at analyzing race bias and the problematic power of written (over oral) representations predate current cultural anthropology's attention to such issues by many decades.

JOHN G. NEIHARDT met Nicholas Black Elk for the first time in August 1930 on the Pine Ridge Sioux Reservation. Neihardt was in South Dakota researching a narrative poem about the rise of the Ghost Dance Movement of the late 1880s and the massacre at Wounded Knee. Black Elk was a man who had participated in the "Messiah craze" of the Ghost Dances and who had fought at Wounded Knee. Returning in the spring of 1931, Neihardt spoke with Black Elk for three weeks. With Black Elk's son Benjamin acting as translator and Neihardt's daughter Enid acting as stenographer, the transcription process proceeded slowly. However, once he began writing, Neihardt finished *Black Elk Speaks: Being the Life Story of a Holy Man of the Oglala Sioux as Told Through John G. Neihardt* by October 1931, and it was published early the next year.[3] The book was soon out of print; it was the early 1970s before *Black Elk Speaks* "exploded into surprising popularity."[4]

To this day, *Black Elk Speaks* is one of the most popular and often studied American Indian narratives, yet there remain significant critical disagreements over its interpretation. In his introduction to the most recent (1979) edition, Vine Deloria writes that "present debates center on the question of Neihardt's literary intrusions into Black Elk's system of beliefs." Deloria continues: "Can it matter? The very nature of great religious teachings is that they encompass everyone who understands them and personalities become indistinguishable from the transcendent truth that is expressed. So let it be with *Black Elk Speaks*" (xiv). Several critics over the years have concurred with Deloria's affirmation of the book's greatness.[5]

More recently, however, there has been a strongly stated challenge to these laudatory assessments. Arnold Krupat wrote in 1985: "In opting for ignorance, Deloria, like all those who would prefer not to inquire, chooses the status quo: accepting *Black Elk Speaks* with no questions asked, Deloria accepts John Neihardt's version of and prescription for the Native American future."[6] According to Krupat, "Even had Neihardt somehow been willing and able to grasp and to credit the continuous nature of Black Elk's revivalistic efforts," that is, efforts to renew the Lakota traditional religion, "he could not have structurally represented them in narrative," both because "Neihardt seems to have had no interest whatever in formal experimentation" and because "Western narrative has no convention for the representation of the ongoing and un-ended."[7]

To date, scholars have not made substantive efforts to reconcile these debates. Rather, the focus of critical activity has been on whether *Black Elk Speaks* is faithful or untrustworthy, a "singularly complete account of a holy man's vision, the ceremonies performed in reenacting the vision, and the powers held by the person who had the vision" or "an act of ventriloquism, told not by Black Elk through Neihardt but vice versa."[8] The literary reputation of *Black Elk Speaks* has been seriously and directly diminished by such debates.[9] Thus, the position of Krupat (and others) – that Neihardt misrepresented Black Elk's words and that, in any event, there are no narrative conventions or structures to represent those spoken words accurately – demands examination. If the text is a failure (or a fraud), that failure in part originates in the writing process. What Neihardt wrote is not always what Black Elk spoke. The question is not whether this matters, but *how* it matters.

My argument is that *Black Elk Speaks* acknowledges that speech *cannot* be fully represented in a written text, and thus its "failure" becomes an effective and *necessary* narrative strategy that redirects authority from writing to speech. Rather than assert its superiority over oral tradition, the act of writing that foregrounds its own incompleteness affirms that oral tradition. Viewed from this perspective, the "failure" of *Black Elk Speaks* yields new interpretations.

Black Elk Speaks is a miswritten narrative, one that does not accurately represent the words and ideas of a Native American speaker. This is strikingly evident in the book's famous climactic speech about the massacre at Wounded Knee. The words written by Neihardt were never spoken by Black Elk. Perhaps partially inspired by W. B. Yeats's poem "The Second Coming," the text places eloquent final words into an American Indian's mouth:

> I did not know then how much was ended. When I look back now from this high hill of my old age, I can still see the butchered women and children lying heaped and scattered all along the crooked gulch as plain as when I saw them with eyes still young. And I can see that something else died there in the bloody mud, and was buried in the blizzard. A people's dream died there. It was a beautiful dream . . . for the nation's hoop is broken and scattered. There is no center any longer, and the sacred tree is dead. (270)

These words demonstrate that Neihardt, unlike Black Elk, believed that the Lakota religion had lost its power to save the Sioux people. In his essay on the theology of *Black Elk Speaks,* Clyde Holler observed that while "Neihardt created a genuine literary work of art," his "literary reshaping of the Black Elk interviews . . . sacrificed strict reporting of Black Elk's theological convictions in order to express his own." Specifically, Holler argued that "Neihardt found it possible to accept that Black Elk possessed supernormal power, but he found it impossible to accept that Black Elk's rituals had power, for the relational meaning of ritual, and its transforming power, was largely lost on Neihardt."[10]

While this criticism is serious and legitimate, *Black Elk Speaks* does continually attempt to communicate one crucial aspect of Black Elk's religious understanding: the sacred qualities inherent in speech.[11] As an oral narrative, the methods of *Black Elk Speaks* "reinvent," in the English language, some representation for the sacred qualities attributed to Lakota utterance.[12] *Black Elk Speaks* introduces this concern in its opening pages with a story about the peace pipe and its origins, a legend that is ultimately about the nature of truth. When two scouts encounter a sacred woman, one foolishly thinks impure thoughts about her and is transformed into a skeleton covered with worms. The other scout does as the woman requests; he returns to his village and gathers his people together to await her arrival. When she arrives, she sings a song.

This is the first poem in *Black Elk Speaks,* and it can be read as an allegory for the spiritual power inherent in utterance:

> With visible breath I am walking.
> A voice I am sending as I walk.
> In a sacred manner I am walking.
> With visible tracks I am walking.
> In a sacred manner I walk.[13]

This legend has been rearranged from the midst of the steno-graphic transcript to the published manuscript's beginning and thus suggests miswriting.[14] Yet this opening prayer also expresses the hope that the text's "visible tracks" will be faithful to the sacred "voice" of the Lakota Sioux oral tradition. For the Lakota, as for many Native American peoples, breath is life, and as Paula Gunn Allen has declared, "The intermingling of breaths is the purpose of good living."[15] Sending a voice, or telling the stories of one's people, is, as Simon Ortiz said, "the way we create the world."[16] Black Elk's prayer sanctifies the imperfect transforma-tion of evaporating oral traditions into a permanent written form that will document his memories of the living world. By opening with this poem, Neihardt underscores that visible text is not sacred speech, nor should it pretend to be. Rather than "take possession" of spoken memories, then, *Black Elk Speaks* directs attention to the primary authority of the Lakota Sioux speakers.

The story continues as the sacred woman gives a peace pipe to the Sioux chief and says, "Nothing but good shall come from it" (4). The text reads, "This they tell, and whether it happened so or not I do not know; but if you think about it, you can see that it is true" (5). This opening tale illustrates that faith in spirit creates truth. It suggests that faith *is* truth, and it challenges Western "secular" convention that truth resides only where objective (or rational) explanations are offered. It also suggests that after an experience passes into history, spoken recountings are themselves original. Speech becomes an original act that (re)creates truth, belief, and history. Thus, the reproduction of speech in text is neither accurate nor inaccurate; writing's relationship to speech is, in all events, a secondary one. It is from speech that power comes.

Black Elk Speaks repeatedly refers to itself as a text centered around an oral culture's dilemma when it is confronted by writing. This process inescapably involves loss of meaning, change in language, and the potential for misunderstanding and misstatement. Miswriting – or the failure to communicate the "whole" of an experience or memory – rather than misrepresentation – the document's insistence on its own capacity to reflect reality completely – provides *Black Elk Speaks* with the techniques to represent the necessarily flawed bridge between spoken word and written text. Whereas one critic finds Neihardt's own admission that he invented sections of *Black Elk Speaks* both "devastating" and "especially ironic," it is neither.[17] That some memory must be lost through writing, rather than that all should be lost through silence, is a major theme of *Black Elk Speaks*. On the one hand, the text articulates a conviction that the writing is truthful: "If you will read again what is written, you will see how it was" (205). Yet the text also recognizes that writing erases the power of oral tradition: "It has made me very sad to do this at last . . . But I think I have done right to save the vision in this way" (205–6). Thus, the text dramatizes this oppositional tension between two choices available to an oral rememberer: partial preservation or total loss.

References to the writing process play repeatedly on the *differences* between the original speech act and its representation in narrative. For example, the text refers to "where we are now" (181) and how "we looked toward where you are always facing (the south)" (191). Or concerning Black Elk's vision, the text reads: "I had never told any one all of it, and even until now nobody ever heard it all. Even my old friend, Standing Bear, and my son here have heard it now for the first time when I have told it to you" (205). When Black Elk discusses a bullet wound received in battle, the listener sees what the reader cannot: "I will show you where the bullet struck me sidewise across the belly here (showing a deep scar on the abdomen)" (266). That "we" are blind to what "you" can see illustrates the disjunction between the activities of listening and reading. These references to a "present" place and time, while a specific "you" sits with a specific "I" who speaks words never uttered before, highlight the singularity and originality of a speech event and the inevitable reduction that occurs through writing. Furthermore, passages that acknowledge that there is a listener present underscore the text's dialogic and inevitably filtered process of construction.

In this way, *Black Elk Speaks* represents the dual processes through which a memory of a people's history and a history of an individual's memory are always in tension, just as the tragic evaporation of oral culture and the flawed solidification of written memory are in tension. Structurally, these tensions are represented in the text through an equally unresolved opposition between linear (or tragic) and circular (or revivalist) movement. Michael Castro has written that *Black Elk Speaks* "is tragedy in the greatest sense − a moving human story of declining fortune and ultimate fall from power" as Black Elk tells the losing struggles of his people for control over their lands.[18] On the other hand, Paul Olson has stressed that the movement of *Black Elk Speaks* is an effort "to bring into history the ritualistic forces that will stop history itself as the white man has shaped it and restore to the Sioux people the old ritualistic and cyclical year which gave them their strength."[19] Although scholars tend to choose one of these two interpretations of the text's movement, both are present.

From its early pages, *Black Elk Speaks* recounts the steady encroachment of white settlers into Sioux territory. Black Elk's childhood is characterized by fear, famine, and bloodshed. The text's trajectory from freedom to subjugation is directly linked to the Indians' loss of their "Mother Earth" (6) and their dispossession onto "little islands" (9), or reservations. It is precisely this loss of Sioux land that apparently prompts Black Elk to teach a non-Indian so that his memories will be more widely disseminated. But the text does not promote a solely tragic version of history.

There are attempts at revivalist and circular movements in *Black Elk Speaks* as well, especially in the entire frame of the narrative that suggests its beginning in its end. For example, the text's introduction and postscript circle back to the "present" moment. It is also significant that on the book's final page, Black Elk performs a ceremony that calls for rain. Calling for rain is a traditional revivalist ritual that indicates Black Elk's continued commitment to the old ways. Although the text states that "what happened is, of course, related to Wasichu readers as being merely a more or less striking coincidence," it does begin drizzling (271). There are further passages that represent how circular movement contains the Sioux spirit and power, qualities again linked to the land:

> You have noticed that everything an Indian does is in a circle, and that is because the Power of the World always works in circles, and everything tries to be round. In the old days when we were a strong and happy people, all our power came to us from the sacred hoop of the nation, and so long as the hoop was unbroken, the people flourished . . . Our tepees were round like the nests of birds, and these were always set in a circle, the nation's hoop, a nest of many nests, where the Great Spirit meant for us to hatch our children.

Black Elk continues: "But the Wasichus have put us in these square boxes. Our power is gone and we are dying, for the power is not in us any more" (194–6). Thus, the narrative returns to a tragic line, deriving its climactic conclusion from events at Wounded Knee in December 1890, the most devastating of Sioux historical memories.

Looking backward, what *Black Elk Speaks* encapsulates is a straight arrow moving toward loss, suffering, and a failed vision. Yet the text also represents an attempt to communicate what has been sustaining and redemptive about the traditional ways. Most specifically, its "story of all life that is holy and is good to tell" includes a vision of interracial cooperation that directly challenges all differences derived from skin color (1). Despite the horrors perpetrated by whites on the Indians, *Black Elk Speaks* does not categorically condemn white people. The term used is always "Wasichu," those people who "would sell their Mother Earth" (135), put the Indians in "square boxes" (196), and sell "the yellow metal" that "they worship and that makes them crazy" (9). It is not a racial or ethnic distinction, but "a term used to designate the white man, but having no reference to the color of his skin" (8). Therefore, the text can refer to the "black Wasichu" (104) who fought with the U.S. Cavalry and to an Indian who could "make himself over into a Wasichu" (141). Race, then, is itself represented as a construction of the Wasichu imagination; real differences between peoples lie elsewhere. These differences are actually based on an attitude toward the earth, toward life, and, perhaps most significant here, toward speech.

The contrast between the sacred power of utterance and the "forked tongue" (214) of Wasichu speech (and the relationship of both to written expression) forms one unifying theme for *Black Elk Speaks*. What almost destroys the Sioux people is their innocent acceptance of the promises made by "the gnawing flood of the Wasichu" who were "dirty with lies and greed" (9). One characteristic passage reads: "The Wasichus had slaughtered all the bison and shut us up in pens. It looked as though we might all starve to death. We could not eat lies" (230). In Black Elk's view, a Wasichu is one who deliberately defiles the sacredness of utterance and thus deceives others for selfish advancement. In the final analysis, *Black Elk Speaks* proposes that the Siouxs' (ultimately naive) faith that all humans use speech in a sacred manner was the cause of Black Elk's and his people's systematic dispossession by Wasichu America. This is a tragic history lesson. But by its insistence on characterizing the differences between people in terms of ethics rather than race, *Black Elk Speaks,* in effect, revives yet another sustaining piece of Black Elk's vision.

"It was my function to translate the old man's story, not only in the factual sense – for it was not the facts that mattered most – but rather to re-create in English the mood and manner of the old man's narrative."[20] So Neihardt introduced the 1972 edition of *Black Elk Speaks.* He thereby confirmed again how much *Black Elk Speaks* was a product of the thirties, both in its method of interviewing and in its aim of preserving the stories of the dispossessed. Simultaneously, Neihardt's statement demonstrates how deliberate his "miswritings" of Black Elk's words were, while insisting upon his faithfulness to the spirit of Black Elk. The text reveals that faithfulness particularly in its analysis of race bias and its self-reflexive undermining of literate cultures' authority over oral traditions. Furthermore, *Black Elk Speaks* defied the tendency of nearly all political camps in the thirties to patronize the lives of dispossessed subjects. For these reasons, Neihardt and Black Elk's collaboration also transcends its time and speaks to ongoing political and cultural concerns.

WILLIAM RALGANAL BENSON was the child of Addison Benson, a "squaw man," that is, a Gold Rush settler who married an Indian woman and lived with his wife's tribe. Benson married into the Pomo tribe, which lived in Lake County on the shores of Clear Lake, about one hundred miles north of San Francisco, and his son William Ralganal was born around 1863. A few years later the father died, and as a result, his mixed-blood son grew up speaking mainly the Pomo language, while "his knowledge of English was picked up almost entirely by ear."[21] Nevertheless, as an adult, Benson's bilingual and bicultural abilities proved invaluable to any number of ethnographers and anthropologists who traveled to Lake County to research Indian culture and society. For Alfred L. Kroeber, Stephen M. Barrett, and others, Benson served as interpreter and informant, a service that at least in one instance earned him coauthorship for an article on the Pomo Indian's creation myth.[22] The only known example of Benson's own writing is "The Stone and Kelsey 'Massacre' on the Shores of Clear Lake in 1849 – The Indian Viewpoint." It first appeared in the *California Historical Society Quarterly* in 1932 and was not reprinted for fifty-five years.[23]

This short text depicted a trauma that had been documented in white history books, but never before by those Indians who survived. In order to prepare the narrative, Benson interviewed several elderly Pomo men and women about the Gold Rush days of 1849, eighty years earlier, and specifically about the murder of two white men, Stone and Kelsey, by a group of Pomo Indians. Stone and Kelsey were gold prospectors who had used the Indians as virtual slaves; they starved and whipped them. This treatment led to the murders of Stone and Kelsey by the Pomo, which were followed (a year later) by a reprisal attack on the Pomo by white soldiers outraged by the "massacre." The bloodshed left a deep and unhealed wound on the Pomo people. It was this series of memories, told expressly from the Pomo perspective, that emerged so vividly from Benson's narrative.

The narrative has received almost no attention from literary critics and other scholars in part because it is not easily classifiable. Scholars such as David Brumble, Gretchen Bataille, Kathleen Sands, and Hertha Wong have devoted extensive attention to early Native American autobiography, or what Arnold Krupat named "original bicultural composite composition."[24] However, there is considerable work to be done in terms of analyzing the "literariness" of Native American oral literature; Brian Swann, for example, argued that "it is about time that we begin to study this literature as seriously as we study Faulkner and Hemingway."[25] It may also be that Benson's narrative eluded careful analysis because it is not autobiography and because it is seemingly "semiliterate"; that is, it disregards grammatical rules of standard English.[26] For example, a representative passage reads:

> about 20 old people died during the winter from starvetion. from severe whipping 4 died. a nephew of an indian lady who were lieving with stone was shoot to deth by stone. the mother of this young man was sick and starveing. this sick woman told her son to go over to stones wife or the sick womans sister. tell your aunt that iam starveing and sick tell her that i would like to have a handfull of wheat. the young man lost no time going to stones house. the young man told the aunt what his mother said. the lady then gave the young man 5 cups of wheat and tied it up in her apron and the young man started for the camp. stone came about that time and called the young man back. the young man stoped stone who was horse back. rode up to the young man took the wheat from him and then shoot him. the young man died two days after. (744)

The repetitive usage of words like "starvetion," "starveing," and "sick" sets up the tragic vignette that follows, even as it emphasizes that this particular account could not or would not represent impartiality. What is seen and heard is entirely from "the Indian viewpoint," as the narrative's original subtitle indicates. The devotion of the unnamed young man who listens to his mother and rushes to tell his aunt is evocatively and simply expressed, as are the details of the aunt's responsiveness as she takes the wheat and "tied it up in her apron" for her nephew to carry. Further, Benson's writing of Pomo speech remembered, retold, and translated into English ("tell your aunt that iam starveing and sick tell her that i would like to have a handfull of wheat") recreates something heavily mediated and subjected to the shifting sands of oral remembering, yet it does so in prose that evokes the speaker's presence with a nearly poetic intensity. The white man, Stone, on the other hand, speaks only through the barrel of his gun.

Is the Benson narrative thus hopelessly biased? Is it reliable? Can such a subjective recounting of Native American experience, based entirely on interviews with other Indians many years after the events, be useful in reconstructing history? In fact, far from being a "semiliterate" document, in the customarily demeaning sense of this term, "The Stone and Kelsey 'Massacre' " responds to these important questions by foregrounding its own oral subjectivity and by making an inventive point about the tensions that writing inevitably provokes for a community entirely dependent on preliterate folkways for preserving memory.[27] This foregrounding is accomplished in a number of ways. First, Benson's history of working together with white ethnographers indicates that he could easily have asked any one of them to assist him in presenting "the Indian viewpoint" in standard English. He could have made a similar request of his editors at *California Historical Society Quarterly*. That he did not, that he chose to have the narrative printed in a form uniquely uncharacteristic of written English, reinforces an interpretation that preserving the primacy and immediacy of the speech of those who suffered (and remembered) called for a form of writing unaltered by white collaborators. Whether the editors' lack of intervention reflects their keen sensitivity that these Pomo memories should not be filtered, "cleaned up," or prettified in any way, or whether it indicates their charmed fascination with a picturesque "Red English" text is unknown.[28] But this is less at issue here than the remarkable complexity of Benson's narrative strategies for representing speech, both Indian and white.

The survival of historical memory (despite intervening years) and Benson's struggle to write it down call into question all nonnative representations of Indians that ignore the oral perspectives Benson has collected.[29] The narrative's placement in an academic journal meant its audience was educated, specialized, professional, and overwhelmingly white, a group that routinely delegitimized and subordinated all firsthand oral sources (especially those from "unreliable" Indians with a score to settle) in favor of secondhand written histories.[30] To all such (inherently ethnocentric) hierarchies of knowledge, especially in light of what Benson's informants told him, "The Stone and Kelsey 'Massacre' " is a direct rebuke.

A further strategy for validating the Indian perspective is evident in the narrative's structure. Benson's tale of approximately four thousand words is divided into five paragraphs; the third is the longest, accounting for more than half of the story. Significantly, there is no separate paragraph that discusses only Indian violence toward whites. The one moment of Indian violence is deeply embedded in the context that made it necessary. The editor who first introduced Benson's document suggested that the elderly Pomo Indians Benson interviewed inaccurately fused two separate historical events into one: first the killing of Stone and Kelsey (which took place in the autumn of 1849) and the sadistic reprisal attack by white soldiers (which took place almost a year later in 1850).[31] This "misremembering," which reflects memory's unreliability and ought to undermine the text's worth as historical corrective, occurs in the narrative's instrumental third paragraph. However, precisely this "misremembering" points to a larger truth. After Stone and Kelsey were killed, the text reads: "so the indians lived fat for a while" (746). Then an infantry of white soldiers approaches the Indian village, intent on revenge, and the passage of many months is compressed into a single phrase. While this has been interpreted as the Indians' inaccurate conflation of two distinct historical moments, this is not the case. Rather, what Benson's informants did is properly connect what all "official" accounts made obscure: the suffering they experienced before the "massacre" with the brutality that occurred much later.[32]

The central third paragraph opens with this statement: "the starvetion of the indians was the cause of the massacre of stone and kelsey" (744). The paragraph then devotes considerable space to describing the tribal plan to find a temporary remedy for their hunger. They "hired" two men "name of Shuk and a nother man by the name of Xasis. to kill a beef for them" (744). In order to accomplish this task, the two men steal Stone and Kelsey's horses for a night, hoping to catch an ox and return the horses before daybreak. But the plan goes wrong, they catch no oxen, and one horse gets away. In the middle of the night, tribal leaders convene an emergency meeting to discuss what should be done next:

> Shuk and Xasis wanted to kill stone and kelsey. they said stone and kelsey would kill them as soon as they would find out that the horses was taken with out them known; one man got up and suggested that the tribe give stone and kelsey forty sticks of beades which means 16000 beads or 100 dollars. no one agreed. another man suggested that he or Shuk. tell stoneor kelsey that the horse was stolen. no one agreed, and another man suggested that the other horse should be turned out and tell stone and kelsey both horses were stlen. no one agreed. every thing looks bad for Shuk and Xasis. no one agreed with Shuk and Xasis to kill the two white men. (745)

These written memories document collective voices in past tense ("no one agreed"), narrative commentary in present tense ("every thing looks bad for Shuk and Xasis."), and the likely outcome if no actions are taken in a sort of "future subjunctive" ("stone and kelsey would kill them as soon as they would find out"), awkward shifts that fuse individual memories with an immediacy of intensity sustained over decades into a tribal experience of almost mythic significance. Benson narrates what happened through strategies suggesting events that are both timebound and timeless for these Pomo speakers. This passage also works to "set the record straight" about the Indian people's propensity to violence. It is clear that the majority of the men preferred some form of accommodation or subterfuge to murder.

The text also includes the actual murder of Stone and Kelsey the next morning in this third paragraph, and its recounting provides a remarkable "inner" look at how Benson's informants reconstruct history. Here, for the first time, Stone and Kelsey are represented as speakers, but they speak as remembered by the Pomos who felt driven to kill them. Benson's narrative of Pomo oral remembrances places these white voices within a context that is entirely Pomo in perspective, thus making strange what in any other context (such as an official white narrative history) might seem utterly ordinary:

Stone came out with pot full of fire which was taken from the
fireplace. and said to the indians. whats the matter boys you came
Early this morning. some thing rong; the indians said. O nothing
me hungry thats all. Qka-Nas: or cayote Jim as he was known by
the whites: Qka-Nas said to the men. I thought you men came to
kill this man; give me these arrows and bow. He jerk the bow and
the arrows away from Shuk and drew it and as he did.Stone rose
quickly and turned to Qka-Nas and said what are you trying to do
Jim, and as Stone said it. the indian cut loose. The arrow struck
the victim.pith of the stomach. the victim mediately pull the arrow
out and ran for the house. fighting his way.[33]

Benson's narrative may have been written by a man whose
"knowledge of English was picked up almost entirely by ear,"
but it is not simply "writing by ear." The writing here cannot be
dismissed as primitive. To the contrary, Benson's use of punctuation, for example, which at first appears arbitrary, is, upon reex-
amination, quite deliberate. The periods mark pauses for breath,
the colons suggest parenthetical information, and the semicolons
function approximately as semicolons do in grammatical English.
As Alessandro Portelli observed in another context, when the
spoken is written punctuation marks "hardly ever coincide with
the rhythms and pauses of the speaking subject, and therefore end
up by confining speech within grammatical and logical rules
which it does not necessarily follow."[34] Benson's oral narrative,
by contrast, avoids this dilemma through its blatant dismissal
of grammatical rules; its visual form consequently achieves a
remarkable range of rhythms and expressions.

Perhaps most significantly, Benson's narrative realizes the authoritative tone of the white voice versus the more submissive
speech of the reluctant assassins. The first words Stone speaks
are "whats the matter boys," which patronizes the Indian men.
Furthermore, having previously murdered Pomo Indians in cold
blood and treated those remaining as virtual slaves, Stone knows
that there is "some thing rong" even as he asks as a question what
really is a statement. Whether Stone is genuinely ignorant or
simply playing dumb to the reality before him ("what are you
trying to do Jim"), the spoken record of Stone's last moments
reveals a man hoping to subvert his own murder attempt by the
controlling tone of his speech.

In fact, Benson's narrative reverses all negative characteristics

onto whites, even as it works to "set the record straight" in the
more permanent form and structure of a written text. This same
paragraph continues with an elderly woman's oral memories; it is
"one old lady a(indian)" who "told about what she saw while
hiding under abank," and her speech painfully recollects what
occurred during the attacks by white soldiers. Benson writes:

> She said she saw two white man coming with their guns up in the
> air and on their guns hung a little girl. they brought it to the creek
> and threw it in the water . . . alittle ways from her she, said layed
> awoman shoot through the shoulder. she held her little baby in her
> arms. two white men came running torge the woman and baby,
> they stabed the woman and the baby and, and threw both of them
> over the bank in to the water. she said she heared the woman say,
> O my baby; she said when they gathered the dead, they found all
> the little ones were killed by being stabed, and many of the woman
> were also killed stabing. She said it took them four or five days to
> gather up the dead. (747)

This woman recalls the voice of another woman. The narrative's punctuation has changed since the previous passage, becoming more fluid and rhythmic, and this quotation reads more like
one breathless sentence (note the absence of capital letters). The
focus throughout is on what "she said" to Benson more than
eighty years after the event, and Benson's repetitive use of those
two words alerts the reader to the difficulty *and* necessity of
evoking intense experience through the multilayered reconstruc-
tions of memory, speech, listening, and writing. The paragraph
finally ends with a description of an Indian "tied to atree and
burnt to death" by the sadistic soldiers (747).

After a brief fourth paragraph that continues an account of
the assault, Benson's narrative concludes with three eyewitness
testimonies, each of which is recounted in a style and format
similar to the testimony of the old woman. Unlike the representations of multiple and conflicting voices in the Indian men's night-
long debate and in the scene in which Stone and Kelsey are
murdered, the details of the reprisal attacks on the two Pomo
villages are recounted by individual voices in a way that powerfully brings home the effects of these haunting memories for each
and every Pomo. While many non-native narratives treat Native
Americans as an undifferentiated mass, Benson's account empha-

sizes the significance and uniqueness of each individual's suffering. For example, one old man tells how he and another boy were
taken hostage by the soldiers and forced to march barefoot until
their feet bled. When one of the soldiers noticed the open sores,
he "went to abox opened it took a cup and diped something out
of asack" and then "took ahand full of the stuff and rubed it in
the cuts on the bottom of their feet" (748). The "stuff" was salt.
Such painful humiliations could never be forgotten. And they
never were.

Benson's "The Stone and Kelsey 'Massacre' " and its recovery
of Indian spoken memories in order to correct white accounts of
Pomo history are characteristic of American efforts of the 1930s
to "let the subject's mind speak for itself."[35] Benson's account
does not pretend objectivity. It insists upon an inherent authority
to write Indian speech in an ungrammatical (yet nonetheless eloquent) English, and it self-reflexively meditates on the inevitably
limited capacity of a written record to represent a painful reality.
The uniqueness of this narrative's language and grammar, recre-
ated in writing that is itself an "unnatural" medium for an oral
people whose memories are primarily sustained through speech,
mirrors and comments on the "unnaturalness" of the atrocities
that "The Stone and Kelsey 'Massacre' " documented.[36] The dilemmas with which Benson grappled and the creative solutions
he found both mark his account as a cultural product of the
thirties and also underscore its distinctiveness as a literary document.

PUBLISHED in 1936, *The Autobiography of a Papago Woman,*
an account of Maria Chona's life, was one of Ruth M. Underhill's earliest efforts at documenting Papago life, and it provides a third angle on writing Native American speech.[37] Underhill's field research and writing on the Papago Indians of
southern Arizona began while she pursued an anthropology
Ph.D. at Columbia University under the supervision of Ruth
Benedict and Franz Boas. In 1931, Underhill "fell permanently in
love" with the "hard-working but poetic Papagos" after her first
trip to their reservation. Underhill added that she "could have
spent a life among the Papago," but economic (and academic)
necessities led her to move on to study other tribal societies after
two years (x). Nevertheless, Underhill's work on the Papago

continued in one form or another for more than half a century.[38] Today, more than sixty years after Boas first suggested that she study the Papago, Underhill's research in this field stands among the most highly respected and widely admired anthropological efforts at documenting Native American culture and society.

But in her introduction to *Papago Woman,* Underhill specifically cautions her readers that the text's arrangement is her own and not Maria Chona's. "Chona is ninety years old," Underhill writes, "and her memory works with the fitfulness of age, presenting incidents in repetitious confusion." Underhill continues: "The writer felt most deeply the objections to distorting Chona's narrative. Yet if it had been written down exactly as she herself emitted it, there would have been immense emphasis on matters strange to her but commonplace to whites and complete omission of some of the most interesting phases in her development" (33). For alterations like these, Underhill has been criticized.[39] It is also true that Chona did not speak English and Underhill's grasp of Papago language was generally limited; the anthropologist had a number of translators who assisted her in conducting the bilingual interviews, among them a young woman named Ella Lopez Antone.[40] Yet despite the fieldwork activity's cumbersome nature, *Papago Woman* cuts dramatically against the stereotypical grain of Indian woman as passive squaw, long-suffering but silent. This cross-cultural collaboration represents the traditional systems of Papago life while recreating the drama of one woman's emergent selfhood within those traditions.

What, then, of the alterations in the narrative? If Neihardt "miswrites" in order to emphasize the legitimacy of Lakota speech and memory and Benson inserts white speech into a Pomo context, thus privileging the power of Pomo historical memory, how does *Papago Woman* reconcile writing's inevitable falsifications with efforts to recollect the past? The answer lies partly in Underhill's choice of a narrative structure to represent Chona's life. Underhill herself announces that "the arrangement [of Chona's memories] . . . is the writer's," not the speaker's (33). Yet while the structure of *Papago Woman* works to correct the "fitfulness" of an old woman's memory as she retells the oral traditions of her people, it also recreates the patterns of Chona's life.

There are two structural motions that *Papago Woman* follows, both of which serve to replicate the movement of Chona's life from early childhood through to old age. First, there is a repetitive cycling through the four seasons. For example, the text repeats accounts of Chona's and her tribe's winter trek to Mexico to find work – even as it adds incremental detail when it is retold. The narrative also dwells twice on the time of the year when the tribe drinks cactus liquor and sings for rain. In this latter example, the rain songs reappear in the text at both points; the passages are not, however, verbatim repetitions since the songs are variations of one another, as songs almost always are in oral cultures.[41] Similar descriptions of the tribe dancing all night long also accompany both passages. Still, while the seasonal rituals repeat, the text also relates the different activities Chona participates in as she matures. The first time, Chona describes the drinking ceremonies that surround singing for rain:

> I was too little to drink. They put me on the house top with my older sister. Our jars of liquor were up there, too. The house top was the only safe place. (40)

The second time Chona is married with children:

> [My husband] held my hand to keep me safe, and I had the baby on my back and one little child by the hand. The big ones we left home on the housetop as my mother had done. When we came to a house, the people held out the gourd to us. We drank it all and then we covered it with a song: that is what we call it. (70–1)

As part of a narrative strategy that connects Chona's identity to the seasonal rituals of Papago culture, this structural recurrence also illustrates her shifting tribal status as she comes of age within her society.

Closely related to this, though perhaps more significant, is the second structural movement in *Papago Woman*. This movement follows Chona's memories through the decades as she develops an individual sense of identity, one that is both wholly within and yet recognizably distinct from her tribal or collective Papago identity.[42] The opening page of the narrative immediately introduces this movement; *Papago Woman* begins with memories drawn from Chona's early childhood, descriptions of the land on which the Papagos lived, the fruit and nuts they ate, and the grass houses in which they slept. Everything is narrated in unindividualized and communal terms, as if the experience of one Papago child in one family speaks for children in all Papago families. There is no "I" in sentences such as "Right above us was Quijotoa Mountain, the one where the cloud stands up high and white when we sing for rain" (34).

From this communal portrait, the narrative's subsequent movement to the specific conditions of Chona's life emerges subtly within the retelling of a simple yet thematically crucial memory. Here Chona recollects being a small child, awakened in the pre-dawn hours by her father's voice. This speech is the first voice represented within the text; it emerges disembodied out of the darkness, and it sets the scene that introduces the text's first use of an "I":

> Early in the morning, in the month of Pleasant Cold, when we had all slept in the house to keep warm, we would wake in the dark to hear my father speaking.
>
> "Open your ears, for I am telling you a good thing. Wake up and listen. Open your ears. Let my words enter them." He spoke in a low voice, so quiet in the dark. Always our fathers spoke to us like that, so low that you thought you were dreaming.
>
> "Wake up and listen. You boys, you should go out and run. So you will be swift in time of war. You girls, you should grind the corn. So you will feed the men and they will fight the enemy. You should practice running. So, in time of war, you may save your lives."
>
> For a long time my father talked to us like that, for he began when it was black dark. I went to sleep, and then he pinched my ear. "Wake up! Do not be idle!" (35)

Chona's father repeats the words "open your ears" until he finally must pinch the ears to get a sleepy child out of bed. Throughout the early pages of the narrative, the young Chona continually hears speech that instructs (from various adult speakers). It expands into a chorus of instruction that she listens to about the mores and customs of her people. In a preliterate culture like this Papago community, what adults tell children is a unifying social force through which customs are reaffirmed and transmitted. Much later, Chona recalls the words of caution and instruction she gave her own daughter about preventing illness. Hence, the oral process of conveying Papago customs is again reaffirmed. In this manner, *Papago Woman* documents the movement of a certain

traditional cycle that involves the initiation of children into tribal
ways.

And yet the text holds the cyclical motion of tradition in tension with another countervailing motion. It is the movement
from one who remembers her childhood as a girl indistinct from
her community to one who, at the narrative's conclusion, speaks
about her own distinctive qualities and her impending mortality
as an elderly woman:

> I like to work at my daughter's house, at the Burnt Seeds. She has
> cornmeal there and cactus seeds. I can eat when I live there, and
> every year I go with her to the drinking ceremony. They want
> me, for I can sing. But when I go to someone's house I have to
> stay a long time before I can walk back. It is not good to be old.
> Not beautiful. When you come again, I will not be here. (86)

Papago Woman's structure and movement involve not only repetition, variation, and the emergence of the individual voice out
of a collective tribal chorus, but also outright contradiction. The
narrative places individual statements that do not agree side by
side. For example, when Chona as a young girl witnesses a
woman threatened with punishment because she is too frightened
to sleep beside her new husband at night, Chona's mother tells
her daughter: "It's right to be afraid of men. All good girls are"
(55). But when Chona is old enough to have her own marriage
arranged, her mother tells her: "If he wants anything, don't be
afraid of him. That's why we are having you marry" (63). Also,
her father tells Chona about her new responsibilities as a man's
wife: "That husband of yours, listen to him. Don't talk when he's
talking, for he is like a chief to you. Don't beg him to take you
with him here and there, but if he wants you to go, go whether
you feel like it or not . . . Don't think you can get mad and run
home" (62). Later Chona states categorically that "no woman
questions her husband among our people" (74). Yet, when she
discovers that her husband has taken a second wife (customary
for medicine men among the Papago), Chona herself runs home:
"I piled my clothes in a basket, and I put in a large butcher knife.
I thought if he followed, I would kill him. Then I took my little
girl and went away" (76). And her family *does* take her back. In
general, Chona repeatedly comments that her own ability to retell

old stories is excellent: "Some women are thinking only of bas-
kets and they do not remember such things. But I remember"
(49). Her strength of memory is significant to her; inconsistencies
among the stories she remembers are not.

Perhaps, however, these narrative inconsistencies are themselves an "invented" *textual* strategy, one that deliberately works
to approximate orality. Contradictory statements recreate the op-
erations of all oral remembering, not simply a "memory [that]
works with the fitfulness of age." The retelling of oral tradition
changes with the context of what is both present (the time now)
as the speaker speaks and past (the time remembered), when the
speaker first spoke or heard what is being recollected. So when
Chona recalls her mother telling her "good girls" are afraid of
men, the child she was while her mother spoke shapes what is
remembered. When her mother tells her "don't be afraid" of her
new husband, Chona's perspective has shifted; she is older and
the culture now sees fit to have her married.

Speech repeats – it also contradicts, just as speech often does in
conversation. Underhill could have smoothed out these details,
but these meanderings and shiftings of meaning reflect a search
for a written form that approximates the workings of a voice
sorting through the memories of a long life. It is a process not too
dissimilar from a modernist aesthetic, but a process that also calls
attention to the difficulties of representing non-Western experience within the conventions of Western narrative strategies.

Throughout *Papago Woman,* there is a continual suggestion that
translation across cultural differences is made easier when the
ethnographer and the native are both women. In *The Changing
Culture of an Indian Tribe* (1932), Margaret Mead makes a point
about the significance of women anthropologists who interview
native women:

> A woman from another culture can enter a primitive society and,
> as soon as she can speak a few words, can find a hundred points of
> interest to discuss with the native women. It may be months
> before a man can establish a similar rapport because the male
> investigator has first to get by heart the peculiar cultural preoccu-
> pations which distinguish one culture from another and which are
> of so much more importance to the men than are the routine affairs
> of domesticity.[43]

Papago Woman does indicate the "rapport" of two women who can seemingly "get by heart" over cultural barriers, especially when they discover that they may not be so different after all. This is a sign of what James Clifford has called "the romantic mythology of fieldwork rapport."[44] If there is a textual failing here, it is that Chona and Underhill's relationship sounds too good to be true.

However, Underhill's text also foregrounds the difficult process of turning speech into text, an imperfect process embedded in subtle relations of power, relations that even a shared gender cannot transcend. The memories of an oral culture cannot be recorded without the presence of a listener to write them, and inevitably the listener reshapes what is spoken.[45] The text deals with this dilemma in a number of ways. For example, rather than conceal her editorial hand, as one critic has argued she does,[46] Underhill's narrative highlights her own presence by incorporating moments when Chona speaks directly to the Columbia University anthropologist. The native speaker (Chona) repeatedly addresses a non-native listener (Underhill), asking her questions, provoking comments, seeking to know whether she is making herself understood. During a discussion of a specific ritual, Chona asks whether Underhill's experience among the Papago has included such an event: "Have you heard the rattle when our people come up in the night to dance? Ah, good!" (64). At another moment, the text suggests a physical gesture Chona makes to clarify a verbal point: "Leaf Buds' husband went out to meet my father and led him to a mesquite tree far away so that his power would not come near us. He hung his bow and arrows on that tree, and my father sat down under it. So! Do you see?" (44). No: The limits of writing and reading are here dramatized. No reader can "see" because speech demands presence, and no text can recreate a living voice, and so, like *Black Elk Speaks*, *Papago Woman* (by demonstrating the limits of the text's power) asserts the spoken word's primacy over writing.

Underhill writes that *Papago Woman* is "an Indian story told to satisfy whites rather than Indians" (33). This indicates interventionist efforts by Underhill to make accessible what would otherwise be obscure. Yet the text *also* highlights Chona's active participation in the cross-cultural translation-transcription process. Chona herself is an ethnographer of sorts; she is not just the passive subject Underhill examines. Chona also "studies" white culture (with Underhill *her* subject) by asking questions and requesting information. The narrative repeatedly tells of "gaps" in Chona's understanding as to whether or not white life experiences are different from those of Indian people: "When I was nearly as tall as my mother, that thing happened to me which happens to all our women though I do not know if it does to the whites; I never saw any signs" (57). Or when Chona recalls the moment she learned that her first husband of many years had died, she felt such deep sorrow she almost wanted to die herself: "He almost took me with him. Does that happen to the whites?" (78). The text of *Papago Woman,* then, documents two individuals engaged in exploration of one another's culture, not simply one culture taking possession of another.

Within the confines of an ethnographic model, Underhill's aim was the preservation of an American Indian woman's oral memories. As in the case of *Black Elk Speaks,* Underhill's narrative represents a self-consciously incomplete effort at reconstructing through writing what can only be appreciated most perfectly through dialogue. The alterations in *Papago Woman* illustrate an acute awareness of orality's irretrievability and reflect efforts to "invent" narrative strategies in order to capture the peculiarities of oral history telling. Part of the larger urge in the thirties to capture the voices of marginalized peoples, Underhill's account nevertheless refuses to portray Chona in the oversimplified, sentimentalized terms so prevalent in cultural products of that decade. Instead, what Chona and Underhill's narrative achieves is very possibly the most telling and unsentimental portrait we have of nineteenth-century Native American womanhood.

THE TASK of transforming Native American speech into written text impelled several writers to break free from the narrative conventions and rhetorical strategies employed by most ethnographers, journalists, and documentarians in the thirties. Hardly passive or pitiable victims, the Native American subjects actively assisted their collaborators in reformulating ethnographic methodology and contributed skills and ideas to their listeners. In turn, the writers sought to affirm the legitimacy, dignity, and power of the speakers.

Through a variety of narrative structures and strategies, then, the three ethnographic writings examined in this chapter all question their own (always problematic) authority, foreground their own partiality, and self-reflexively acknowledge their own limits as "factual" sources while at the same time urgently insisting on the validity of their subjects' perspectives. The texts reflect a recognition that writing the "truth" in fieldwork activity is a complex (and perhaps perpetually failing) enterprise, a project inevitably compromised by the relations of power in which the writer and speaker are enmeshed. However, despite ethnographic narrative's complicity in the distortions that accompany all representations, making these distortions a central theme in the recollection and representation of Indian speech can accomplish a partial (textual) reversal. This reversal works to delegitimate the usual position of privilege accorded to the writer and directs attention back to the speaker. Closer analyses of texts such as the three discussed here should thus encourage more qualified conclusions concerning the demarcation between an "old" and "new" ethnographic form. As a stage in the development of Native American narrative, and as a corresponding stage in the development of the ethnographic genre, these narratives stand at a literary and historical crossroads.

4

Zora Neale Hurston:
Talking Black, Talking Back

IN 1925, Professor Howard W. Odum, author of numerous widely respected scholarly articles and books on black folklore, described a black chain gang as it worked and sang outside his home in Georgia. He had thought the workers "oblivious" to his presence. So he sat on a rock wall and attempted to write down their work songs. This is what he heard:

> White man settin' on wall,
> White man settin' on wall,
> White man settin' on wall all day long,
> Wastin' his time, wastin' his time.[1]

The moment's irony encapsulates much of the troubled history of writing black speech in the United States in the early twentieth century. While the 1920s and 1930s witnessed intensive investigations into and fascination with the folkways of black Americans, few who recorded black speech were themselves black.

The most remarkable exception to this rule was Zora Neale Hurston. As an ethnographer, folklorist, and documentarian starting out in the late 1920s, Hurston confronted a reading public attuned to the Uncle Remus tales of Joel Chandler Harris, as well as the "poetic sociologies" of other white collectors of black folklore, including Odum, Julia Peterkin, Roark Bradford, and DuBose Heyward.[2] But as Hurston's biographer Robert Hemenway comments, "white collectors, no matter how earnest, liberal, kind, sympathetic, and well meaning, were always – by definition of race – outsiders looking in."[3] By contrast, as a southern black woman collecting southern black folklore, Hurston faced her own particular problem, that is, "by definition of race," she was an insider looking out, for she consciously sought and addressed a wider white audience.[4] In 1928, driving her Chevrolet across Florida, Hurston's search for black folklore held great promise if only she could surmount the difficulties. The result of her search was the 1935 collection of more than seventy black folktales in *Mules and Men*.

In recent years, there has been a dramatic shift away from the uncritical acceptance of methods and strategies conventionally employed in ethnographic writings. A close examination of Zora Neale Hurston's *Mules and Men* reveals that it needs to be understood both as an important counterexample to the scholarly practice of anthropology as it was evolving in the 1930s, and as a significant forerunner to the experimental ethnographies being written since the early !980s. Through its innovative use of African-American storytelling strategies, *Mules and Men* indirectly debunks the social scientific practice of anthropological research so pervasive during the thirties; situating Hurston's text within contemporary theoretical discussions about the ethnographic genre reveals *Mules and Men*'s notable critical prescience.

This chapter will begin by analyzing the general difficulties confronting Hurston as she sought to document black speech, and then examine the ways in which she broke with ethnographic and folkloristic convention in order to convey the vitality of black rhetorical strategies in written form. *Mules and Men* has received its share of critical attention, but the extant analyses have not addressed its narrative strategies for writing black speech.[5] My contention is that *Mules and Men* becomes a narrative that self-reflexively invents literary strategies for documenting black speech by adopting, or adapting, the very rhetorical language that is its subject. In this way, black vernacular strategies, particularly varieties of "signifying," not only are the subject, but simultaneously become the means through which the forms and the messages of "talking black" are documented.[6]

More important, however, and of greater relevance to my book's overall argument, is that *Mules and Men* has not been analyzed as an experimental ethnographic text that engages with and comments on certain key ethnographic paradigms in anticipation (by several decades) of such experiments in recent years. It does so in at least four ways. First, Hurston's ethnography comments ironically on the paradigm of a stable and exotic otherness whose "inner life" remains "hidden" and "invisible" until such time as the enterprising social scientist shows up from "outside" and "discloses" those secrets, making them "visible." Instead, it is seldom precisely clear who is "inside" and "outside" the narrative frame. Second, Hurston's narrative plays against the "scientific" ideas of objectivity and impartiality prevailing in her day by demonstrating repeatedly how the presence of the ethnographer shapes what gets told and what each story "means." Most meanings in *Mules and Men* remain incomplete, indeterminate, and ambiguous. Indeed, significantly, the meanings derived also often depend on the reader's position in relation to the subjects.

Hurston's strategy not only suggests multiple (rather than fixed) meanings, but also – and this is my third point – continually calls attention to the power relations between reader, author, and subjects. These relations of power are highlighted precisely by the aforementioned ways in which *Mules and Men* addresses the (mostly white) readers outside its margins by adapting into written form the African-American storytelling techniques that are its subject. Finally, *Mules and Men* challenges the ethnographic convention by which the ethnographer is made to disappear from the overall tale being told, even though the subjectivity of the ethnographer inevitably constitutes the organizing consciousness of an ethnographic text. The book not only acknowledges what most ethnographies of its time suppressed, but does so in the most hyperbolic and melodramatic fashion possible. The narrative increasingly adopts a theatrical mode – with "Zora" as the star – turning the text as a whole into a mock(ing) ritual reenactment of standard fieldwork methods. Simultaneously, by deliberately omitting puzzle pieces required for a fuller understanding of this climactic melodrama, *Mules and Men* again subverts the notion of a clear demarcation between text and social context. The text is staged as a live performance, interdependent with and in dialogue with the world around it.

Mules and Men engages the ethnographic paradigms of its day in ways that not only "talk black," but also talk back at white readers and collectors of black folklore. As much as *Mules and Men* may appear to be about folktales in which animals speak, people climb up to Heaven to chat with God, and the Devil intervenes in human affairs, it can also be read as an act of careful resistance against whites' intrusions into black affairs. Readers may fathom some of these meanings, but not all. The narrative frames itself as a challenge to its readers (most especially its white readers) to examine their own motives for tackling a black folklore text. As this chapter argues, the narrative's multiple levels and frames skillfully signal various messages, depending on how well readers read and whether or not they can detect (what one informant calls) "de inside meanin' of words."[7]

DURING THE TWENTIES and thirties, black authors who documented black speech confronted a myth that dated back as far as the late eighteenth and early nineteenth centuries: that the ways blacks spoke English reflected deficient intellectual capacities. As John Edgar Wideman puts it, black people have almost always been defined in writing by how they spoke. "Negro dialect," Wideman writes, "lacked proper grammar, its comic orthography suggested ignorance, its 'dats' and 'dems' and 'possums' implied lazy, slovenly pronunciation if not the downright physical impossibility of getting thick lips around the King's English."[8] Thus, in recreating the speaking voices of black people in their prose and poetry, black authors faced a peculiar dilemma: if they wrote black speech as it was often spoken, they ran the danger of perpetuating assumptions about black inferiority. On the other hand, if they wrote black speech as educated whites supposedly spoke English, they confirmed another problematic myth: that blacks demonstrated equality with whites only by rising above their own cultural heritage.

Perhaps the most troubling hurdle for a black ethnographer to overcome during the early decades of the twentieth century was the widespread "scientific" perception that the cultural heritage of black Americans, including their speech and folklore, was a crude derivation of a "standard" white culture. This perspective posited, for example, that American blacks had adapted white English speech patterns, oral traditions, and folksongs through a long process of simplification. Thus, it was relatively commonplace for the most respected social scientists, like Edward Sapir, to conclude that there was "no doubt the African tradition as such was entirely lost or nearly so" on American shores.[9] Stripped of its African roots, at least in the eyes and ears of "science," black culture and, by extension, black consciousness were thought to lack genuine originality or humanity. Considered respectable "science" in the early twentieth century, for example, were these crass observations by the folklorist Odum, written in 1910, concerning black folk music: "It is a marvel of the Negro's mental tendency that he can keep together such a vast heap of moral refuse and filth . . . These songs come ill-harmonized to the soft, stirring melodies of a folk-life; and sadder is it to know that the song reflects his true nature."[10] Thus, it would not have been possible to address the concerns of black culture as a black ethnographer working within the framework of the social sciences without confronting contentious debates surrounding race, culture, and society.

During the thirties, the perspective of white ethnographers that black Americans spoke a "nonstandard" dialect because they had managed to acquire only an imperfect English, persisted largely unchallenged. The resulting ethnographic studies of the period betrayed attitudes about black speech that were based more on this racial fantasy than on empirical fact. One noted ethnographer in 1930 wrote that blacks, having learned English from whites who had spoken to them as simpletons, now articulated like backward children. The dialect blacks spoke resembled "the peasant English of two centuries ago, modified to suit the needs of the slaves" and "the 'baby talk' used by masters in addressing them."[11] The position of ethnographic research toward black English throughout the thirties reveals, as one recent critic comments, "a tone of condescension as the white scholar bends over backward to compliment the black by telling him he has learned his adopted language, the language of the master class, very well, and, like a good immigrant, appropriately forgotten his African linguistic past."[12] Indeed, the white scholars of the period held that black dialects deserved to be documented precisely because those dialect differences ought to be eliminated. Only when all blacks spoke English just like whites, they argued, would claims that essential differences existed between the races become more difficult to justify. This view, deemed "liberal" in its day, dominated the social scientific fields of anthropology, sociology, and ethnography at least until 1941, when Melville Herskovits's seminal study, *The Myth of the Negro Past,* challenged any conclusions concerning black English that did not take into account its continuities with various African languages.[13]

Yet the years prior to 1941 found proponents of racial equality on the defensive. In a 1927 article entitled "Fallacies of Racial

Inferiority," which Hurston helped research while she was at Barnard College, Dr. Franz Boas argued, for example, that "we may not say that a certain size of the brain of the negro is racially determined as against the brain size of Europeans, for the reason that a very large number of individuals are found in both races which have the same brain size."[14] Another "liberal" commentator on "racial adjustment" declared, "It is known that there are differences in the native mental ability or intelligence of the two races, but just what these differences are, in quantity or in quality, is not known."[15] As these comments indicate, those advocating greater equality operated within the same tautological frame regarding race as their opponents. Supposed biological difference signaled black deficiency, so the goal was to "prove" either that no differences existed or that they were surmountable.[16] Among the studies of black culture proliferating in the thirties, no matter what their conclusions, the "scientific" methods used to ascertain whether black people, already defined as racially different, also had inferior mental capacities and characteristics all started with the same false premise. As historian Barbara Jeanne Fields observes, "A commonplace that few stop to examine holds that people are more readily oppressed when they are already perceived as inferior by nature. The reverse is more to the point. People are more readily perceived as inferior by nature when they are already seen as oppressed."[17] Inadvertently, to be sure, Boas and other "liberal" racial theorists sustained and helped entrench deeply problematic assumptions about what race was and what it potentially meant in terms of culture and society.[18]

The ethnocentrism of thirties "scientific" arguments concerning race and culture circumscribed all aspects of the debates, as anthropologists, sociologists, and folklorists calculated, categorized, and collated their data to validate this or that argumentative position. It was what one folklore scholar has called a " 'Mason jar' approach to folklore study," and it reigned supreme during the period Hurston conducted her fieldwork and ethnographic writing.[19] With rare exception, writes Adrienne Lanier Seward, the "emphasis on collecting and classifying" in folklore "science" was "guided by the discipline's nineteenth-century character, which was oriented toward recording and preserving traditions thought to be dying rather than exploring them from a point of view reflecting their vital functions and dynamic mutability."[20]

Ripped from the context of everyday life, collections of black oral storytelling tradition became rarified specimens fit for an exoticized museum display. But that was not all. In addition, many progressive-minded observers believed that any affirmation of black folklore only slowed the "uplift" of the race. Typical in this regard is the response of one angry Communist (and white) critic to the images professional folklorists recorded of "the Negro's supposed incompetence and unthinking amiability . . . If the Negro ever hoped for salvation through his culture, he should be thoroughly disillusioned by the status of the race during this particular phase of American capitalism."[21]

Black critics and intellectuals were less prone themselves to such judgments, especially after influential figures like W. E. B. Du Bois and James Weldon Johnson had so celebrated black folk songs in their writing.[22] Yet the few blacks trained as folklorists in the twenties, like Arthur Huff Fauset, faced a double dilemma. First, to engage in folklore study meant risking comparison with the popular (though dubious) standards set by Joel Chandler Harris and his Uncle Remus stories. Second, to affirm black oral heritage meant utilizing the aforementioned "scientific" methods of ethnographic fieldwork. On the first problem, Fauset wrote in 1925 with characteristic insight that "the Harris variety of the Negro folk tale assumes to interpret Negro character instead of simply telling his stories. The result is a composite picture of the ante-bellum Negro that fits exactly into the conception of the type of Negro which so many white people would like to think once existed, or even now exists."[23] However, on the second matter, Fauset was unwilling to identify his professional methods as part of the problem for the black folklorist. Instead, he argued for a "strong need of a scientific collecting of Negro folk lore before the original sources of this material altogether lapse."[24] Fauset's position suggested the cultural schizophrenia of a black folklorist who knew, in vernacular terms, that the big house could not interpret the cabin. Yet, at the same time, Fauset's acceptance of white "scientific" methods for documenting a black culture falsely presumed to be "dying" left him to struggle within a discourse that inherently denied the legitimacy, vitality, and wholeness of black culture.

Undoubtedly, these debates concerning culture and race weighed heavily on Hurston as she set out to record and interpret black folktales in 1928. Returned to Eatonville, Florida, where she was born and raised, Hurston had schooled out and come home, to use her own allegorical expression, but could not keep the cow from rearing and pitching and kicking over the milk pail. In other words, given the lack of precedent for what she attempted, Hurston's anthropological training did *not* prepare her for successful fieldwork among her own people. Hurston went much further than Arthur Fauset in her rejection of folklore "science" and its questionable methods. *Mules and Men* is best understood as a text that uses its fluency with an academic discipline and its generic conventions to debunk that discipline's underlying assumptions and to stretch the boundaries of the ethnographic genre.

The strategies and structures *Mules and Men* adopts to address the difficulties of formal ethnographic convention cannot be understood without a grasp of what is meant by "talking black," specifically the rhetorical technique known as "signifying." In black folklore studies, numerous scholars – including Hurston – have, for the last half-century or more, identified and debated the meanings of signifying, though all agree that it represents one of the most diversely applied and pervasive strategies for expression within the black vernacular tradition.[25] And in recent years, perhaps most especially due to essays by Henry Louis Gates, Jr., the relationship between signifying and black literature has begun to be explored in greater depth.[26] Signifying is an indirect way of speaking in which that which is spoken encodes one message or meaning even as it more explicitly states something else entirely. In some instances, signifying can be "the verbal art of insult in which a speaker humorously puts down, talks about, needles – that is, signifies on – the listener."[27] In other cases, it is "a language of implication" or a "technique of indirect argument or persuasion."[28] Claudia Mitchell-Kernan writes that whether designed to insult or persuade, signifying "is clearly thought of as a kind of art – a clever way of conveying messages."[29] Mitchell-Kernan continues:

> The black concept of signifying incorporates essentially a folk notion that dictionary entries for words are not always sufficient for interpreting meanings or messages, or that meaning goes be-

yond such interpretations. Complimentary remarks may be delivered in a left-handed fashion. A particular utterance may be an insult in one context and not another.

In short, "Meaning conveyed is not apparent meaning"; rather, the "reference must be processed metaphorically."[30] As portrayed in *Mules and Men,* one power that blacks have is the ability to talk back at the world of whites' assumed superiority. They have the power to turn the world over through black rhetorical strategies, notably through the power of signifying on white authority.

Signification is almost all about power. Part of that power is the option to deny it happened at all, since its indirection leaves open the possibility that what is interpreted as signification may not have been intended that way. In folktales where slaves signify on their masters, the whites reveal a chronic inability to get what is meant by what is said. Although the master retains the authority to bring physical harm to his supposed inferior, he can seldom outduel his slave verbally. That he not know he has been outfoxed (until it is too late) can be a crucial part of the message and meaning of the folktale. Furthermore, as it is embedded in a black speech event, the white dialogue naturally comes from a black teller's mouth, so it is always framed by what blacks think or imagine or know whites are. In a world of dramatic power imbalance between whites and blacks, signifying works to reverse those power relations. It may not change social conditions, but it can frame those conditions within the terms of black culture.

One folktale in *Mules and Men* concerns how white people pray to God, and it provides an excellent example of signification at work:

> Well, it come a famine and all de crops was dried up and Brother John was ast to pray. He had prayed for rain last year and it had rained, so all de white folks 'sembled at they church and called on Brother John to pray agin, so he got down and prayed:
> "Lord, first thing, I want you to understand that this ain't no nigger talking to you. This is a white man and I want you to hear me. Pay some attention to me. I don't worry and bother you all the time like these niggers – asking you for a whole heap of things that they don't know what to do with after they git 'em – so when I do ask a favor, I want it granted. Now, Lord, we want some

rain. Our crops is all burning up and we'd like a little rain. But I don't mean for you to come in a hell of a storm like you did last year – kicking up racket like niggers at a barbecue. I want you to come calm and easy. Now, another thing, Lord, I want to speak about. Don't let these niggers be as sassy as they have been in the past. Keep 'em in their places, Lord, Amen." (88–9)

This storyteller skillfully conveys an indirect message veiled behind irony and humor. Through its white speaker, this story signifies on whites who use Christianity to justify their oppression of African Americans. For one thing, it could only trouble a white that God might mistake him for a black, if God is actually blind to color. For another, the folktale relates the last time this preacher prayed for rain and got more than he bargained for; it was so loud a rainstorm, it sounded like "niggers at a barbecue." This signifies on whites by suggesting that they just don't know how to loosen up, preferring something "calm and easy" to the "racket" blacks make when they're having a good time. Finally, the tale tells how blacks ask God "for a whole heap of things that they don't know what to do with after they git 'em," suggesting that the prayers of "sassy" blacks do get answered. The ones kept "in their places," then, are whites who falsely presume their faith will serve them ahead of those who are more deserving. If signification is "a language of implication" and if it ought to be, as Geneva Smitherman says, "teachy but not preachy," then this folktale surely signifies.[31]

Yet if, as Smitherman adds, a signifying story is "directed at person or persons usually present in the situational context (siggers do not talk behind yo back),"[32] then as an oral folktale, told by a black to black listeners, this story would not signify. However, once written, it *becomes* signifying; as I read it, it is me who is signified on – its white reader. What *Mules and Men* innovatively achieves – and Hurston's text was the first to use signifying as both subject and literary strategy, although it is a strategy used by many black American authors since 1935 – is the transformation of an oral language *into* the written form. This transformation has been, as Michael Awkward puts it, one way black authors have represented the "inspiriting influences" of their black cultural heritage.[33] But more than that, by adding the layer of writing (which expands the performative context to include readers), *Mules and Men* beautifully demonstrates by example one of signifying's main attributes: how the meanings of words change, depending on the context in which they are spoken.

Rather than lament the presumed demise of black oral tradition or the near impossibility of writing black speech effectively, *Mules and Men* puts literacy at the service of orality. It builds on writing's possible applications, and it illustrates through example how writing can add layers of meaning through further expanding the situational context. As opposed to the "Mason jar" approach favored by her contemporaries, then, Hurston aims in her text to represent black speech as an ongoing process, embedded in various historical situations and relations of power, not a dead, isolatable specimen.

In order to accomplish her goal of presenting black oral traditions as vital and legitimate, Hurston had to do more than document the telling of tales; she had to address the entire complex of problems surrounding ethnography as a scholarly and a political enterprise evolving in the thirties. In the introductory pages of the book, Hurston tackles head-on the inevitable complexities and ambiguities of the ethnographer's role. Subsequently, the opening folktale in the first chapter subtly but unmistakably comments on the central dilemmas of ethnography itself.

More conscious than her contemporaries of the always difficult and complicated three-way relationship between ethnographers, subjects, and readers, Hurston was particularly aware of her own duality as a black ethnographer, a figure both inside and outside the world of her subjects and the world of her readers.[34] In exploring the ambiguities of her own position, Hurston reconceived the significance of a well-known historical concept of black duality, one that had been most eloquently described by W. E .B. Du Bois in 1903. The American black, Du Bois wrote, "ever feels his twoness, – an American, a Negro; two souls, two thoughts, two unreconciled strivings; two warring ideals in one dark body, whose dogged strength alone keeps it from being torn asunder."[35] From its opening pages, *Mules and Men* plays critically on the Du Bois idea.

At face value, Franz Boas's brief three-paragraph preface could be read as simply a generous endorsement of the text that follows, which is how it was most likely intended. But Boas cannot escape focusing on the peculiarity of Hurston's blackness. First, Boas praises Hurston by setting her work apart from all previous writings on black folklore, notably the Uncle Remus books of Joel Chandler Harris. "Ever since the time of Uncle Remus," Boas writes, "Negro folklore has exerted a strong attraction upon the imagination of the American public," yet such prior accounts have outlined "the intimate setting in the social life of the Negro . . . very inadequately" (xiii). Second, Boas indicates that it is Hurston's black skin that allows her "to penetrate through that affected demeanor by which the Negro excludes the White observer effectively from participating in his true inner life" (xiii). In this way Boas argues for the intrinsic and original value of Hurston's writing. Before the preface ends, Boas repeats himself for emphasis: "Miss Hurston's work [makes] an unusual contribution to our knowledge of the true inner life of the Negro" (xiii). In response, and perhaps for good reason, Hurston's own introduction cannot resist putting on a black mask by signifying on Boas.

Hurston's introduction opens with Dr. Boas telling the author, "You may go and collect Negro folklore." Hurston states how she expressed immediate excitement and decided to study Eatonville, Florida, where she was born and raised, for "when I pitched headforemost into the world I landed in the crib of negroism." Yet, Hurston adds, as a child she never knew her culture's special qualities; she could only learn to "see myself like somebody else" once she had left home, and "then I had to have the spy-glass of Anthropology to look through" (1). Adopting a personal tone in an introduction had long been "a conventional component of ethnographies"; as Mary Louise Pratt argues, the invariable inclusion in an introduction of such subjective commentary "anchors" what follows "in the intense and authority-giving personal experience of fieldwork," and "it mediates a contradiction within the discipline between personal and scientific authority, a contradiction that has become especially acute since the advent of fieldwork as a methodological norm."[36] The difference in *Mules and Men* is that Hurston problematizes her own subjective position.

Hurston's introduction focuses on the contradictions inherent in seeking to establish the ethnographer's authority by raising questions about who is inside and who is outside the culture under study. While Boas assumes that the fact of Hurston's blackness would easily establish her as a cultural insider, Hurston disagrees: "I knew that even *I* was going to have some hindrance" conducting fieldwork (3). Her blackness would not in itself prevent her from being dismissed by the residents of Eatonville. If she tried to impress the town, Hurston writes, "somebody would have sent me word in a match-box that I had been up North there and had rubbed the hair off of my head against some college wall" (2). Although an insider by birth, Hurston's education and ambitions have made her an outsider by "form and fashion"; a wrong gesture or word and Eatonville would "stand flat-footed and tell me that they didn't have me . . . And that would have been that" (2). Indeed, as the text tells its readers later on, Hurston must finally lie about who she is and what she's doing in order to gain her subjects' trust. In this way, *Mules and Men* relates the anxiety of "Zora" over how she will be identified and how she must position herself in various roles to fit a variety of specific circumstances. The important issue, however, is not whether Hurston is who she says she is, but rather that she analyzes how a shared blackness in no way guarantees seamless mutual understanding *and* how she signifies on what her readers expect her to be.

Hurston's introduction soon reverses itself, moving quickly from an anxiety over identification as an outsider to self-assurance about her status as an insider. Readers are told how underprivileged blacks are "most reluctant at times to reveal that which the soul lives by," so that they offer instead "a feather-bed resistance." The tensions between personal and scientific authority are again thematized as the text describes how this "resistance" works:

> Folklore is not as easy to collect as it sounds. The best source is where there are the least outside influences and these people, being usually under-privileged, are the shyest. They are most reluctant at times to reveal that which the soul lives by. And the Negro, in spite of his open-faced laughter, his seeming acquiescence, is particularly evasive. You see we are a polite people and we do not say to our questioner, "Get out of here!" We smile and tell him or her something that satisfies the white person because, knowing so little about us, he doesn't know what he is missing. The Indian resists curiosity by a stony silence. The Negro offers a feather-bed resistance. That is, we let the probe enter, but it never comes out. It gets smothered under a lot of laughter and pleasantries.

> The theory behind our tactics: "The white man is always trying
> to know into somebody else's business. All right, I'll set some-
> thing outside the door of my mind for him to play with and
> handle. He can read my writing but he sho' can't read my mind.
> I'll put this play toy in his hand, and he will seize it and go away.
> Then I'll say my say and sing my song." (2–3)

This "theory" could be read in several ways. On the one hand, it
indirectly suggests that the book that follows will give readers an
"insider's" look in a way all previous scholarship could not,
because the anthropologist is black. On the other hand, by calling
"feather-bed resistance" one of "our tactics," it also suggests that
this book will engage in "resistance" toward its white readers,
thus keeping them "outside the door" of the black community.
In fact, the book does both.

The passage more than intimates that its author has "solved"
the difficult task of getting "inside" black folklore culture. Other
(read: white) ethnographers have only deceived themselves if they
think their black folklore collections are definitive. "We let the
probe enter, but it never gets out," Hurston writes, playing on
the Boas argument that only an "insider" (read: black) who "goes
native" can document "blackness" successfully. The passage also
shamelessly indulges in caricature of blacks, stating, for example,
that blacks love to laugh and smile, even while indicating that
black laughter is only a mask put on for white observers. The
seemingly gratuitous reference to the Indian's "stony silence"
further foregrounds the caricaturing process at play.

A healthy dose of self-promotion pervades these lines, as Hurston trumpets her "blackness" as her great asset. Yet this passage
also teases with ambiguities. It treats "whiteness," meaning the
power to interrogate, and "blackness," meaning the obligation to
respond (however disingenuously), metaphorically as the narrator
represents her own ever-shifting positions toward her subjects
and her readers. The text dramatizes these double reversals most
effectively in the shifts between "Ah" and "I," the two pronouns
Hurston uses as narrator. To her Floridian informants, *Mules and
Men* quotes Hurston as saying: "Ah come to collect some old
stories and tales and Ah know y'all know a plenty of 'em and
that's why Ah·headed straight for home" (8). To her readers, the
text typically reads: "I hailed them as I went into neutral" (7). The
narrative constructs Hurston's "I" as mediating between different

worlds, one black and oral and one (presumably in large part) white and literate. Ironically, perhaps, readers accept Hurston's authority as narrator because she writes a "white" English, while her informants accept Hurston as native because she speaks a black dialect. In the passage quoted, then, there is a crucial irony in the way the "theory" is voiced by an "I" and not an "Ah." Furthermore, the passage contains an odd and seemingly out-of-place reference to writing: "He can read my writing but he sho' can't read my mind." Given black oral tradition, the sentence ought to read: "He can hear my voice but he sho' can't read my mind." These details indicate that the entire narrative of *Mules and Men* may itself be "a play toy" set "outside the door of my mind for [the white man] to play with and handle."

Finally, whereas Du Bois had bemoaned the "double-consciousness" of the American black in "a world which yields him no true self-consciousness, but only lets him see himself through the revelation of the other world,"[37] Hurston's "double-consciousness" does not represent "two warring ideals in one dark body," but revises that idea into a potentially liberating ability to see and understand more about one's human condition. According to *Mules and Men,* life behind a mask facilitates self-awareness through performance and through knowledge about one's oppressor.

As a self-conscious ethnographer, Hurston not only had to address her relationship with her mentor, her subjects, and her potential readers early on in the text, but also needed to call attention to the peculiarities of the ethnographic project as a whole. The very first folktale in Chapter 1 – about John, the great hero of African-American folklore, and his white owner, Ole Massa – does precisely this. It is a story that all previous scholarship on *Mules and Men* ignores, perhaps because it does not appear to have any special significance:

> It was night and Ole Massa sent John, his favorite slave, down to
> the spring to get him a cool drink of water. He called John to him.
>   "John!"
>   "What you want, Massa?"
>   "John, I'm thirsty. Ah wants a cool drink of water, and Ah
> wants you to go down to de spring and dip me up a nice cool
> pitcher of water."
>   John didn't like to be sent nowhere at night, but he always tried

to do everything Ole Massa told him to do, so he said, "Yessuh, Massa, Ah'll go git you some!"

Old Massa said: "Hurry up, John. Ah'm mighty thirsty." John took de pitcher and went on down to de spring. There was a great big ole bull frog settin' right on de edge of de spring, and when John dipped up de water de noise skeered de frog and he hollered and jumped over in de spring.

John dropped de water pitcher and tore out for de big house, hollerin' "Massa! Massa! A big ole booger done got after me!"

Ole Massa told him, "Why, John, there's no such thing as a booger."

"Oh, yes it is, Massa. He down at dat Spring."

"Don't tell me, John. Youse just excited. Furthermore, you go git me dat water Ah sent you after."

"No, indeed, Massa, you and nobody else can't send me back there so dat booger kin git me."

Ole Massa begin to figger dat John musta seen somethin' sho nuff because John never had disobeyed him before, so he ast: "John, you say you seen a booger. What did it look like?"

John tole him, "Massa, he had two great big eyes lak balls of fire, and when he was standin' up he was sittin' down and when he moved, he moved by jerks, and he had most no tail." (9–10)

The story provides an allegory of the expectations surrounding the ethnographic project. After all, it is Ole Massa (and not John) who gets fooled, not by what he has seen, but by the lies he has heard. (Note that John succeeds in not having to return to the spring a second time.) The inclusion of the folktale foregrounds black self-awareness (and resistance) within the pages of a book addressed to a readership that will prove the folktale's thesis precisely by missing its point: Because Ole Massa exoticizes John, John can present something terribly familiar as something utterly strange, and he communicates that strangeness so successfully that Ole Massa begins to have doubts himself.

Mules and Men not only uses African-American signifying strategies to mock ethnographic paradigms of exotic "others," it also suggests that the problems of formal ethnographic conventions can be turned around and made into partial solutions. Discarding the "Mason jar" methodology, *Mules and Men* represents black speech as embedded in the context of everyday experience and complicated power relations. Rather than working strenuously to assert the neutrality of her position as an observer and the objective truth of her findings, Hurston's text repeatedly foregrounds the impact of the ethnographer's presence and documents how the meanings of stories change depending on the contexts in which they are told.

Many of the folktales Hurston includes and the ways she positions them in the text illuminate how urgent was the need to break with ethnographic convention in order to provide more sophisticated understandings of black storytelling traditions. This need was particularly pressing when it came to addressing the evident tradition of self-denigration within black culture. Perhaps because it developed within a social context of adversity and hatred, black folklore often reflected a self-deprecating humor.[38] But when specific folktales are recognized as existing within a larger context, one that acknowledges Hurston's presence in her subjects' midst as well as the white readership outside the narrative's frame, a different reading of the tales is possible.

For example, on the question of why black people have been made to work so hard for white people, *Mules and Men* offers this tale:

> God let down two bundles 'bout five miles down de road. So de white man and de nigger raced to see who would git there first. Well, de nigger out-run de white man and grabbed de biggest bundle. He was so skeered de white man would git it away from him he fell on top of de bundle and hollered back: "Oh, Ah got here first and dis biggest bundle is mine." De white man says: "All right, Ah'll take yo' leavings," and picked up de li'l tee-ninchy bundle layin' in de road. When de nigger opened up his bundle he found a pick and shovel and a hoe and a plow and chop-axe and then de white man opened up his bundle and found a writin-pen and ink. So ever since then de nigger been out in de hot sun, usin' his tools and de white man been sittin' up figgerin', ought's a ought, figger's a figger; all for de white man, none for de nigger. (74–5)

Because the black man is quicker, he is given the first choice. But what he sees is size; what he cannot see is that size bears an inverse relationship to power. Allegorically, the size of the bundle contrasts two differing relationships to the world. The black man in the story accepts a literal and objective reality, apparently unaware that what something appears to be need have no direct bearing on its abstract powers. The white man in the tale recognizes abstract powers, especially the tools needed to render a literal reality meaningless through writing. The folktale thus represents black people as somehow "naturally" incapable of abstract thought, the domain of white people. On this level, the story expresses a troubling degree of self-deprecation.

However, another reading is also suggested. This folktale reverses the lazy and shiftless qualities stereotypically ascribed to blacks onto the white man while it affirms the strength and hardworking character of black people. It also asserts the arbitrariness of race differences, suggesting that if the black had been the one to pick up the writing pen and ink, the power imbalance between whites and blacks might have been other than what it has been. Furthermore, the folktale indicates that literacy is a primary tool empowering whites with claims of superiority over blacks. It suggests that the "rational" skills that European peoples claimed to have developed have been applied in a hypocritical fashion. Reworking and redefining reality in the most self-serving manner imaginable, the white man uses writing to take everything and leave nothing. The folktale concludes that the tools of literacy represent nothing more than a means to justify inequality and racism. Finally, as a written folktale within the pages of a book, this story develops one further level of interpretation. It signifies on white readers as they read about how literacy skills bear a direct link to the institutional history of racism.

In short, in keeping with the practice of signifying, the folklore stories in *Mules and Men* do not convey only one straightforward message. The narrative's contextual aspect, that is, the ways its shifting contexts inform shifting meanings, illustrates the richness and vitality of black culture. The folktale can be taken literally. It can be interpreted figuratively. It can be understood in relationship to the specific communal setting and speech event where it is told. It can be seen as a performance in light of Hurston's presence as ethnographer, and it can be understood in relationship to potential readers. Indeed, there are at least four levels of reference, and depending on which level is emphasized, the folktale takes on a different meaning.

Take, for example, another tale in *Mules and Men* that appears to denigrate black people. It tells the story of the origins of color for human beings. On the morning God set to give out color, everybody showed up "to git they color except de niggers. So

God give everybody they color and they went on off" (29). Hours passed and "no niggers," so God sent his angels to find them: "They hunted all over Heben till dey found de colored folks. All stretched out sleep on de grass under de tree of life." The angels wake them up, say God wants to see them, and a commotion breaks out:

> They all jumped up and run on up to de th'one and they was so skeered they might miss sumpin' they begin to push and shove one 'nother, bumpin' against all de angels and turnin' over footstools. They even had de th'one all pushed one-sided.
>
> So God hollered "Git back! Git back!" And they misunderstood Him and thought He said, "Git black," and they been black ever since. (29–30)

Taken literally, this folktale "explains" very little. That black people are "black" both before and after God makes them black is incongruous; it mixes up causes and effects. Is it that they behaved "black" first and that's why they became black? Is it that blackness results from a spoken word collectively misheard, which suggests the importance of listening closely? Taken figuratively, however, this is another signifying tale; it signifies on white preconceptions of black inferiority, pointing at whites' continual confusion of cause and effect in the development of racial inequality. It indirectly expresses outrage at the idea that blacks "deserved" their "blackness" in the encoded sense that "blackness" means a history of oppression. The tale mocks the existing order of things precisely because within that order whites have come to define "whiteness" as "superior." That the tale relies on circular logic is part of its bitter humor and signifying message.

Positioned within the world of its immediate listeners, however, the tale takes on a quite different meaning. Gold, a woman who has been disputing all afternoon on the store porch with Gene, is the one who tells this tale. Clear from the context is that Gold is a better storyteller than Gene. It is also apparent from the context that Gold can play games of ritual insult as well as any man and is more than willing to play with Gene.[39] Here is a typical exchange:

> Then Gold spoke up and said, "Now, lemme tell one. Ah know one about a man as black as Gene."

"Whut you always crackin' me for?" Gene wanted to know. "Ah ain't a bit blacker than you."

"Oh, yes you is, Gene. Youse a whole heap blacker than Ah is."

"Aw, go head on, Gold. Youse blacker than me. You jus' look my color cause youse fat. If you wasn't no fatter than me you'd be so black till lightnin' bugs would follow you at twelve o'clock in de day, thinkin' it's midnight."

"Dat's a lie, youse blacker than Ah ever dared to be. Youse lam' black. Youse so black till they have to throw a sheet over yo' head so de sun kin rise every mornin'. Ah know yo' ma cried when she seen *you*."

"Well, anyhow, Gold, youse blacker than me. If Ah was as fat as you Ah'd be a yaller man."

"Youse a liar. Youse as yaller as you ever gointer git. When a person is poor he look bright and de fatter you git de darker you look." (28–9)

When Gold then tells the folktale about the origin of black people, Gene responds: "Now Gold call herself gettin' even wid me – tellin' dat lie. 'Taint no such a story nowhere. She jus' made dat one up herself" (30). This is a crucial moment for understanding *Mules and Men*'s rhetorical methods. Gene hears the folktale as directed at him, that is, he believes that Gold is signifying on him with this tale suggesting that blackness resulted from sloth. That Gold had commented earlier on the laziness of black men ("Dat's all you men is good for – settin' 'round and lyin.' ") also seems part of the relevant context for the tale (24). The accusation of signifying results from the sense Gene gets that this folktale is (as Mitchell-Kernan has put it) "too timely and selectively apropos to segments of [the] audience."[40] To accuse Gene directly of laziness, for example, would not achieve the same effect. If Gold is signifying, and there is every reason to suspect that she is, then she successfully forces Gene to confront her and risk additional embarrassment.

Note, too, that Gene attempts to defuse the signifying impact of the tale by accusing Gold of originality. In folkloristic terms, Gene takes this line of argument because a story Gold invents would have less validity and power than one that had been passed on as a collective inheritance. Fittingly, another woman comes to Gold's defense: "Naw, she didn't [make it up]. Ah *been* knowin' dat ole tale" (30). Another oral culture-bearer attests to the *lack* of originality and thus the genuineness of Gold's folktale. Gene has been verbally dueled and soundly defeated.

Gene's comment that " 'taint no such a story nowhere" makes special sense in light of Hurston's presence. He knows that she has come home to document genuine black folklore. That he denigrates Gold by accusing her of originality takes on significance because if her story is original (and not traditional), then Hurston as narrator would have little reason to record it. But what Gene fails to grasp is that Hurston got exactly what she wanted by being able to show how a folktale could be improvised so that it may signify on one or more members of the audience. These passages about Gene and Gold illustrate Hurston's message that black oral tradition is a collective undertaking with ongoing and multiple applications.

The meanings of the folktales in *Mules and Men* change when the context used to interpret them changes. Not only does the framing narrative comment on the folktales told within its context, but looking at the text as a whole adds a further dimension of complexity to this equation. Hurston is the ethnographer and author of the narrative, but as "Zora," she also becomes its central figure.

A S JAMES CLIFFORD has made clear, ethnographies stereotypically begin with a brief recounting of the ethnographer's initial attainment of expert status: a "fable of rapport" that "permits the writer to function in his subsequent analyses as an omnipresent, knowledgeable exegete." Clifford goes on to say that the standard ethnographic convention is to separate the rest of "the research process . . . from the texts it generates" and to filter out "the actuality of discursive situations." The ethnographer, in Clifford's words, "disappear[s] into his rapport." Clifford and many other recent scholars have criticized this disappearing act as a disingenuous veiling of the actual "tactical dissimulations and irreducible violence of ethnographic work."[41] *Mules and Men* diverges from such standard formats and formulas in dramatic and provocative ways.

Conscious of her role as observer-participant, Hurston makes clear early on in the text that her presence in the town of Eatonville reshapes how and why people say what they do, even if on the surface the talk appears to have nothing to do with her. But the people of Eatonville do speak with her. Later in the narrative, however, when she travels to the living quarters at the Everglades Cypress Lumber Company in Polk County, Florida, matters deteriorate for the ethnographer. Now everyone treats her with a cordial distance, and the scholar in search of folklore complains that "here was I figuratively starving to death in the midst of plenty" (60). Hundreds of southern blacks "all thought I must be a revenue officer or a detective of some kind," and they "set me aside as different" (60–1). Then one Saturday night after pay day, people gather to dance, tell stories, and pair off and things begin to change.

Hurston's goal is to break down the aforementioned "feather-bed resistance" confronting her. She does this, first, by telling a lie about her reasons for being at the quarters. She lets it be known "that I was also a fugitive from justice, 'bootlegging.' They were hot behind me in Jacksonville and they wanted me in Miami. So I was hiding out" (61). Then she lies about the expensive dress from Macy's she is wearing: "Mah man brought me dis dress de las' time he went to Jacksonville. We wuz sellin' plenty stuff den and makin' good money. Wisht Ah had dat money now" (64). Assuming a false identity distinct from her "real" identity helps Hurston win the trust of the men on the job. No doubt, being female and black makes the task that much easier. But she must also speak in terms these potential informants understand before she can proceed to collect their stories. Convincingly, *Mules and Men* suggests that telling the men the truth about her ethnographic fieldwork would not have allayed anyone's suspicions.

However, Hurston is too good at telling lies to allow only one interpretation. The lumber workers are not the only ones getting conned here. While telling lies to the men wins their trust, writing lies into the narrative wins the readers' trust. If readers accept that Hurston's lies get her beyond the "too-ready laughter and aimless talk" that was "a window-dressing for my benefit," then *Mules and Men* tricks on two levels (62). Seemingly mediating between two "worlds," one black and the other (to no small degree) white, *Mules and Men* establishes itself as the only conduit between this and that "other" world. As in the paired introductory materials by Boas and Hurston, the text plays off the prevailing idea of the black ethnographer as perfect mediator, even as it puts on readers who accept that the narrator is on the level, rather than deceiving on dual levels at once.

Established as someone she is not, Hurston steps outside "to join the woofers, since I seemed to have no standing among the dancers. Not exactly a hush fell about the fire, but a lull came" (62). Since silence is an ethnographer's nightmare, Hurston awaits the opportunity to initiate contact. It comes in the person of a Mr. Pitts who woofs – or "half seriously flirts," as Hurston defines it (247) – with her to see how she responds:

> Then Pitts began woofing at me and the others stood around to see how I took it.
> "Say, Miss, you know nearly all dese niggers is after you. Dat's all dey talk about out in de swamp."
> "You don't say. Tell 'em to make me know it."
> "Ah ain't tellin' nobody nothin'. Ah ain't puttin' out nothin' to no ole hard head but ole folks eyes and Ah ain't doin' dat till they dead. Ah talks for Number One. Second stanza: Some of 'em talkin' 'bout marryin' you and dey wouldn't know whut to do wid you if they had you. Now, dat's a fack."
> "You reckon?"
> "Ah know dey wouldn't. Dey'd 'spect you tuh git out de bed and fix dem some breakfus' and a bucket . . . If you wuz tuh ast dese niggers somethin' dey'd answer you 'yeah' and 'naw.' Now, if you wuz some ole gator-black 'oman dey'd be tellin' you jus' right. But dat ain't de way tuh talk tuh nobody lak *you*. Now you ast *me* somethin' and see how Ah'll answer yuh."
> "Mr. Pitts, are you havin' a good time?"
> (In a prim falsetto) "Yes, Ma'am. See, dat's de way tuh talk tuh *you*."
> I laughed and the crowd laughed and Pitts laughed . . . They were afraid of me before. My laughing acceptance of Pitts' woofing had put everybody at his ease. (64)

This is another instrumental passage because it introduces several important black rhetorical strategies and it gets Hurston further into "the talk" with the men. The self-appointed role of Pitts is to monitor Hurston's speech and evaluate whether or not she belongs. The role of Hurston is to take his talk and turn it back, demonstrating that she is who she says she is – that is, one of them. Pitts accomplishes his role in at least three ways. First, he sounds or woofs, that is, he engages in indirect banter that Hurston must respond to in an appropriate fashion. Second, he talks about what others have said about Hurston, a friendly variation of loud-talking an audience, that is, speaking so that those who stand nearby can overhear, but cannot properly respond.[42] Third, the "yeah" and "naw" Pitts speaks mark that audience, that is, they imitate "not only what was said, but the way it was said."[43] Pitts tests whether Hurston knows what he is doing, and through her responses she indicates that she does. In the end, Pitts marks who he thought Hurston was, that is, a well-spoken, nicely dressed black woman driving a shiny car. He does this by speaking in "a prim falsetto." As Mitchell-Kernan observes, "Individuals who are characterized as 'trying to talk proper' are frequently marked in a tone of voice which is rather falsetto."[44] This mockery is the final test to see whether Hurston knows what Pitts means by how he has said it. With her laughter, she demonstrates that she knows what Pitts is doing and that she will get into it with him. As Roger D. Abrahams suggests, "the social boundaries between the in- and out-groups are nowhere so clearly focused as in this kind of context-situation" in which the styles of black speech determine status.[45] The appreciative laughter of the crowd signals that she has been taken in, at least on a provisional basis.

Yet the verbal contest for full acceptance is hardly over and it quickly recommences. In this instance, acceptance to the "inner circle" of storytellers must be earned through Hurston's proven willingness to perform successfully. The narrative reads:

> James Presley and Slim spied noble at the orchestra. I had the chance to learn more about "John Henry" maybe. So I strolled over to James Presley and asked him if he knew how to play it.
>
> "Ah'll play it if you sing it," he countered. So he played and I started to sing the verses I knew. They put me on the table and everybody urged me to spread my jenk, so I did the best I could. Joe Willard knew two verses and sang them. Eugene Oliver knew one; Big Sweet knew one. And how James Presley can make his box cry out the accompaniment!
>
> By the time that the song was over, before Joe Willard lifted me down from the table I knew that I was in the inner circle. I had first to convince the "job" that I was not an enemy in the person

of the law; and, second, I had to prove that I was their kind. "John Henry" got me over my second hurdle.

   After that my car was everybody's car. James Presley, Slim and I teamed up and we had to do "John Henry" wherever we appeared. We soon had a reputation that way. (65)

"John Henry" is a song Hurston discusses throughout *Mules and Men,* and collecting new stanzas of the ballad typically sung by railroad tunnel gangs was one of her fieldwork goals. That Hurston's initiation back into the oral culture of her upbringing comes with a performance of "John Henry" is a striking coincidence, since the folk song also addresses an initiation into a new world. In brief, the ballad tells the story of a legendary steel-driver who witnesses the introduction of the steam drill and tells his captain that he and his nine-pound hammer can outwork any machine the company installs. The ballad is a bittersweet comment on the tension between preindustrial and industrial realities: After an hour of fierce steel-driving, John Henry collapses and dies from exhaustion.[46] *Mules and Men* includes a version of the ballad in its appendix. One verse reads:

> John Henry told his Captain,
> Man ain't nothing but a man,
> And 'fore I'll let that steam drill beat me down
> I'll die with this hammer in my hand,
> Die with this hammer in my hand. (251)

What *Mules and Men* does not include, however, are the more bawdy versions of "John Henry" available to Hurston and her informants during the late twenties, versions that suggest "that the steel-driver's demise resulted not from too much work but from too many women."[47] As Lawrence Levine comments, while "John Henry" may not customarily be labeled a lewd folk song, "sexual innuendo and metaphor were constantly present in the songs of tunnel gangs, and *John Henry* was no exception."[48] Two sample stanzas Hurston might have heard in the twenties went like this:

> When John Henry was a little boy,
> Sitting on his papa's knee,
> Looking down at a piece of steel,
> Says "A steel-driving man I will be."

John Henry hammered in the mountains
Way in the north end of town.
The womans all laid their heads in the windows
When he laid his hammer down.[49]

The significance of "John Henry" as a ballad with erotic potential is not addressed directly in *Mules and Men,* and by including only a sanitized version in the appendix, Hurston does not help out her readers. Yet the world within the narrative makes little sense unless the reader brings to the text an understanding of "John Henry" that includes a grasp of its bawdiness. This interpretation is reinforced by the sexual overtones in the way that Hurston advances on James Presley and Slim Ellis, the way the crowd encourages her to "spread my jenk" (which an accompanying footnote blandly translates as "have a good time"), and the fact that all three end up together night after night singing "John Henry" "wherever we appeared."

When this background context is understood, it makes far more sense that this performance of the ballad sets into motion a story that reads like overwrought melodrama, with the author in the plot as a pivotal character: a story that ends with Hurston threatened by an enraged woman named Lucy at knife point. But even this is not enough, for making sense of the melodramatic story demands further knowledge that Hurston does not provide in *Mules and Men,* but only in her autobiography, *Dust Tracks on a Road* (1942). The story involves the friendship of Hurston with Big Sweet, a no-nonsense woman who is "shacked up" with Joe Willard. Willard relates a couple of the text's folktales, is the town's favorite dance caller, and philanders with Ella Wall, "the Queen of love in the jooks of Polk County."[50] As the story unfolds, it becomes increasingly clear that Big Sweet has lost her patience with Joe Willard due to his flirtations with Ella Wall.

Into this love triangle steps "Zora," who becomes Big Sweet's most constant female companion. Previously that position had been occupied by the aforementioned Lucy, a woman in love with the Slim Ellis "Zora" had sung with and "who used to be her man back up in West Florida before he ran off from her."[51] As Hurston's autobiography puts it, perhaps a little disingenuously, Slim was "a valuable source of material to me, so I built him up a bit by buying him drinks and letting him ride in my car."[52] Predictably, a jealous Lucy turns against Hurston and Big Sweet in *Mules and Men*. She sides with Ella Wall, telling her everything Big Sweet says. The second love triangle mirrors the first, and Lucy makes it clear that if "Zora" continues to hang around with Slim, she will try to kill her. By the end of the narrative, Lucy makes good on her threat, only to run into trouble with Big Sweet, who has a knife of her own.

This melodrama "Zora" is involved in is not just an elaborate documentation of the role playing an ethnographer inevitably engages in, and it is not only an open and deliberately overdrawn challenge to the mythology that an ethnographer has no impact on the culture he or she is studying. It is actually also yet another example of the way Hurston's text replicates, through a written strategy, the oral storytelling traditions of its subjects. As Abrahams has pointed out, the good African-American storyteller tells more than a story; he or she becomes

> master of the situation he is narrating, director of the heroes' lives in the narration. He achieves this kind of control . . . through the creation of a narrative persona which I call, for want of a better term, the "intrusive I" . . . This "intrusive I" . . . allows the narrator two personae at the same time, his own as narrator or commentator and that of the hero . . . Even when the narrator's persona retreats from that of the hero or main character, the narrator remains, intruding as a commentator. The "I" never disappears completely, though it may recede temporarily. Thus any of the battles won, physical or verbal, are won by both the hero and the narrator . . . He directs this battle as well as wins it.[53]

Clearly, then, while the consequences of "Zora's" romantic entanglements in *Mules and Men* have been interpreted as signs of "the dissolution of the fieldworker's control," attention to African-American storytelling traditions suggests the opposite.[54] Indeed, appropriating aspects of these traditions allowed Hurston to develop partial and experimental solutions to a prevalent ethnographic pitfall.

In allegorical form and content, the climactic melodrama in *Mules and Men* also bears more than a passing resemblance to the famous "toast" (or narrative poem) of black folklore about "the Signifying Monkey." The Signifying Monkey is a popular hero among black storytellers, and the one with whom they share identification. The rhyme contains countless variations, and though there is no known fixed text, the situation it tells usually concerns a trouble-making Monkey who wishes to beat the Lion in order to get back for a past beating. To this end, the Monkey signifies on the Lion, by telling him lies:

> The Monkey and the Lion
> Got to talking one day.
> Monkey looked down and said, Lion,
> I hear you's king in every way.
> But I know somebody
> Who do not think this is true –
> He told me he could whip
> The living daylights out of you.
> Lion said, Who?
> Monkey said, Lion,
> He talked about your mama
> And talked about your grandma, too,
> And I'm too polite to tell you
> What he said about you.[55]

Provoked by the Monkey to fight the Elephant, the Lion does so only to find himself stomped nearly to death. Realizing that he has been tricked into fighting the wrong foe, the Lion goes in search of the Monkey who can be found gloating from the safety of his tree:

> Monkey rapped, Why, Lion,
> You look more dead than alive!
> Lion said, Monkey, I don't want
> To hear your jive-end jive.
> Monkey just kept on signifying,
> Lion, you for sure caught hell –
> Mister Elephant's done whipped you
> To a fare-thee-well![56]

In this version of the toast, the Monkey accrues power through his rhetorical skills that overwhelm the Lion and get him to get himself into serious trouble, leaving the Monkey the clear victor. As Mitchell-Kernan comments, "The monkey and the lion do not speak the same language; the lion is not able to interpret the monkey's use of language, he is an outsider, un-hip, in a word. To anyone in the know, the monkey's intent should be transparent. If the lion were hip, he could not have been duped."[57] And as Gates adds, "The Monkey speaks *figuratively,* in a symbolic code; the Lion interprets or 'reads' *literally* and suffers the consequences of his folly, which is a reversal of his status as King of the Jungle. The Monkey rarely acts in these narrative poems; he simply speaks."[58] Once again *Mules and Men* makes clear that black speech is about attaining power and knowing how to employ it against more powerful foes. Stories of the Signifying Monkey can be found on records as far back as 1930, and there is evidence that this toast existed at least since the turn of the century.[59] It thus stands to reason that Hurston, raised and schooled in black folklore, knew the toast of the Signifying Monkey, even though *Mules and Men* makes no direct reference to it.

The ballad of "John Henry" and the toast of the Signifying Monkey are thus two further elements of black oral tradition Hurston manages to weave into *Mules and Men.* Significantly, both tell tales well known to have multiple versions, many of them obscene. Taken together, the veiled references to them make sense of the drama of which "Zora" makes herself the star.

Hurston must have recognized that singing "John Henry" with Slim Ellis signaled erotic intentions to the community and would provoke Lucy to seek revenge:

> Lucy came in the door with a bright gloat in her eyes and went straight to Ella. So far as speaking was concerned she didn't see Big Sweet, but she did flirt past the skin game once, overcome with merriment.
>
> "Dat li'l narrer contracted piece uh meatskin gointer make me stomp her right now!" Big Sweet exploded. "De two-faced heifer! Been hangin' 'round me so she kin tote news to Ella. If she don't look out she'll have on her last clean dress befo' de crack of day."
>
> "Ah'm surprised at Lucy," I agreed. "Ah thought you all were de *best* of friends."
>
> "She mad 'cause Ah dared her to jump *you*. She don't lak Slim always playing JOHN HENRY for you. She would have done cut you to death if Ah hadn't of took and told her."
>
> "Ah can see she doesn't like it, but –"
>
> "Neb' mind 'bout ole Lucy. She knows Ah backs yo' fallin'. She know if she scratch yo' skin Ah'll kill her so dead till she can't fall." (149)

That this passage oddly capitalizes "JOHN HENRY," whereas elsewhere the text does not, suggests the central importance of the ballad for explaining developments in the narrative. It was

"Zora" playing "John Henry" with Slim that ultimately set Lucy on a collision course with Big Sweet's pocket knife, even though "Zora" here positions herself as the innocent bystander. While it would be overly simplistic directly to equate Lucy with the Lion, Big Sweet with the Elephant, and Zora with the Signifying Monkey, such parallels are intimated. The rude description of Lucy in Hurston's *Dust Tracks* suggests that there existed a lasting animosity between the two.[60] Furthermore, the passage stresses Big Sweet's size in relation to Lucy. Lucy is "dat li'l narrer contracted piece uh meatskin" and Big Sweet wants to "stomp her right now!" And finally, given the context, Zora's comment at this moment that "Ah thought you all were de *best* of friends" is pure disingenuous provocation in the best Signifying Monkey tradition.

MULES AND MEN experiments in innovative ways with the difficulties of documenting storytelling strategies that have been, as the text states, "colored by the negro mouth" (45). The move toward fiction is part of *Mules and Men*'s overall strategy of replicating its subjects in its methods. While initially "Zora" says simply that she wishes to "set down" the oral folktales of black Floridians "before everybody forgets all of 'em," this statement cannot be taken at face value, for ultimately *Mules and Men* achieves something far more complex: a meditation on the processes of field research and writing that raises questions relevant to all those who collect stories from real people, be they ethnographers, documentarians, oral historians, or journalists (8).

The well-known criticisms of her contemporaries for Hurston's supposedly inadequate attention to white racism and the notorious political conservatism increasingly evident in Hurston's work in the years after *Mules and Men* and *Their Eyes Were Watching God* were published, as well as the problematic nostalgic and romanticizing tendencies recently identified by Hazel V. Carby already in these early texts, make it all the more crucial to complete the currently evolving picture of Hurston by examining closely the messages encoded in the individual tales collected in *Mules and Men,* as well as its overall narrative structure.[61] By placing Hurston's efforts in the context of the peculiar dilemmas facing a black collector of black folklore in the thirties and by analyzing *Mules and Men*'s mockery of a white readership, it becomes apparent not only how incisively Hurston dissects white racism, but also how sophisticated and innovative her reworkings of ethnographic paradigms actually are.

When *Mules and Men* is understood as not only about, but also an extended example of, African-American storytelling strategies – in other words, when it becomes clear that Hurston should not be read too literally – it becomes apparent that Hurston not only reproduces assumptions of exotic otherness, but also ridicules them, that she appropriates the self-authorizing language of an "objective" science only to debunk it, and that concerns about the power imbalance between her subjects and her readers were at the center of her efforts. It is precisely her engagement with the traditional storytelling techniques of her subjects that provides her with the tools for the beginnings of a revitalized ethnography. The experimental hybrid genre created by Hurston foregrounds, rather than suppresses, the impossibility of neutrality and objectivity, and continually calls attention to the ways the ethnographer's presence affects the tales being told and the tale-tellers themselves. *Mules and Men* acknowledges the role playing at the heart of the ethnographic process and leaves open-ended the meanings of the stories within its pages. It demonstrates constantly that shifting performative contexts generate shifting meanings, invites readers to bring outside knowledge to the text rather than accept it as a definitive substitute for the culture it describes, and proves by example that the culture it represented was hardly fit for a museum display, but rather provided critical insights that remain pertinent to this day.

5

Tillie Olsen and the Communist Press: Giving the People Voice

"M Y VISION is very different from that of most writers," Tillie Olsen said in 1974. "I don't think in terms of quests for identity to explain human motivation and behavior. I feel that in a world where class, race, and sex are so determining, that that has little reality. What matters to me is the kind of soil *out* of which people have to grow, and the kind of climate around them; circumstances are the primary key and not the personal quest for identity."[1] In Olsen's case, the "soil" from which her writing grew was unmistakably red. When she was eighteen, Olsen (then Tillie Lerner) joined the Young Communist League, the youth organization of the Communist Party. Eventually, political involvement brought her from her native Omaha, Nebraska, to the West Coast, where she became actively involved in the San Francisco General Strike in the summer of 1934. By 1934, Olsen also wrote whenever she could find the time and that year published a number of pieces in the *Partisan Review,* the *New Republic,* the *Young Worker,* and the *Western Worker,* among others.[2]

Yonnondio: From the Thirties is Olsen's most significant accomplishment from that decade, although it was not published until 1974. Prevailing scholarship on Olsen's thirties career focuses on whether her engagement with communism helped or hindered the novel's effectiveness as literature. In a pioneering early critical assessment of Olsen's Depression-era work, Deborah Rosenfelt concluded that "on the whole, in spite of the Left's demands on her time and energies, the prescriptiveness of its more dogmatic criticism, and the androcentrism or outright sexism of many of its spokesmen, there is no doubt but that Olsen's Marxian perspective and experience ultimately enriched her literature."[3]

More recent scholarship has been less sanguine about the role

110

radical politics played in Olsen's early writing. Paula Rabinowitz, for example, arguing that "scholarship about the 1930s has reproduced the conditions of 1930s criticism, which inscribed gender by maintaining its absence,"[4] believes that Olsen was not able "to disentangle her Party responsibilities from those necessary for her writing" and "as a woman worker and writer" was "multiply pulled by the often dichotomized positions operating within the Left."[5] Similarly, according to Constance Coiner, there are, in Olsen's dual loyalties to communism and an emerging feminism, "conflicting impulses" that are readily apparent when one compares Olsen's "openly tendentious" published writings from the thirties – writings that are "marked by an uncontested authorial voice and a completion and closure of meaning" – with *Yonnondio* itself, in which "Olsen strains away from her early 1930s 'official' proletarian literature" and consequently displays both an "evolving lyrical style" and "the complexity, susceptibility, and potential of human consciousness."[6] Finally, Alan Wald cites *Yonnondio* as one of a few worthy literary achievements by pro-communist authors of the thirties, but then adds: "It is possible to recognize such accomplishments without indulging in a policy of celebrating a writer's book simply because he or she adheres to a certain political line or comes from a certain class background."[7] In sum, these latter three scholars suggest (despite the diverse nuances of their points) that the strengths of Olsen's writings need not be interpreted as the fruit of communist conviction, although their limitations most assuredly can be. A commitment to U.S. communism, once perceived as a vivifying force in Olsen's development as a writer, is thus now interpreted as largely a problem she had to overcome.

Without wanting to minimize the serious problems thirties communists had with gender politics, or the extent to which Stalinism distorted their vision in general, this chapter's argument deals little with whether or not Olsen's adherence to Communist Party (CP) policies did or did not assist her literary talents. Rather than focusing on the relationship between politics and art, what this chapter seeks to demonstrate is the considerable extent to which Olsen's writings from the thirties need to be understood as wrestling with many of the same dilemmas evident in the CP press of her day and, moreover, that these dilemmas are quite similar to the ones exercising ethnographers and documentarians.

Yonnondio, I am arguing, needs to be understood as part of a
literary genre I call persuasive literature, one that has been almost
entirely neglected by scholars of the thirties. Like ethnography
and documentary, persuasive literature also strives to represent
lived reality in writing in ways that will change readers' minds
about social conditions.

Even while Olsen has insisted that her early writings were
not determined by communist imperatives regarding proletarian
literature, it remains incontrovertible that these writings were
produced within a communist context.[8] Not only does the revolutionary fervor of both Olsen's nonfiction and fiction from the
mid-thirties suggest quite strong parallels between her work and
the literature in CP periodicals, but there are also numerous moments in Olsen's prose when she engages with the particular
problems facing CP authors in a variety of experimental ways.
Indeed, while there has been a growing consensus that the thirties
were the decade Olsen began to move away from communist
commitments, her recently recovered column for the *People's
World* from the spring and early summer of 1946 strongly suggests the persistence of her involvement in communist causes.[9]

In order to illuminate how embedded both Olsen's nonfiction
and fiction were in communist concerns, this chapter will first
chart the tensions evident in the CP press of the thirties over
how best to represent people's voices and how to persuade their
audiences. As will be elaborated, there was a close connection
between CP press efforts to persuade its readership and its insistence on relaying the real voices of real people. Then I will turn
to Olsen's own nonfiction from the thirties to explore how it
grappled with these same conundrums. And finally, I will turn to
Yonnondio itself.

Throughout my analysis of Olsen's work, I will try to show
how – precisely because of her engagement with politically persecuted and marginalized peoples – she was acutely aware of a
phenomenon that has become a central preoccupation for cultural
critics in the 1980s and 1990s: the difficulty of adjudicating among
competing versions of reality. How to persuade readers to care
about the lives of the poor despite the proliferation of conflicting
narratives about those lives (especially in light of the frequent
power imbalance between readers and subjects) raised pressing
questions about how best to authenticate, and thereby authorize,

one's own perspective. My contention is that because of the pecu-
liarly powerful synecdochic qualities associated with the notion of
"voice" – the ways voices are conventionally understood to be
the most direct conduits to the lives they derive from and express – representing the voices of the persecuted and marginalized
became a central task for CP writers.

D OCUMENTING the voices of disenfranchised peoples was
a main aim of the CP press during the thirties. This intention was reflected in the mastheads of Communist periodicals,
which identified themselves as, for example, "The Voice of
Women Workers" or, in another case, "The Voice of Militant
Labor."[10] In addition, CP publications frequently included regular letters columns entitled "Woman's Voice," "Voices of the
Workers," "Voices from Prison," or "Voices of Protest."[11] The
CP press seldom questioned that voices mattered and usually
made room in their pages for them. For example, the *Labor
Defender*'s column, "Voices from Prison," routinely labeled individual letters with such captions as "A New and Militant Voice,"
"A Hero Speaks," "Answer this Voice," "An Inspiring Voice
from Sacramento," "Help Us Answer Their Cry," and "A Voice
from the Isle of Torture."[12] And *Working Woman* solicited its
readers to write to its "Woman's Voice" column by declaring,
"We want you to get together and give voice to the problems
confronting you."[13] The insistence that what they were representing were actual voices signaled the presumed authenticity of the
experiences and perspectives expressed. Furthermore, the focus
on voices, particularly in the letters columns, grounded abstract
discussions of "the masses" in the specific situations of individual
lives. Finally, the CP was clearly convinced of the need for individuals to articulate their own perspectives: Speaking out, speaking for oneself – these were crucial aspects of politicization.[14] For
example, this is how the "Woman's Voice" column sought to
encourage and empower its readers:

> Here are a few suggestions about what to write.
>   What kind of work are you doing? What are the conditions of
> the speed-up, the wage-cuts, and various difficulties on your job?
> What is your home life like? What steps, if any, are being taken in
> your neighborhood to fight these conditions?

These ideas are not intended to cover all the points which you
can write about. Write as you wish. Do not worry about not
"being a writer."[15]

In short, for these and other reasons, "giving the people voice"
was a central component of the CP's efforts at political persuasion.

Most letters to the CP press expressed not only clear support
for the struggle of working people, but also explicit support for
CP goals. Typical examples were the letters from striking workers who criticized the way their "local papers did not print one
line" about their demands and who warmly thanked the Communist press for its support.[16] Another typical letter from a prisoner
convicted of criminal syndicalism in California ended her remarks
this way: "I am proud to be a Communist, to be an I.L.D. [the
CP's International Labor Defense] member and that I carried the
Red Flag representing the solidarity of the workers and farmers
on the last International Labor Day, May First."[17] And one
"Mollie K." wrote that the "job of the women is to fight with
the men against wage cuts, come out with him in the front
on the picket line, [and] enlist in the unemployed council."[18]
The sentiments of the CP could not have been expressed more
succinctly, and like-minded letters dominated all CP "voices"
columns.

"Giving the people voice" could thus mean providing a forum
for airing grass-roots sentiments and individual workers' demands. But it could also involve sliding too easily from letting
the people speak to speaking for the people, thereby reducing the
cacophony of individual concerns to a univocal party analysis.
This tension lay at the heart of the CP's efforts, since – for the
tasks of persuasion and mobilization – either dimension would
have been insufficient without the other.

The tension was particularly evident in the way readers' letters
were framed. Occasionally, for example, editorial comments
were appended to a letter so that its persuasive message could not
be mistaken. After one such letter, the editors wrote: "Your letter
speaks not only for yourself" but echoes "the voice of millions."[19]
Another letter anonymously signed "Southern Textile Worker"
stated that its author was "writing in a little wooden shack with
the wind blowing through all the corners." Making a fire, she
added, "was a problem this morning because finances nowadays

around here don't come up to the high point needed to keep the
house in matches." There was "not a cent of cash in this house
and a heap of others like it." Perhaps uncertain how such poi-
gnancy and despondency contributed to furthering communism
in America, a clarifying note followed: "This letter shows how
the Southern textile workers are starving while working. You can
imagine what happens to the unemployed."[20] With the barest
hint of disrespect for its readers' intelligence, in these instances
CP periodicals attempted to balance self-articulation and pro-
grammatic analysis.

At times, though, the balance was disrupted, as it was in
"Voices of the Workers," a regular column appearing in *Labor
Unity,* published monthly by the Trade Union Unity League, a
CP-led industrial union whose sectarian loyalties were reflected in
its slogan: "Class Against Class."[21] For a time in *Labor Unity,*
readers' voices were carefully reconstructed – selectively quoted
and deliberately framed – by anonymous staff writers so that
every letter without fail opened with the "correct" politics. A
typical first sentence ran: "The Northwest lumber workers,
writes O. R. from Astoria, Ore., are fast waking up to the fact
that the only answer to the low wages and intolerable conditions
is STRIKE."[22] In general, it is difficult to read these "voices"
without suspecting that they have been revised for maximum
rhetorical effect:

> Last week, writes J. N., the Mercury Mill in North Charlotte,
> N.C., announced they were putting through another 10 per cent
> wage cut. This last one makes the fifth one in two years. All the
> men and women are against this new cut and are very hot about it.
> Then why don't you all stand up and do something about it?[23]

Yet another role played by voices in CP writings emerged in
simulations of workers' dialogues with one another. Just as the
combination of editorial remarks and readers' letters created a
dialogue of sorts between the party and the people it was trying
to mobilize, so also individual politicization was understood to
emerge from dialogues between party members and other workers they were trying to convert. In short, drawing people into
the movement was thought to depend to a significant extent on
individual conversations.[24] In order to instruct its readers on how
the process of persuasion should work, one paper, the *Young
Worker* (a weekly publication of the Young Communist League)

ran a regular fictional series entitled "Sez Pat to Andy." The column lasted from October 1933 to February 1934, and its favorite targets were the New Deal policies of President Roosevelt. Anonymously written, the column consisted of an imaginary conversation between two men, represented solely by their spoken words – much like a radio script. The only introduction was provided at the beginning of the first installment. "It may surprise you off-hand to learn that our friend Pat is Irish and Andy is a Swede, fresh from the farm," the introduction explained. "The repartee may not be so ripping now [and] then," the author acknowledged, "but the boys are merely exercising their inalienable right of expressing their opinions."[25] The potential benefits of enacting partisan instruction through a fictional dialogic encounter were obvious. Not only was the experiment in vernacular a means of inviting "ordinary" readers to engage with a debate they might otherwise find uninteresting. Even more importantly, "mistaken" notions could be represented and seemingly given their due, and then immediately be discredited. Indeed, as it quickly turns out, Andy is more than a bit naive, unable to grasp how or why Pat is so hard on the policies of President Roosevelt. For example, the dialogue opens with a vaguely favorable comment by Andy about Roosevelt: "Did you hear the speech made by F. D. to the Legion in Chicago? He sure put it over." In reply, Pat sneers: "Put it over is right. That's his specialty – putting them over." Andy is baffled: "I don't like the way you said that. It sounds kind of sarcastic like." Whereupon Pat condemns the National Recovery Act and ends with a jab at Andy: "That [Roosevelt] speech also was to get suckers like you all ready to go to another war."[26]

In the weeks following, Andy tells Pat that "the way you speak someone might think you were a Russian and not an American." Like some fed-up character in a Clifford Odets agitprop production, Pat responds smoothly: "Let me tell you a couple of things. I speak that way just because I am an American and I'd like to see this country run the way it should be. But right now neither you or I have anything to say about how this country is run. Only the bankers and bosses have that right."[27] Pat's bitterness and anger continue unabated in his conversations with Andy. Andy never seems able to keep up. In one discussion on a proposed government plan to help labor relations, Pat comments that working people will "get plenty out of it. But that ain't saying that it's going to be good. The more I think of it, the more it looks to me like we're going to get too much out of it." Confused by Pat's sarcasm, Andy responds: "There you go – always talking in riddles. To get anything straight out of you is like getting milk out of a bull. You're like the preacher back home was."[28] As this encounter indicates, the column's built-in dilemma was that Andy had to remain slow-witted for the column to perpetuate itself.

Trying to demonstrate by example how political conversation should persuade, "Sez Pat to Andy" could not represent the process of persuasion as it occurred without writing itself out of existence. Apparently unwilling to accept this possibility, the column persisted in setting Andy's innocent voice against Pat's savvy one. Far from being persuaded, Andy (after four months) ended just as stupidly as he began, and Pat remained locked into his own role as know-it-all. In response to one last question from Andy, Pat would conclude the column with this speech:

> In order to smash the rackets, you got to smash the political machines that support them; in order to smash the political machines you got to smash the big bosses that run them. Then you'll have something altogether different. You'll have the country run by workers.[29]

An appropriate coda for a column that had been repeatedly concerned with attacking not only capitalism ("the big bosses") but also the American political system, these ultra-left sentiments – throwing out the government and instituting a workers' state – represent a rhetoric that would have had little place in the reformist era ushered in by the People's Front the following year. Such soon-to-be-outdated notions may have been one more reason "Sez Pat to Andy" vanished from the *Young Worker*.

Yet there is at least one other moment that may have foreshadowed the impending collapse of the column. It concerns an episode dealing with events following the mysterious burning of the Reichstag in Berlin and, most specifically, the staged Nazi show trial of Communists accused of the crime. In the midst of Andy's typical blunderings and Pat's customary party-line pontificating, Andy blurts out a question that is not out of character, but does not reflect his usual innocence either: "Say, Pat," he asks, "is that really true about Hitler?" What follows is a rare moment of self-reflexive CP fiction:

> Pat: What do you mean by "that"?
> Andy (blushing): Aw, you know what I mean – what every-body has been saying about him.
> Pat: I still don't get you.
> Andy: Jesus Christ! Ever since they started printing damn near everything I say, I don't know what to do. I'm just afraid to open my mouth, and I have to count ten before I let a word slip out. Even when I cuss to myself, I look around to make sure nobody is spying on me. But as for this Hitler – is it – is it – is it really true he's queer?
> Pat (laughing): Queer! My God! Is Tammany crooked? Is the NRA hard on the workers? Is Mae West an angel? Is Hitler queer? Naw, he's just "one of those" that spends his time waiting for a street car. Why do you think the official anthem of the storm troopers is "Who's Afraid of the Big Bad Wolf"?
> Andy: You don't have to get so worked up about it, I just wanted to know, that's all.[30]

Mentioning "that" leaves Andy blushing and Pat confirming that Hitler was indeed " 'one of those.' " In a surprising conjunction, the column's sole moment of self-reflection ("they started print-ing damn near everything I say") coincides with the inclusion of an utterly superfluous discussion of Hitler as "queer." At all other points, "Sez Pat to Andy" had stuck closely to a standard (one might say exceedingly dry) CP critique of the New Deal and its failures. Yet when it turns to fascism, the text ruptures and turns homophobic, conflating homosexuality with a kaleidoscope of cultural references, all of which symbolize (to the CP) capitalism's decadence: political boss corruption, New Deal reform policies, and an openly sensual movie star.[31] Invoking the "specter" of gay sex, "Sez Pat to Andy" illustrates what it perceives as the thin line between capitalism and fascism, and a caption notes, "For once the boys agree and no wonder, the topic is – Nazis." Fur-thermore, Andy's curious articulations suggesting how he has been manipulated all along in a column intent on slamming home a CP line breaks the illusion of verisimilitude the column had been trying to create by calling attention to the very process of representation. The excess of the passage makes no sense, except as a signal of the constraints that would soon thereafter contribute to the column's demise. Andy's one attempt to escape the character for which he was slated highlights the impossible corner into which the party had cordoned itself. "Letting the people speak" (however unappealingly) was incompatible with sustaining a strict adherence to the party line.

More self-consciously aware than the *Young Worker* was of the problems that faced writers who sought to educate and radicalize working-class readers, other CP periodicals sought to prescribe possible solutions to these problems. These prescriptions suggested that there was a right and a wrong way to persuade through writing, a right and a wrong way to represent in writing the struggle for a revolutionary America. And throughout, whether proposing strategies for nonfiction or fiction, the CP press insisted on the importance of maintaining a firm connection to the real, to the actual experiences of working people – best expressed through those people's own words. More persuasive than omniscient narration, the Communist press clearly felt, the inclusion of seemingly unmediated voices would work to collapse the distance between subject and reader, and thus authorize the writing's persuasive messages.[32]

Despite the heightened self-awareness in some CP journals, however, the same seemingly inescapable tension recurred between letting people speak freely and providing an analysis that would, it was hoped, lead to transformed conditions. Typical examples of self-consciousness about this dilemma emerge in prescriptive writings from the *Western Worker,* a San Francisco-based CP newspaper with which Tillie Olsen had close ties. For example, between August and November 1935, the paper ran a ten-part series, "Manual for Field Writers," intended "to help our writers and worker correspondents achieve the best results in reporting for the Western Worker. Clip them and save them. Keep them on hand to instruct new forces as they are drawn into the movement."[33] Concerned that "the affairs of life" in the "capitalist press" are presented "as a confused and unintelligible welter" and that "history is presented as a jumble of a thousand unrelated incidents," the series insisted that the working-class press must recast the world so that "the worker can see it all as a related whole."[34] Still, the series instructed potential writers to "go easy on editorializing and philosophizing," since there were more effective ways to persuade people.[35] For example:

> If you tell a story about a worker fired out of a plant for union activity, you don't have to tell the reader that this is a "vicious persecution." Make the facts carry their own conclusions . . . If you tell the story and then tell the reader what to think about it and how to feel about it, he gets aggravated and you can't blame him.[36]

The series seemingly could not stress this point enough. "The best written news story puts down occurrences so clearly that the reader draws his own correct conclusions," emphasized a later article in the series on how to report conventions and union meetings. "The poorly written news story seeks to inform the reader what to think about it."[37]

Significantly, the series insisted that particular attention be paid in revolutionary reportage to the question "What are the people saying?"[38] The series underscored the importance of interviews and urged reporters to "go into hotel lobbies, pool rooms, lunch counters – all of the places people gather and talk."[39] The series also stressed that the reporter ought not to "go in as a reporter. Join in their conversations merely as an interested person. Point out stories in the local papers and get their opinions. Advance such remarks as, 'Well, I don't go much on what you read in this paper, it's owned and controlled by . . .' Almost all people are disgusted with the capitalist press and it makes a good opening."[40] In brief, the series concluded:

> The working class press must be continually reporting the remarks of street car conductors, factory hands, laborers, elevator men, mechanics – workers of every sort. Anything these workers say is news in our press. This is the way to report REAL public opinion – not the insincere mouthings of silk-hatted leeches.[41]

This focus on reporting reality, especially on documenting actual and unguarded speech as the best means to that end, was also central in the prescriptions for revolutionary fiction. Further remarks in the *Western Worker* indicate that the newspaper sought "stories of struggle and experience written from one fellow worker to another." Its stories needed "to convey the essential ideas of the revolutionary movement to workers who do not yet fully understand the issues before them." Most especially, the *Western Worker* requested stories that "set down the dialog between yourself and the last fellow worker you recruited to the party . . . this alone would be a story that would be a valuable aid to other comrades, would convince hundreds of others, and would be filled with humor and interest."[42] Real conversation was the key to political persuasion, and writing those conversations could accomplish the same goal for its readers.

Yet many would-be writers who sought to express themselves in the Communist press had a difficult time finding their way into print. They found themselves denied a forum because they were not saying what the party wanted to hear in the ways the party wanted to hear it. For example, one intriguing sequence of columns in the *Western Worker* began on March 5, 1934, under the headline "Writers!! Workers!!", a front-page advertisement promoting "a contest in short stories dealing with struggles of the working-class [*sic*], preferably in the western states."[43] *Western Worker* promised that "a new [story] will appear every week until the end of the contest, June 18th."[44] However, on May 7, the newspaper ran an article chiding its would-be fiction writers: "No short stories have appeared in the Western Worker for the past two weeks. There are still over twenty on hand, but they have not been printed because for various reasons they fail to furnish the real picture or to inspire workers to struggle."[45]

After criticizing the various stories that had come in, the article tried to end on a more positive note:

> A proletarian short story is not a mere description of bad conditions. It is not an abstract discussion of the evils of capitalism. It should give a real and vivid picture of the fact that the workers and poor farmers are awakening and fighting. It should show militant struggle or the value of mass action, not just by mentioning these things, but by describing an incident in which they are used . . . Let's all try again.[46]

Six weeks later, however, "The Western Worker Short Story Contest" again announced that "many of the contestants have not taken sufficient care in preparing their stories, and others have written about situations and events with which they are obviously unfamiliar."[47] *Western Worker* had made it clear that the goal of revolutionary literature was to be convincing, to balance somehow verisimilitude with Communist didacticism. Yet here a commitment to publishing the voices of people in order to further their self-empowerment clashed with the desire for voices to operate as instruction and persuasion.

The Communist press always stated that it knew what it wanted from its readers, but like shifting markers on a playing field, what it said it wanted didn't stay quite still. This meant that "giving the people voice" took on multiple (and subtly contradictory) meanings during the early thirties. Writing voices could serve to instruct and persuade through the representation of dialogic encounters, as in "Sez Pat to Andy." Writing voices could also work to individuate the experiences of working people, as happened more or less effectively in some (though not all) letters columns. Furthermore, these same columns, along with the short story contests, encouraged real people to speak out, in the hope that this would be a first step on the path to self-empowerment and feelings of dignity for the otherwise silenced. Likewise, such letters and stories, along with reports on "REAL public opinion," would serve as a means to authenticate the sufferings of working people and thus to authorize the CP in its efforts to contest the representations of the working class in more popular and mainstream media. In this contest, the CP also hoped that the inclusion of "actual" voices would collapse the distance between subject and reader and encourage direct identification with the disinherited and working American. Yet for many, as the preceding discussion of nonfictional and fictional prescriptions suggests, in order to create the illusion of authenticity and immediacy, a painstaking artificiality was often demanded.

FROM THE BEGINNING of the economic crisis in 1929 until 1933, the Communist Party of the United States (along with Communist movements worldwide) resisted all cooperation with democratic or reform activities and insisted on separate organizations operated and led solely by CP members. Known as the third period, this historical moment was characterized by the isolation and marginalization of Communist activities and resulted in the party's general inability to expand its membership or establish its strength among workers. By 1933, some frustrated Communist leaders articulated the beginnings of a new position, which would permit more broad-based coalitions with democratic reform movements. With a People's Front, these reform-minded Communists hoped to appeal more widely to workers and intellectuals alike. But the People's Front did not become official party policy until the summer of 1935. Thus, the period from 1933 until mid-1935 can be understood as a transitional period in Communist history that gave evidence of many contradictory cultural and political impulses.[48]

It was during this transitional period that Tillie Olsen achieved a degree of prominence as writer and spokesperson for the Young Communist League. As one recent historian has noted, "during the early years of the depression a new generation of militants, mostly native born ethnics, joined either the Party or the Young Communist League," and while an older generation had been "more concerned with guarding orthodoxy than leading social struggles, for these young men and women the formative political experience which shaped their development was their activity on the forefront of the struggles of the early 1930s."[49] Tillie Olsen was one of this new generation, and her career as a young writer and militant can be understood as of a piece with the rapidly shifting tides in CP analysis during the mid-thirties.

"What are the people saying?" the *Western Worker* had asked its writers to find out. In her article on the events surrounding July 5, 1934, or "Bloody Thursday," Olsen provided one answer.[50] This is how she recounted an incidental moment after state police opened fire on striking maritime workers in San Francisco, killing two men:

> The man stopping me on the corner, seeing my angry tears as I read the paper, "Listen," he said, and he talked because he had to talk, because in an hour all the beliefs of his life had been riddled and torn away – "Listen, I was down there, on the waterfront, do you know what they're doing – they were shooting SHOOT-ING – " and that word came out anguished and separate, "shooting right into men, human beings, they were shooting into them as if they were animals, as if they were targets, just lifting their guns and shooting. I saw this, can you believe it, CAN YOU BELIEVE IT? . . . as if they were targets as if . . . CAN YOU BELIEVE IT?" and he went to the next man and started it all over again.[51]

In one grammatically impossible sentence, this passage highlighted the tension between one who knows what she believes and responds with grief and anger and another who has had his liberal notions shattered because of an eyewitness experience. Through the representation of this man's fractured speech, Olsen's prose emphasized the urgent power of experience as it ripped through the consciousness of a man presumably not inclined to accept the Communist cause. His liberal arguments for reform stripped bare by bloodshed, the man echoes his incredulity again and again to one and then another anonymous person on the street. Olsen is herself mute. Her framing narrative underscores that what is past ("he talked because he had to talk") is also present ("the man stopping me on the corner") and that experiences like this never fade, are not forgotten. Brutality is stressed through repetition and uppercase lettering ("shooting SHOOTING"), and dashes and ellipses represent fragmented incomprehension. Partisan readers have their opinions confirmed, while more conservative readers might have their convictions challenged. By documenting a moment of conversion, of persuasion, the text undidactically expressed the hope that others might be persuaded, too. How a reader responded to the rhetorical question "CAN YOU BELIEVE IT?" would indicate where that reader stood in relation to the events unfolding in San Francisco.

Olsen's article further tells of "a night that was the climax of those first days," when twenty thousand longshoremen and Communists listened impatiently to the mayor of San Francisco as he attempted to break the momentum building toward a general strike. Again using ellipses to represent forgotten (or perhaps forgettable) speech, this passage describes the mayor as he addressed the auditorium:

> "Remember, I am your chief executive, the respect . . . the honor . . . due that office . . . don't listen to me then but listen to your mayor . . . listen," and the boos rolled over him again and again so that the reptile voice smothered, stopped. He never forgot the moment he called for law and order, charging the meeting with not caring to settle by peaceful means, wanting only violence, and voices ripped from every corner. "Who started the violence?" "Who calls the bulls to the waterfront?" "Who ordered the clubbing?" – and in a torrent of anger shouted, "Shut up, we have to put up with your clubs but not with your words, get out of here, GET OUT OF HERE."[52]

Five people speak in this brief passage, first the mayor's "reptile voice" and then a sequence of anonymous workers who are tired

of listening to it. The mayor insists that he is "your chief execu-
tive" and therefore is deserving of "respect" and "honor," but
the audience is utterly unpersuaded. The mayor's attempt to turn
the world on its head by claiming that the workers did not care
"to settle by peaceful means, wanting only violence," is what
causes the crowd to respond with its rhetorical questions, expressed with a collective fury.

Significantly, this contest between mayor and audience is over
power and representation, over who has, and who should have,
the authority to represent the world in words. It attests to the idea
that the power of language in shaping perceptions of the world is
a critical tool in shaping a public's opinion, and it addresses how
that power operates on two levels. First, there is the confrontation
between the mayor and his audience; it is crucial that Olsen's
article pits the insidious voice of elected authority against the
righteous indignation of the masses and shows that that authority
can be shouted down. But implicitly present is also the encounter
between Olsen's version of these events and how mainstream
and more conservative newspapers might have described them.
Olsen's inclusion of multiple workers' voices anticipates, and
urgently seeks to counter, "more objective" reports, whose
"balance" between the mayor's and the longshoremen's perspectives might have failed to portray accurately the actual
imbalance of power between the weight carried by each side's
words.

Olsen returned to the subject of the general strike in San Francisco for a second article, "Thousand-Dollar Vagrant," which
tells of the treatment she and three other CP members received
during a raid on party headquarters and their subsequent arrests.
In certain passages, as when Olsen listens to her comrades being
questioned in an adjoining room, another contest over power is
represented, this time over the need to be heard if communist
voices are to make a difference. However, here the contest is also
about the failure of authorities to listen and the subsequent threats
of violence made against the silenced:

> They tell me to go in the other room. I am glad to sit down. I
> know why they want me out of the kitchen. I hear the questions.
> "Where were you born? In Russia?" Silence, a thud of something
> soft on a body. "What you doing here?" Silence. A thud. "Who's
> the girl?" Silence. A thud. "Where do you live? You? How many
> times you been arrested? Who's the head guy around here? What

nationality are you? Come on . . . we know you're all Jews or greasers or niggers. Who do you live with?"

The gorilla leaves the others to do the questioning and the slugging and comes into the other room. "What's your name?" "Teresa Landale." "Your address?" I can't give mine. "37 Grove," I answer. "What?" he bellows, "that's the Western – Western Striker address." (Western Worker.) "What do you do for a living?" "I'm a writer." "A writer?" He calls over to a weasel-faced bull – "Hey, we got the editor of The Western Striker." I protest. In vain. From now on I am editor of The Western Striker. "You married?" I don't answer. "You're Jack Olson's [sic] girl aren't you? Aren't you?" I don't answer. "What you doing here?" "I came to do a little typing." "Ever been arrested before? . . . Who's the other guys? Who got away? You're a Communist, ain't you? You know what would've happened if we wouldn't 've come. You'd probably been raped. Don't you know these guys aren't any better than niggers?"[53]

Only their own questions matter to these police officers. They hear what they want to hear from Olsen and the others, and they believe what they want to believe. Their hostile questioning of those arrested (along with the text's clear suggestion that the three men are getting beaten) leaves little or no room for Olsen or the others to respond. The only strategies available are to remain quiet or to lie, and Olsen uses both. Only through writing down afterward the grossly unequal dialogue are the acts of cruelty and injustice, racism and anti-Semitism established. Only in the text, by presenting the competing versions of reality through voices and silences, does Olsen have the power to represent the police as they really were. The very act of (hi)story telling becomes a crucial political activity.

This intense interest in the relationship between language and power, especially in how best to represent voices, is also reflected in Olsen's choice of the other major subject in her thirties nonfiction: the circumstances surrounding the prosecution of eighteen CP members as a result of involvement with an agricultural workers' strike in the San Joaquin Valley. Charged with criminal syndicalism, the eighteen men and women were imprisoned for five months before trial and for four additional months during their trial. Eight were subsequently convicted of criminal syndicalism and sentenced to one to fourteen years in prison.[54] Olsen's first of two pieces on·this case discussed the grand jury proceedings against the labor organizers, with special attention paid to the inconsistent testimony of state witnesses against them. Entitled "The Yes Men of the Sacramento C.S. Frame-Up," Olsen's article reveals previously untapped skills at satire, and again the text's representation of voices figured prominently as a strategy for political persuasion:

> Did you ever hear him advocate the overthrow of our government by force?
> By force of arms, yes.
> Did you ever hear him advocate the overthrow of our industrial system?
> Yes.
> Did you ever hear him advocate general strikes?
> Yes.
> Did you ever hear him advocate resistance of officers with arms?
> Yes.[55]

Here the questioning of a prosecution witness by the prosecuting attorney explains the article's choice of title. The passage then notes how this same witness against the Communists "slipped up a little" when "he'd think he was still yessing and answer yes to questions like 'where did you hear him speak?' " Sarcastically, the text remarks that "you get to feel pretty sorry for ex-District Attorney McAllister by the time you've waded through the 160 page transcript of grand jury proceedings" since "all along he had to be extra careful to ask his questions in such a way that the witness would only have to say yes, and lots of times he had to break right in the middle to keep them from saying the wrong thing." Since court transcripts reinvent a version of historical experiences within the terms of the legal system and so become incredibly important methods for casting the "truth" of those experiences in terms acceptable to that system, Olsen's article's focus on an incisive reading of those court transcripts makes excellent political sense.[56] Her text offers up a "reading" of the court's version of events as if it was itself a work of fiction, which is precisely what the Communists believed the prosecution's case to be. In all, Olsen's article is entirely damaging in its portrait of how the law in California worked in 1934 to protect the interests of the empowered against everyone else.

"Yes Men" particularly, and irreverently, explores how difficult the prosecution's case was to prove despite all the built-in advantages it had been given by the court system. "Fake Witnesses Stutter Their Parts Despite Many Careful Rehearsals," reads a subtitle over the text. The article also attacks the second chance given witnesses for the prosecution who had failed the first time in their efforts to be cooperative, noting how the prosecuting attorney was given the right to "call a special second jury session to have them 'remember" more testimony, and fix it up about the pictures of the defendants which had strangely been wrongly identified."[57] "Yes Men," as in Olsen's other reportage from the thirties, works to correct official written records with a record all its own and approaches its responsibility with a clear recognition that language, however untruthful, can undeniably reshape reality and thus have real consequences, especially when it is backed by institutional authority.

Despite the fact that (at least in Olsen's version) the state witnesses were not telling the truth, it was the prosecuting attorney's version that became the one that mattered most. Not surprisingly, given the account in Olsen's article, the Sacramento grand jury indicted the Communists on criminal syndicalism charges, and Olsen returned to write a second piece on the case, though in a far different manner. Entitled "Why They're Trying Don," it focuses on the life of twenty-three-year-old Donald Bingham, whose mother "with the lint of the South Carolina cotton mills strangling in her lungs, coughed to death one night, leaving him an orphan." Now Bingham "is in the county jail of Sacramento, coughing and feverish with T.B.," but as Olsen adds, "Donald got his cough, not in a three year slavery in the cotton mills, but in the leaky, stinking jail of Fairfax, where he was railroaded in 1932 for leading a hunger march." Olsen's article notes that the "lessons that have brought [Bingham] today to membership in the Young Communist League (and to the Sacramento jail) have been of every kind." The account traced Bingham's life from his days working as a nine-year-old child laborer and fourteen-year-old vagrant to his early involvement with unions, where he "learned how corrupt unions can be." Later, in Oregon, Bingham joined the International Workers of the World. But "instead of a militant group that organized the workers and had an answer to how to go about eliminating the rottenness Donald found about him, he found instead a few bellyaching oldsters living on past glories who sneered at him for being young. Donald tore up his card." When the Depression hit, "Donald saw human beings starving," though he "kept trying to find a way out for all this." Finally in 1931 in Oakland, California, Bingham joined the Young Communist League. Olsen writes in undisguised triumph: "Donald had gotten his answer. He had found there was a real working class organization – and that what was more all the things he had suffered and seen around him, did not need to be." The article concludes with Bingham as an increasingly active and effective political organizer and "the growers and industrial associations that are behind the C.S. frameups knew that," and that "was why they had Donald indicted with the other 17. Because they knew he was organizing the youth to fight against them."[58] "Why They're Trying Don" is the most stridently polemical article Olsen published during the thirties, as it turns the life of one young man into a case study of radicalization.

Strikingly, the article includes not one direct quotation from Bingham. Instead, it rewrites the experiences of his life so that they form a straight line from impoverished childhood to imprisonment due to political activism. The article lacks the inventiveness more characteristic of Olsen's other essays from the thirties, and it resorts to more conventional methods in order to state its persuasive purpose. Olsen's essay on Bingham blocks out all competing voices and perspectives in a manner quite unlike her other articles from the era. For the first time, and at first glance, here is an article that suggests how capably Olsen could write standard CP news reports when called on to do so, even as it indicates the limitations of those standardized strategies.

In all her other nonfiction pieces from the thirties, Olsen had used competing voices to represent the competition of social class against social class, the struggle that lay at the center of the Communist analysis. Liberals babbling in shocked disbelief, pompous elected officials who demanded order, brutal police officers who asked red-baiting questions, and prosecution witnesses who said yes but didn't listen were all bit players in Olsen's journalistic world from 1934. Set these alongside the silenced and imprisoned Donald Bingham, whose life had been one of near-constant struggle for self-affirmation, and the pieces begin to fall together. Time and again, Olsen's journalism examined the repeated failure of conscience by various members of the power elite – their lies, half-truths, manipulations, and conniving cruelties – in short, a pattern of behavior that added up to one answer for Olsen, and that meant an unwavering support for the ideals best represented by the example of Donald Bingham, an unbowed member of the CP. Olsen's nonfictions recognized the powers not only of the spoken word, but also of the written, as a means for the redress of past grievances, as well as the need not only to criticize corruption and injustice, but also to affirm alternatives. In contrast to her dissections of mainstream and right-wing talk elsewhere, then, the celebration of a leftist activist in "Why They're Trying Don" relied on a different strategy. Attempting to avoid overt subjectivity, Olsen instead sought authority through omniscient narration. In short, viewed collectively, Olsen's nonfictional work did not stick with any one persuasive method, but instead shifted between methods precisely because none were or are completely satisfactory. Far from providing a sharp contrast to *Yonnondio,* then, the nonfictional pieces in a multitude of ways actually anticipated that great unfinished experiment of Olsen's career as a revolutionary writer.

I WAS WRITING about human beings and the circumstances in which they find themselves," Olsen told me about *Yonnondio,* the unfinished narrative she had begun in 1932 and set aside in 1936 or 1937. "I was writing about how circumstances shape people and how children are formed and deformed. My writing came out of what I knew and saw in other human beings." Of the migrant family whose life the novel chronicles, Olsen added: "It is *all wrong* that people have to live in such circumstances when they are capable of so much. The Holbrooks were who I would be if I had led that life. You feel such respect when you know them and the agony of their defeats. They never realize what possibilities there could have been."[59]

Yonnondio tells the story of an impoverished midwestern couple, Jim and Anna Holbrook, and their struggle to find a home and a dignified existence for themselves and their children. In its unfinished state, the narrative follows this family through a trilogy of locations as they migrate in search of better work: from Wyoming mining town to Dakota farming community to an unspecified city where most everyone works in slaughterhouses.

In each setting, individual family members display an almost transcendent capacity to endure both petty and not-so-petty hardships with remarkable strength and resolve, though they are also damaged by their experiences. In each place, this family bent on improving its lot is confronted with oppressive realities that make it impossible to break even, let alone find a new and better life.

As a persuasive narrative derived from the experiences of working people, *Yonnondio* extends and amplifies the recurrent concerns with voice expressed in Communist periodicals. Just as the CP press had done, Olsen's novel suggests the ongoing tensions between letting the people speak and speaking for the people. *Yonnondio* also employs people's voices in ways quite similar to those attempted in CP periodicals from the same era: as a mechanism for providing explicit class-based analysis, as a tool enabling worker self-articulation, as a means toward authenticating real lives and experiences while insisting on the individual conditions of workers as a supplement to abstract discussions, and as a method for collapsing the distance between subject and reader and creating a sense of immediacy and intimacy. But to the considerable extent that *Yonnondio* self-consciously engages with the dilemmas of how best to represent reality for the purpose of persuasion – and that it explores its own dissatisfaction with existing methods – Olsen's narrative goes much further than other CP literature.

Thus, in *Yonnondio,* the difficulties of representing voices for the purpose of persuasion are handled in a self-reflexive fashion. To a degree perhaps unrivaled in revolutionary fiction from this era, and only surpassed by the monumental nonfictional efforts of *Let Us Now Praise Famous Men, Yonnondio* becomes a narrative about being a novel about the uses of voice to persuade readers to care more about the American underclass. It is a book that does not take its task lightly, aware of the challenges and pitfalls that face any such attempt. Indeed, the text of *Yonnondio* switches almost ceaselessly from one narrative strategy for representing voice to another (and then another), thereby reflecting an urgency befitting its ambitious aim. This aim was clearly to make a politically persuasive statement about social conditions for working-class Americans, silenced and neglected by government, businesses, schools, media, and all other established agencies and institutions purportedly designed to serve the people's needs.

The novel's self-critical commentary on how to write a novel about unjust working and living conditions begins with a direct expression of rage against a readership that might get absorbed too easily into the writing's poetry. In much the same manner as *Let Us Now Praise Famous Men, Yonnondio* disrupts and thwarts readers' expectations and efforts to empathize too quickly with its characters. An early passage tells of a serious mining disaster in a Wyoming mining town and describes "tearless" miners' wives who watch "frightened men" emerge from the earth while "the rest [were] sealed in an open grave."[60] The language is lyrical and evocative: "The shattered dusk, the mountain of culm, the tipple; clean lines, bare beauty – and carved against them, dwarfed by the vastness of night and the towering tipple, these black figures with bowed heads, waiting, waiting" (20). When the narrative line breaks, it is to ask readers a bitter question: "And could you not make a cameo of this and pin it onto your aesthetic hearts?" (20). When it turns to critique itself, the narrative mockingly meditates on its own portrait of this tragic scene: "So sharp it is, so clear, so classic" (20). Turning back to the reader, the text states about itself that "surely it is classical enough for you" and "surely it is original enough" (20). In highlighting its own fictive efforts to render the harsh world of reality in language, the voice of self-reflection (and self-mockery) postulates how representations cannot substitute for the real thing any more than caring about characters can replace actual concern for actual people.

As with *Famous Men, Yonnondio* insists on a heightened commitment from its readers, one extending beyond an appreciation for poetic language and poignant moments. To this end, voices intervene repeatedly in the narrative, articulating radical anger or advancing political arguments. Just as "Pat" told "Andy" exactly what the CP believed, so also characters in *Yonnondio* voice CP-style analyses of working conditions in a manner designed to be more persuasive than if the perspectives had been expressed by the narrator directly. For instance, one day after work Jim Holbrook sits on the steps of his home and talks with his friend Kryckszi and another man, whom the text describes as having "something wrong with his shoulders, so he hunched over, misshapen" (70). Kryckszi asks Jim whether he's still eager to get out of sewering into the meatpacking plants: "You not try to get on at the yards any more, Holbrook?" Jim responds:

"Naw."

"Today they hire."

"Damn shame you aint a nigger," the other man interrupted. "If you was you could get on in a minute."

"Today they hire," Kryckszi said again. "They think you are scissors bill maybe they take you too – that is why they taking blacks – they think they scab if there is strike – *have* to scab, how else they get job?" (70–1)

It is not only "realism" that dictates the inclusion of dialogues like this one, which incorporate a taste of working-class racism, not just a response to the CP's stated question "What are the people saying?" It is also an example of how Olsen has managed subtly to embed an instructive political point about employers' racism and ability to play black and white workers off against each other into a simple, casual conversation. At another point in the text, Anna Holbrook speaks of a friend whose husband was killed in a mine blast and tells how she "talks about the coal. Says it oughta be red, and let people see how they get it with blood" (2). And a South Dakota farmer concludes that tenant farming is "the only thing worse than farmin your own. That way you at least got a chance a good year, but tenant farmin, bad or good year, the bank swallows everything up and keeps you owin 'em" (29). Similarly, letting one of the Holbrook children describe the odor of a midwestern meatpacking town – "does too smell like vomit, worse'n vomit, worse'n dead dogs and garbage, worse'n the crap can" – carries more weight, through its "subjectivity," than a straight description could (56). Likewise, six-year-old Mazie Holbrook's curious question, "Pop, does the boss man honest have a white shiny tub bigger than you and he turns somethin and the water comes out?" conveys class injustice more movingly and pointedly than a narrator's recitation could (9). But finally, when a doctor insists that Anna Holbrook needs expensive medicines after her miscarriage, Jim's despairing words get appended with editorial commentary, not unlike people's voices sometimes were in the Communist press: "The doctor says she needs everything she cant get, tells me everything she needs, but not how to get it (cry from a million swollen throats), everything she needs but not how to get it" (78). The integration of voices frustrated and angry with the existing economic and social arrangements into daily conversation is clearly not only an effort to persuade through seemingly nondidactic methods; it also works to represent the nascent groundswell of discontent and yearning radical movements could draw on if they only knew how.

Yonnondio also deploys voices of authority in such a way that they undermine themselves and, through the innovative juxtaposition of various modes of address, are revealed as deeply callous and self-serving. In one instance, after a mine blast, "the statement the company already is issuing" is released even before the dust settles. The narrative represents the text of this statement elliptically, with much the same disdain Olsen showed the San Francisco mayor's words in "The Strike": "Unavoidable catastrophe . . . (O shrink, super's nephew, fire boss that let the gas collect) . . . rushing equipment . . . bending every effort . . . sparing no expense . . . to save – or recover the bodies" (20). Here parenthetical information tells the real story, pointing to the actual perpetrator of the crime, as does the final dash (substituting "recover" for "save"), embedding the workers' truth within the fiction of an "official" report. As so often in *Yonnondio,* alternative truths crack through. Rather than express genuine concern or acknowledge guilt, the official narrative had reconstructed unpleasant events in terms that denied all responsibility. Olsen's juxtapositions, then, educate readers to recognize that the effort to represent the world as it actually is, is forever contested.

Similarly, when a conveyor belt breaks in a meatpacking plant where Jim Holbrook works under insufferable conditions, the manager blames his workers: " 'Fined, fined for carelessness,' yells Bull Young. 'What jammed the convey?' " (125). And when a steam pipe breaks, scalding several women with boiling water, and horrified workers move to help, the manager again blames his workers: "Stay where you are . . . Carelessness. Nobody's getting away with nothing. You'll be docked for every second you aint workin. And fined for carelessness" (126). Empowered voices can always reconstruct events so that the real responsibility for economic violence is obscured, falls in some neutral terrain, or ends up with the victims themselves. According to management, accidents caused by half-hearted inspection of faulty equipment or by a grueling speedup system are never their responsibility, rather it was "unavoidable" or due to workers' "carelessness."[61]

Indeed, rewriting reality is a major activity of those who are in power throughout *Yonnondio,* and the dispossessed are often unable to resist. When a doctor examines Anna after her miscarriage, the narrative strategically divides his voice into halves – the said and the unsaid – so that his pathetic social Darwinism is represented and revealed:

> "How old's the baby?" (Damn fools, they ought to sterilize the whole lot of them after the second kid.)
> "Four months, mm. You remember how long your wife's been feeling sick?" Of course not. These animals never notice but when they're hungry or want a drink or a woman.
> "Hmmmm. Yes." She took the ergot down quietly, but moaned at the hypo. "So you had intercourse before, it wasn't only the fall." (Pigsty, the way these people live.) "And she's been nursing all along? We'll have a look at the baby." (Rickets, thrush, dehydrated; don't blame it trying to die.) "Viosterol is what it needs – and a dextri-maltose formula." (77)

The horridness of this voice needs no supplementary explication – it speaks for itself – and its evil is further amplified by the complete silencing of Anna and Jim. These strategies forcefully convey *Yonnondio*'s unequivocal condemnation of those whose professional credentials give their versions of reality "official" status, however undeservedly.

There is also Mazie Holbrook's public school teacher, a woman the text uncharitably caricatures as one who "waddled and held her head like a duck" (34). But the teacher is also discredited through her own words – for example, when she asks Mazie with a "wheezing horror" how it was possible that she was "eight years old and can't read yet" (34). One verbal slap is followed by another, and the narrative registers its disgust by running together the teacher's comments (to stress their fakey, formulaic quality) when she introduces Mazie and her brother, Will, to the rest of the class: "MazieandWillHolbrookhavecomefromthecountry wheretheygrowthecornandwheatandallourmilkcomesfromsayhelloToMazieandWillchildren" (49). It is further significant that afterward, during recess, a boy taunts Mazie – "So ya come from the country where our milk comes from; ya learn about bulls?" – and then hits her hard in the stomach (50). As before, so here again, Olsen has counterposed voices and description so as to establish a direct relationship between "official" talk and its material consequences: scalded flesh unattended to, a fist in the gut.

Outraged that those who speak falsely are empowered, the novel contrasts their voices with the painful silencing of the poor. There are several moments in which central characters, like Mazie and her mother Anna, are at a loss for words, and the consequences of oppressive economic and social circumstances on the consciousness of the poor is perhaps most effectively represented through their inarticulateness. Portrayed as someone of great sensitivity and imagination – stars, for example, are like "splinters offn the moon" or "lamps in houses up there" – Mazie's emotional well-being appears to depend on an ability to speak and to know the meaning of what she sees (32). "I know words and words," Mazie says in *Yonnondio*'s opening pages – "Tipple. Edjication. Bug dust. Supertendent" (4). But the words, like the world from which they arise, are disjointed pieces of a whole whose meaning eludes the young girl, and quite often, "the question she had meant to have answered could not be clamped into words" (9–10). When Mazie sings it brings to mind "a longing, a want undefined, for something lost, for something never known," and though she tries she cannot express that feeling: "Oh, singin is like . . . Mazie, broken, searched for the word, feeling tears stand behind her eyelids. Singin is like . . . But no right words would form" (53).

When Mazie attends school for the first time and rapidly learns to read, "the crooked white worms of words on the second-grade blackboard magically transforming into words known and said" (34), her schooling also brings with it a new shame: "For the first time, Mazie was acutely conscious of her scuffed shoes, rag-bag clothes, quilt coat" (35). Furthermore, when her mother falls ill, and the eight-year-old is forced to take over maternal tasks ("Git to that tub of diapers. Yes, Ma."), Mazie has increasing trouble: "You will recite, Mazie. A hushed voice, faltering, that was she. We will have a test. And her pencil would move over the paper, separate from her guidance and her body" (58). The result is a "failure report" (67).

Similarly, Anna loses her voice when she permits herself to feel the multitudinous difficulties confronting her. "O Momma, what's the matter?" Mazie asks her. The text continues:

> "Nothing, Mazie." Kneeling down on the floor alongside to reassure her; smiling a tormented smile. "I've got to . . ." her throat constricting, "do something."

"What, Momma?"

"I dont know," twisting and twisting the rompers, "I dont know." (88–9)

These stammered speeches do not push a political program in the same way that other more openly didactic articulations in the narrative do. Rather, they appear as part of a self-conscious awareness that genuine authenticity would have to reflect an increasingly shaky confidence just as much as increasing rebellion. Yet this too is a political point, for it is clearly the circumstances that cause the silence. Throughout, then, *Yonnondio* implicitly underscores the importance of self-articulation for empowerment.[62]

At other moments, however, *Yonnondio* makes clear that self-articulation is not nearly sufficient for engendering social change. In focusing on the relationship between struggles for individual self-respect and a collective struggle for social justice – for example, in recounting an incident at Jim Holbrook's sewering job – the narrative makes that point on two levels. Through the representation of dialogues between Holbrook and his co-workers and his manager, an individual speaking out and rebelling alone is portrayed as deluded. Not content to let the dialogue alone communicate this message, however, Olsen also ultimately intervenes with her own voice. The incident begins with a conversation between Jim Holbrook and a co-worker, Jim Tracy. Tracy is a big talker, a young man who keeps up a steady string of complaints about the job they do. "I'll make a kick with that bastard today," Tracy promises one day after work, predicting that the contractor will order a speedup (59). An exhausted Holbrook responds, "Put on the low needle and give our ears a vacation" (60). When the contractor "came in, puffed up like a balloon, with a smaller red balloon of a face wobbling on top," he does in fact demand a speedup, just as Tracy anticipated (60). Like all managers in Olsen's novel, this one is incapable of real compassion for his workers: "What I want to know is what the hell you do when you're on the job, suck titty?" (60). The men protest and the contractor threatens to fire them all: "There's plenty good concrete men and muckers with their tongues hangin out for a job" (60–1). When an unbowed Tracy keeps his word and quits ("Not me . . . I'm throwin up this sh——y job"), the contractor lays down a challenge: "Anybody else feel like the breadline?"

(61). But no one besides the unmarried Tracy can afford to speak out and lose his job.

Left at that, the narrative's major argument – that genuine radical action can only be achieved when workers bond together – would potentially be lost. Thus, the narrative abruptly breaks in order to address more precisely what is at stake in solitary choices like Tracy's. Without "a wife and kids hangin round his neck," the narrative informs us, it is easy for Tracy to quit. He is young and so still "believed the bull about freedomofopportunity and a chancetorise and ifyoureallywanttoworkyoucanalwaysfindajob and ruggedindividualism and something about pursuitofhappiness" (62). Then this interruption interrupts itself, this time to speak about Tracy's future, finding him impoverished, panhandling, "nowhere to go, the flophouses, the slophouses, a bowl of misery and a last month's cruller" (63). At the end of this flashforward, Tracy is in his "last hour writhing in the 'piano' in the chain gang down in Florida" (64). Finally, brought back to the present and shifting the mode of address again, the narrator makes even more plain her revolutionary manifesto by speaking directly at Tracy from behind the veil of fictiveness:

> And there's nothing to say, Jim Tracy, I'm sorry, Jim Tracy, sorry as hell we weren't stronger and could get to you in time and show you that kind of individual revolt was no good, kid, no good at all, you had to bide your time and take it till there were enough of you to fight it all together on the job, and bide your time, and take it till the day millions of fists clamped in yours, and you could wipe out the whole thing, the whole goddamn thing, and a human could be a human for the first time on earth. (64)

In short, in its creative and shifting mix of modes of address, the narrative replicates its own persuasive point that one person speaking and acting alone cannot change the world.

Not just in its message, then, but also in its method, *Yonnondio* is best understood as an extension of – and not a break from – concerns and dilemmas expressed in the Communist press of the thirties. Linking individuated accounts of working-class lives to a revolutionary analysis, the novel rewrites the fallacy of a "rags-to-riches" mythology. Demonstrating the uselessness of individual action, the novel emphasizes the necessity of collective organization. Unmasking the claims that managers, doctors, teachers, or anyone else with loyalties to the existing political or economic system genuinely cares about the plight of the working family in America, the novel argues that these individuals represent a class that cannot be trusted to defend or even understand workers' concerns. Directly engaged with the question of how best to use language for persuasive and radicalizing ends and how best to articulate the relationship between writing and reality so that social change could be engendered, *Yonnondio* concluded that letting the people speak was simply not enough; sometimes it must speak for the people. Written from within a revolutionary context, all of Tillie Olsen's fragmentary and experimental nonfictions and fictions from the Depression era reflect an ever-changing methodology developed out of a radical concern with the connections between speech, silence, power, and material conditions.

RECENT feminist and postcolonial critics have agonized over whether the subaltern can speak at all, given the grossly unequal global distribution of power and the ways all representations are enmeshed in those unjust power relations – a question Olsen, in her portrayal of the Holbrook family, clearly confronted as well.[63] Cultural critics in disciplines ranging from literature to legal theory, anthropology, and history have also engaged in heated debates over whether "reality" is accessible, or indeed even exists, outside of its renditions in "texts," for many activists worry that to entertain such thoughts undermines the possibility of making truth claims about that reality. Because of the political struggles in which she was immersed, Olsen anticipated such concerns, and the diverse partial solutions she devised remain instructive.

Rather than assert the necessity for objectivity or lament its loss, Olsen's nonfiction and fiction alike continually and self-reflexively foreground the ways the "text" of working-class people's lives is invariably rewritten by those who are unjustly empowered even as it is still happening. Furiously aware of the futility of social(ist) realism, Olsen's writings grapple with this phenomenon by representing the representations, highlighting the proliferation of versions of reality, intercutting, juxtaposing, interpreting them. Yet these strategies are (crucially) counterbalanced by others. Whether reminding readers that language has material consequences or, like all self-critical ethnographers and documentarians, pushing readers to remember that caring about a representation can never be a substitute for caring and doing something about the real thing, Olsen leaves the responsibility for refusing comfortable solutions to the vexed question of the relationship between reality and representation squarely where it belongs: with us.

Notes

Chapter 1

1. *Black Elk Speaks: Being the Life Story of a Holy Man of the Oglala Sioux as Told Through John G. Neihardt* (Lincoln: University of Nebraska Press, 1979, repr. of 1932), 1.
2. Alfred Kazin, *On Native Grounds: An Interpretation of Modern American Literature* (New York: Doubleday, 1956, repr. of 1942), 383.
3. Ibid., 382.
4. William Phillips and Philip Rahv, "Literature in a Political Decade," in Horace Gregory, ed., *New Letters in America* (New York: Norton, 1937), 173.
5. B. A. Botkin, ed., *Lay My Burden Down: A Folk History of Slavery* (Chicago: University of Chicago Press, 1945), ix.
6. *The Disinherited Speak: Letters from Sharecroppers* (New York: Workers Defense League for the Southern Tenant Farmers' Union, n.d.). While William Stott cites 1937 as the publication date of *The Disinherited Speak,* H. L. Mitchell cites 1938, and the National Union Catalogue lists no date. William Stott, *Documentary Expression and Thirties America* (Chicago: University of Chicago Press, 1986, repr. of 1973), 344, and H. L. Mitchell, *Mean Things Happening in This Land* (Montclair, NJ: Allanheld, Osmun, 1979), 105.
7. W. T. Couch, "Preface" to *These Are Our Lives as Told by the People and Written by Members of the Federal Writers' Project of the Works Progress Administration in North Carolina, Tennessee, and Georgia* (Chapel Hill: University of North Carolina Press, 1939), xiii–xiv.
8. *These Are Our Lives,* 418.
9. Stott, 25.
10. James Clifford, "Introduction: Partial Truths," in Clifford and George E. Marcus, eds., *Writing Culture: The Poetics and Politics of Ethnography* (Berkeley: University of California Press, 1986), 1–26.
11. For some useful discussions of these debates, see Clifford and Marcus; James Clifford, *The Predicament of Culture: Twentieth-Century Ethnography, Literature, and Art* (Cambridge, MA: Harvard University Press, 1988); Micaela DiLeonardo, ed., *Gender at the Crossroads of Knowledge: Feminist Anthro-*

141

pology in the Postmodern Era (Berkeley: University of California Press, 1991); Johannes Fabian, "Presence and Representation: The Other in Anthropological Writing," *Critical Inquiry* 16 (Summer 1990): 753–72; Frances E. Mascia-Lees, Patricia Sharpe, and Colleen Ballerino Cohen, "The Postmodernist Turn in Anthropology: Cautions from a Feminist Perspective," *Signs* 15 (Autumn 1989): 7–33; and Micaela DiLeonardo, "Malinowski's Nephews," *Nation* 248 (March 13, 1989): 350–2. For a discussion of the ways some of Clifford's earlier formulations have been applied by literary scholars, see also the essays in Marc Manganaro, ed., *Modernist Anthropology: From Fieldwork to Text* (Princeton, NJ: Princeton University Press, 1990). Others who address the complexities of ethnographic-style encounters include Alessandro Portelli, *The Death of Luigi Trastulli and Other Stories: Form and Meaning in Oral History* (Albany: State University of New York Press, 1991); Raphael Samuel and Paul Thompson, eds., *The Myths We Live By* (New York: Routledge, 1990); Michael Frisch, *A Shared Authority: Essays on the Craft and Meaning of Oral and Public History* (Albany: State University of New York Press, 1990); Paul Sullivan, *Unfinished Conversations: Mayans and Foreigners Between the Two Wars* (New York: Knopf, 1989); Ronald Grele, *Envelopes of Sound: Six Practitioners Discuss the Method, Theory, and Practice of Oral History and Oral Testimony* (Chicago: Precedent, 1975); Dennis Tedlock, *The Spoken Word and the Work of Interpretation* (Philadelphia: University of Pennsylvania Press, 1983); and Dell Hymes, *"In Vain I Tried to Tell You": Essays in Native American Ethnopoetics* (Philadelphia: University of Pennsylvania Press, 1981).

12. Renato Rosaldo, *Culture and Truth: The Remaking of Social Analysis* (Boston: Beacon, 1989), 30–2.

13. See the excellent synthetic discussion in Mascia-Lees, Sharpe, and Cohen.

14. Marc Manganaro, "Textual Play, Power, and Cultural Critique: An Orientation to Modernist Anthropology," in Manganaro, 19.

15. Henry Louis Gates, Jr., "Writing 'Race' and the Difference It Makes," in Gates, ed., *"Race," Writing, and Difference* (Chicago: University of Chicago Press, 1986), 8. In a similar vein, Trinh T. Minh-ha comments: "The question 'What is oral tradition?' is a question-answer that needs no answer at all. Let the one who is civilized, the one who invents 'oral tradition,' let him define it for himself. For 'oral' and 'written' or 'written' versus 'oral' are notions that have been as heavily invested as the notions of 'true' and 'false' have always been." Trinh T. Minh-ha, *Woman, Native, Other: Writing Postcoloniality and Feminism* (Bloomington: Indiana University Press, 1989), 126.

16. Other such early attempts are the projects conducted in 1927–9 by Andrew P. Watson, a Fisk University graduate student in anthropology under the guidance of Paul Radin, and in 1929–30 by John B. Cade, head of the Extension Department of Southern University in Scotlandville, Louisiana. The Watson interviews focus on religious conversion experiences and are reprinted in their entirety in George P. Rawick, ed., *The American Slave: A Composite Autobiography*, Vol. 19 (Westport, CT: Greenwood, 1972). The Cade interviews have never been published as a whole, but excerpts appear in John B. Cade, "Out of the Mouths of Ex-Slaves," *Journal of Negro History* 20 (July 1935): 294–337.

17. Donald M. Jacobs, "Twentieth-Century Slave Narratives as Source Materials: Slave Labor as Agricultural Labor," *Agricultural History* 57 (April 1983): 223. Books that draw from the Federal Writers' Project Slave Narrative Collection include James Mellon, ed., *Bullwhip Days: The Slaves Remember* (New York: Weidenfeld & Nicolson, 1988); Charles L. Perdue, Jr., Thomas E. Barden, and Robert K. Phillips, eds., *Weevils in the Wheat: Interviews with Virginia Ex-Slaves* (Bloomington: Indiana University Press, 1980); Tom E. Terrill and Jerrold Hirsch, *Such as Us: Southern Voices of the Thirties* (Chapel Hill: University of North Carolina Press, 1978); Botkin, *Lay My Burden Down;* and Georgia Writers' Project, *Drums and Shadows: Survival Studies Among the Georgia Coastal Negroes* (Athens, GA: University of Georgia Press, 1940).

18. Martia Graham Goodson, "The Significance of 'Race-of-Interviewer' in the Collection and Analysis of Twentieth Century Ex-Slave Narratives: Considering the Sources," *Western Journal of Black Studies* 9 (1985): 132.

19. One important exception is B. A. Botkin, "The Slave as His Own Interpreter," *Library of Congress Quarterly Journal of Current Acquisitions* 2 (November 1944): 37–63.

20. Charles H. Nichols, *Many Thousands Gone: The Ex-Slaves' Account of Their Bondage and Freedom* (Leiden: Brill, 1963), xi.

21. Some important entries in the more recent debates among historians surrounding the uses of ex-slave narratives include Norman R. Yetman, "The Background of the Slave Narrative Collection," *American Quarterly* 19 (Fall 1967): 534–53; George Rawick, *From Sundown to Sunup: The Making of the Black Community* (Westport, CT: Greenwood, 1972); John W. Blassingame, "Using the Testimony of Ex-Slaves: Approaches and Problems," *Journal of Southern History* 41 (November 1975): 473–92; Paul D. Escott, *Slavery Remembered: A Record of Twentieth-Century Slave Narratives* (Chapel Hill: University of North Carolina Press, 1979); and David Thomas Bailey, "A Divided Prism: Two Sources of Black Testimony on Slavery," *Journal of Southern History* 46 (August 1980): 381–404. In this context, compare also the essays collected in Deborah E. McDowell and Arnold Rampersad, eds., *Slavery and the Literary Imagination* (Baltimore: Johns Hopkins University Press, 1989).

22. For critical assessments of the routine devaluation of ex-slave narratives, see Charles T. Davis and Henry Louis Gates, Jr., "Introduction: The Language of Slavery," in Davis and Gates, eds., *The Slave's Narrative* (New York: Oxford University Press, 1985), xi–xxxiv; and William L. Andrews, *To Tell a Free Story: The First Century of Afro-American Autobiography, 1760–1865* (Urbana: University of Illinois Press, 1986), esp. 1–31.

23. Ophelia Settle Egypt, J. Masuoka, and Charles S. Johnson, eds., *Unwritten History of Slavery: Autobiographical Account of Negro Ex-Slaves* (Nashville, TN: Social Science Institute, Fisk University, 1945), i. All subsequent quotes are from this edition and will be documented parenthetically in the text.

24. Ulrich Bonnell Phillips, *Life and Labor in the Old South* (New York: Grosset & Dunlap, 1929), 174. Compare also Frederic Bancroft, *Slave-Trading in the Old South* (Baltimore: J. H. Furst, 1931).

25. Davis and Gates, xi.
26. Warren I. Susman, *Culture as History: The Transformation of American Society in the Twentieth Century* (New York: Pantheon, 1984), 183.
27. Lawrence W. Levine, "American Culture and the Great Depression," *Yale Review* 74 (January 1985): 213.
28. Lawrence W. Levine, "The Historian and the Icon: Photography and the History of the American People in the 1930s and 1940s," in Carl Fleischhauer and Beverly W. Brannan, eds., *Documenting America, 1935–1943* (Berkeley: University of California Press, 1988), 22, 16, 20. Also see Lawrence W. Levine, "The Folklore of Industrial Society: Popular Culture and Its Audiences," *American Historical Review* 97 (December 1992): 1369–99, and the responses by Robin D. G. Kelley, "Notes on Deconstructing 'The Folk' " (1400–8), and Natalie Zemon Davis, "Toward Mixtures and Margins" (1409–16), in ibid.
29. Michael Denning, "Towards a People's Theater: The Cultural Politics of the Mercury Theatre," *Persistence of Vision* 7 (1989): 27.
30. Paula Rabinowitz, *Labor and Desire: Women's Revolutionary Fiction in Depression America* (Chapel Hill: University of North Carolina Press, 1991), 4. Also see Constance Coiner, "Literature of Resistance: The Intersection of Feminism and the Communist Left in Meridel Le Sueur and Tillie Olsen," in Lennard J Davis and M. Bella Mirabella, eds., *Left Politics and the Literary Profession* (New York: Columbia University Press, 1990), 162–85, and Charlotte Nekola and Paula Rabinowitz, eds., *Writing Red: An Anthology of American Women Writers, 1930–1940* (New York: Feminist Press, 1987).
31. Stott, 266. For similar conclusions, also see T. V. Reed, "Unimagined Existence and the Fiction of the Real: Postmodernist Realism in *Let Us Now Praise Famous Men*," *Representations* 24 (Fall 1988): 156; Richard H. Pells, *Radical Visions and American Dreams: Culture and Social Thought in the Depression Years* (New York: Harper & Row, 1973); and Kazin, 387. For example, Pells writes that *Let Us Now Praise Famous Men* "managed to summarize and transcend the attitudes and values of an entire generation" (246).
32. Errol Morris's *The Thin Blue Line* (1988), and Jennie Livingston's *Paris Is Burning* (1991), are two excellent recent examples of such films. A notable fictional film that adapts the documentary form as part of its critical engagement with the politics of the relationship between reality and representation is Tim Robbins's *Bob Roberts* (1992).
33. Stuart Hall, "The Determinations of News Photographs," *Working Papers in Cultural Studies* 3 (Autumn 1972): 84.
34. Edward Said, "Representing the Colonized: Anthropology's Interlocutors," *Critical Inquiry* 15 (Winter 1989): 212.
35. Michel de Certeau, "History: Science and Fiction," in his *Heterologies: Discourses on the Other*, trans. Brian Massumi (Minneapolis: University of Minnesota Press, 1986), 203.
36. Charles O. Hartman, *Jazz Text: Voice and Improvisation in Poetry, Jazz, and Song* (Princeton, NJ: Princeton University Press, 1991), 5.

Chapter 2

1. Forsyth Hardy, ed., *Grierson on the Movies* (Boston: Faber & Faber, 1981), 24. Significantly, the Griersonian model of documentary filmmaking almost always included an omniscient voice-over narrator, whose authority to present the lives of the film's subjects was never problematized. On the development of documentary cinema since the 1920s and its relationship to voice, see Bill Nichols, "The Voice of the Documentary," in Alan Rosenthal, ed., *New Challenges for Documentary* (Berkeley: University of California Press, 1988), 48–63.

2. Agee and Evans found Erskine Caldwell and Margaret Bourke-White's *You Have Seen Their Faces* (New York: Viking, 1937) a particularly egregious example of these general tendencies. They considered the book "morally shocking" – "particularly so since it was publically received as *the* nice thing to do, the *right* thing to do. Whereas we thought it was an evil and immoral thing to do. Not only to cheapen them, but to profit by them, to exploit them – who had already been so exploited." Evans quoted in William Stott, *Documentary Expression and Thirties America* (Chicago: University of Chicago Press, 1986, repr. of 1973), 222–3.

3. James Agee and Walker Evans, *Let Us Now Praise Famous Men* (Boston: Houghton Mifflin, 1980, repr. of 1941), 14. All subsequent quotes are from this edition and will be documented parenthetically in the text.

4. For example, see Alessandro Portelli, *The Death of Luigi Trastulli and Other Stories: Form and Meaning in Oral History* (Albany: State University of New York Press, 1991); Cynthia Ward, "The Rising of the Bones: The Oral and the Written," *Modern Fiction Studies* 35 (Spring 1989): 121–35; James Clifford, "Introduction: Partial Truths," in James Clifford and George E. Marcus, eds., *Writing Culture: The Poetics and Politics of Ethnography* (Berkeley: University of California Press, 1986), 1–26; Walter J. Ong, *Orality and Literacy* (New York: Methuen, 1982); Alessandro Portelli, "The Peculiarities of Oral History," *History Workshop Journal* 12 (Autumn 1981): 96–107; Jack Goody, *The Domestication of the Savage Mind* (Cambridge University Press, 1977); and Jack Goody and Ian Watt, "The Consequences of Literacy," in Jack Goody, ed. *Literacy in Traditional Societies* (Cambridge University Press, 1968), 27–68.

5. For an excellent discussion of a contemporary political trial and its relationship to orality, see Alessandro Portelli, "Oral Testimony, the Law and the Making of History: The 'April 7' Murder Trial," *History Workshop Journal* 20 (Autumn 1985): 5–35.

6. See Henry Louis Gates, Jr., "Writing 'Race' and the Difference It Makes," in Gates, ed. *"Race," Writing, and Difference* (Chicago: University of Chicago Press, 1986), 8; Portelli, "Oral Testimony," 12; and Ong, 79.

7. See Daniel Aaron, *Writers on the Left* (New York: Oxford University Press, 1961), 169–73, and Warren Susman, "The Culture of the Thirties," in his *Culture as History: The Transformation of American Society in the Twentieth Century* (New York: Pantheon, 1984), 150–83.

8. John Dos Passos, *The Big Money* (New York: Harcourt, Brace, 1936), 461–2.

9. The argument over the innocence of Sacco and Vanzetti has continued for more than seventy years. Recent books that detail the Sacco–Vanzetti case and argue that the two men were most likely not guilty include Paul Avrich, *Sacco and Vanzetti: The Anarchist Background* (Princeton, NJ: Princeton University Press, 1991); William Young and David E. Kaiser, *Postmortem: New Evidence in the Case of Sacco and Vanzetti* (Amherst: University of Massachusetts Press, 1985); and Brian Jackson, *The Black Flag: A Look Back at the Strange Case of Nicola Sacco and Bartolomeo Vanzetti* (Boston: Routledge & Kegan Paul, 1981).

10. John Dos Passos, *Facing the Chair: Sacco and Vanzetti – The Story of the Americanization of Two Foreign Born Workmen* (New York: Oriole Editions, n.d., repr. of 1927), 45. All subsequent quotes are from this edition and will be documented parenthetically in the text.

11. For example, the work of the Gilder Commission in 1895 and the New York State Tenement Commission in 1901 outlawed dangerous rear tenements, provided for light and ventilation in all tenements built after 1901, and mandated that all buildings over five stories have completely fireproof stairs and hallways. To a large extent, these reforms were the result of Riis's writings. Francesco Cordasco, "Introduction," in Cordasco, ed., *Jacob Riis Revisited: Poverty and the Slum in Another Era* (New York: Anchor, 1968), xx–xxi.

12. Jacob A. Riis, *How the Other Half Lives: Studies Among the Tenements of New York* (New York: Dover, 1971, repr. of 1890), 207.

13. See Jerrold Hirsch, "Portrait of America: The Federal Writers' Project in an Intellectual and Cultural Context," Ph.D. diss., University of North Carolina, Chapel Hill, 1984. Cp. Jerre Mangione, *The Dream and the Deal: The Federal Writers' Project, 1935–1943* (Boston: Little, Brown, 1972).

14. See Michael Schudson, "Objectivity Becomes Ideology: Journalism After World War I," in his *Discovering the News: A Social History of American Newspapers* (New York: Basic, 1978), 121–59.

15. Ibid., 122.

16. Stott, 77.

17. Ibid., xi.

18. For supplementary perspectives on Agee's development, see Miles Orvell, *The Real Thing: Imitation and Authenticity in American Culture, 1880–1940* (Chapel Hill: University of North Carolina Press, 1989), esp. 272–85; T. V. Reed, "Unimagined Existence and the Fiction of the Real: Postmodernist Realism in *Let Us Now Praise Famous Men*," *Representations* 24 (Fall 1988): 156–76; Carol Shloss, *In Visible Light: Photography and the American Writer, 1840–1940* (New York: Oxford University Press, 1987), esp. 179–97; J. A. Ward, *American Silences: The Realism of James Agee, Walker Evans, and Edward Hopper* (Baton Rouge: Louisiana State University Press, 1985), esp. 78–94; Lawrence Bergreen, *James Agee: A Life* (New York: Dutton, 1984); Victor A. Kramer, *James Agee* (Boston: Twayne, 1975), esp. 74–96; and Stott, esp. 290–314.

19. James Agee, "TVA I: Work in the Valley," *Fortune* 11 (May 1935): 142.
20. For the five-year publishing history of *Let Us Now Praise Famous Men,* see Bergreen.
21. *Farm Tenancy: Report of the President's Committee* (Washington: United States Government Printing Office, 1937), 11. All subsequent quotes are from this edition and will be documented parenthetically in the text.
22. See ibid., 106–8, for the complete list.
23. For a fuller discussion of these vignettes, see Michael E. Staub, "As Close as You Can Get: Torment, Speech, and Listening in *Let Us Now Praise Famous Men,*" *Mississippi Quarterly* 61 (Spring 1988): 147–60.

Chapter 3

1. See Frances E. Mascia-Lees, Patricia Sharpe, and Colleen Ballerino Cohen, "The Postmodernist Turn in Anthropology: Cautions from a Feminist Perspective," *Signs* 15 (Autumn 1989): 7–33; Marc Manganaro, "Textual Play, Power, and Cultural Critique: An Orientation to Modernist Anthropology," in Manganaro, ed., *Modernist Anthropology: From Fieldwork to Text* (Princeton, NJ: Princeton University Press, 1990), 19. Cp. James Clifford and George E. Marcus, eds., *Writing Culture: The Poetics and Politics of Ethnography* (Berkeley: University of California Press, 1986); Renato Rosaldo, *Culture and Truth: The Remaking of Social Analysis* (Boston: Beacon Press, 1989); Johannes Fabian, "Presence and Representation: The Other in Anthropological Writing," *Critical Inquiry* 16 (Summer 1990): 753–72; and Micaela DiLeonardo, "Malinowski's Nephews," *Nation* 248 (March 13, 1989): 350–2.
2. For further discussion of related debates in contemporary scholarship on Native American texts, see Susan Hegeman, "Native American 'Texts' and the Problem of Authenticity," *American Quarterly* 41 (June 1989): 265–83.
3. *Black Elk Speaks: Being the Life Story of a Holy Man of the Oglala Sioux as Told Through John G. Neihardt* (Lincoln: University of Nebraska Press, 1979, repr. of 1932). All further references are to this edition and will be documented parenthetically in the text.
4. John G. Neihardt, "Preface: The Book That Would Not Die," in *Black Elk Speaks* (New York: Pocket, 1972), xiii.
5. For examples, see Robert F. Sayre, "Vision and Experience in *Black Elk Speaks,*" *College English* 32 (February 1971): 509–35; Sally McCluskey, "*Black Elk Speaks:* And So Does John Neihardt," *Western American Literature* 6 (Winter 1972): 231–42; Lucile F. Aly, *John G. Neihardt: A Critical Biography* (Amsterdam: Rodopi N.V., 1977), esp. 168–77; Albert E. Stone, *Autobiographical Occasions and Original Acts: Versions of American Identity from Henry Adams to Nate Shaw* (Philadelphia: University of Pennsylvania Press, 1982); esp. 63–76; and Michael Castro, *Interpreting the Indian: Twentieth-Century Poets and the Native American* (Albuquerque: University of New Mexico Press, 1983), 79–97.
6. Arnold Krupat, *For Those Who Come After: A Study of Native American Autobiography* (Berkeley: University of California Press, 1985), 134.

7. Ibid., 129–30.

8. Paula Gunn Allen, *The Sacred Hoop: Recovering the Feminine in American Indian Traditions* (Boston: Beacon, 1986), 108; G. Thomas Couser, "*Black Elk Speaks* with Forked Tongue," in James Olney, ed., *Studies in Autobiography* (New York: Oxford University Press, 1988), 84.

9. The terms of this debate seem to have been first articulated in an article co-written by H. David Brumble III and Karl Kroeber, "Reasoning Together," *Canadian Review of American Studies* 12 (Fall 1981): 253–70. This essay has been reprinted in Brian Swann, ed., *Smoothing the Ground: Essays on Native American Oral Literature* (Berkeley: University of California Press, 1983), 347–64. Roughly speaking, Krupat takes the Brumble position and Kroeber extends Deloria's opinion.

10. Clyde C. Holler, "Lakota Religion and Tragedy: The Theology of *Black Elk Speaks,*" *Journal of the American Academy of Religion* 52 (March 1984): 19–20. Holler continues: "The intention of Black Elk's ritual giving of his vision to Neihardt was to 'make the tree flower.' The message of *Black Elk Speaks,* on the other hand, is that the tree is dead. The deepest and most essential changes Neihardt made in the editing of the transcript express this conviction and suppress Black Elk's continued faith in the efficacy of Lakota ritual" (41).

11. While the sacredness of Lakota language is a complex issue, helpful discussions of Lakota ritual speech and its sacred qualities include Raymond J. DeMallie, ed., *The Sixth Grandfather: Black Elk's Teachings Given to John G. Neihardt* (Lincoln: University of Nebraska Press, 1984), esp. 80–93; James R. Walker, *Lakota Belief and Ritual,* ed. Raymond J. DeMallie and Elaine A. Jahner (Lincoln: University of Nebraska Press, 1980); William K. Powers, *Oglala Religion* (Lincoln: University of Nebraska Press, 1977), 64–7; and Frances Densmore, *Teton Sioux Music* (Washington: United States Government Printing Office, 1918).

12. Indeed, Holler acknowledges the difficulty Neihardt must have faced in achieving such an end: "What was the proper use of this [spoken] material in the very different cultural context of English literature? Black Elk could tell Neihardt of his hopes for the book, but he could not tell him how to realize them in the different context of literate expression." Holler, 28.

13. *Black Elk Speaks,* 4. Compare with the stenographic transcription of Black Elk's speech; it is exactly the same. DeMallie, 284.

14. See DeMallie, 283–5.

15. Allen, 56.

16. Quoted in an interview conducted by Laura Coltelli, in her *Winged Words: American Indian Writers Speak* (Lincoln: University of Nebraska Press, 1990), 107.

17. Couser, 86. For Neihardt's admission, see McCluskey.

18. Castro, 86.

19. Paul A. Olson, "*Black Elk Speaks* as Epic and Ritual Attempt to Reverse History," in Virginia Faulkner with Frederick C. Luebke, eds., *Vision and Refuge: Essays on the Literature of the Great Plains* (Lincoln: University of Nebraska Press, 1982), 22.

20. Neihardt, xii.
21. Max Radin, "Introduction" to William Ralganal Benson, "The Stone and Kelsey 'Massacre' on the Shores of Clear Lake in 1849 – The Indian Viewpoint," *California Historical Society Quarterly* 11 (September 1932): 266.
22. See Jaime de Angulo and William Benson, "The Creation Myth of the Pomo Indians," *Anthropos* 27 (April 1932): 261–74. Also see the oral tale Benson contributed to Jaime de Angulo and L. S. Freeland, "Miwok and Pomo Myths," *Journal of American Folklore* 41 (1928): 244–9.
23. The reprinted version is in Donald McQuade et al., eds., *The Harper American Literature, Vol. 1* (New York: Harper & Row, 1987), 743–8. Further references are to this edition and will be documented parenthetically in the text. The original narrative was published in *California Historical Society Quarterly* 11 (September 1932): 266–73.
24. Krupat, 31. Also see Hertha D. Wong, "Pictographs as Autobiography: Plains Indian Sketchbooks of the Late Nineteenth and Early Twentieth Centuries," *American Literary History* 1 (Summer 1989): 295–316; H. David Brumble III, *American Indian Autobiography* (Berkeley: University of California Press, 1988); and Gretchen M. Bataille and Kathleen M. Sands, *American Indian Women: Telling Their Lives* (Lincoln: University of Nebraska Press, 1984).
25. Brian Swann, "Introduction," in Swann, xv. There has been some excellent (if controversial) work in this area. For example, see Dennis Tedlock, *Finding the Center: Narrative Poetry of the Zuni Indians* (Lincoln: University of Nebraska Press, 1977), and Dell Hymes, *"In Vain I Tried To Tell You": Essays in Native American Ethnopoetics* (Philadelphia: University of Pennsylvania Press, 1981).
26. The exceptions I have found are the two introductory statements: Radin, "Introduction," and "William Ralganal Benson," in McQuade et al., 742–3, which repeats much of the Radin material.
27. For an interesting discussion of comparable concerns in African literature and for an elaboration of the concept of oral subjectivity, see Cynthia Ward, "What They Told Buchi Emecheta: Oral Subjectivity and the Joys of 'Otherhood,' " *PMLA* 105 (January 1990): 83–97. On "preliteracy" in Native American culture, see Hertha D. Wong, "Pre-literate Native American Autobiography: Forms of Personal Narrative," *MELUS: The Journal of the Society for the Study of the Multi-Ethnic Literature of the United States* 14 (Spring 1987): 17–32.
28. For another intriguing example of how "Red English" gets written, see Thomas Abler, ed., *Chainbreaker* (Lincoln: University of Nebraska Press, 1989), a memoir first narrated in Seneca by Governor Blacksnake, then recorded by Benjamin Williams during the early nineteenth century and recently edited by Abler. The validity of reproducing "Red English" is discussed by Anthony Mattina in "North American Indian Mythography: Editing Texts for the Printed Page," in Brian Swann and Arnold Krupat, eds., *Recovering the Word: Essays on Native American Literature* (Berkeley: University of California Press, 1987), 129–48, and in the introduction to

The Golden Woman: The Colville Narrative of Peter J. Seymour, ed. Anthony Mattina (Tucson: University of Arizona Press, 1985).

29. Robert F. Berkhofer points out that the most popular Indian during the thirties was Tonto, the Lone Ranger's companion. Tonto means "fool" in Spanish. See Robert F. Berkhofer, Jr., *The White Man's Indian: Images of the American Indian from Columbus to the Present* (New York: Vintage, 1979), 102.

30. Alessandro Portelli illustrates the general tendency of written cultures to delegitimize oral sources. See especially his "Oral Testimony, the Law and the Making of History: The 'April 7' Murder Trial," *History Workshop Journal* 20 (Autumn 1985): 5–35.

31. See both "William Ralganal Benson" and Radin, "Introduction."

32. See, e.g., *History of Napa and Lake Counties, California* (San Francisco: Slocum, Bowen, 1881), 49–62. This particular account is fascinating because it includes multiple versions of the massacre: a historical report, a statement made by early white settlers, and a "verbatim" account by a Chief Augustine. Responding to the account, Radin questions the "somewhat romanticized versions of the occurrences in question, following approved models and involving a so-called 'chief' Augustine." Radin, 267. There is no Chief Augustine in Benson's account.

33. In the reprinted version, this passage contains typographical errors. I follow the punctuation and spelling from the original. Compare the reprinted version in McQuade et al., 745, with the original in *California Historical Society Quarterly* 11 (September 1932): 270.

34. Alessandro Portelli, "The Peculiarities of Oral History," *History Workshop Journal* 12 (Autumn 1981): 98.

35. *These Are Our Lives as Told by the People and Written by Members of the Federal Writers' Project of the Works Progress Administration in North Carolina, Tennessee, and Georgia* (Chapel Hill: University of North Carolina Press, 1939), 418.

36. Here I have adapted the ideas of Walter J. Ong, "Oral Remembering and Narrative Structure," in Deborah Tannen, ed., *Analyzing Discourse: Text and Talk* (Washington: Georgetown University Press, 1982), 12–24.

37. The original narrative, *The Autobiography of a Papago Woman,* appeared as *Memoirs of the American Anthropological Association* 46 (1936). The 1985 edition of *Papago Woman* includes a foreword written by Ruth Benedict around 1933. Presumably the narrative was completed by that time. See Ruth M. Underhill, *Papago Woman* (Prospect Heights, IL: Waveland, 1985), vii. This 1985 edition is a reprinting of a 1979 edition published by Holt, Rinehart, & Winston. The original narrative appears as Part 2; the other material was appended later. Further references are to the 1985 edition and will be documented parenthetically in the text.

38. For example, see her *Singing for Power: The Song Magic of the Papago Indians of Southern Arizona* (Berkeley: University of California Press, 1938); *Social Organization of the Papago Indians* (New York: Columbia University Press, 1939); *Hawks over Whirlpools* (New York: Augustin, 1940); *Papago Indian Religion* (New York: Columbia University Press, 1946); *People of the Crimson Evening* (Washington: U.S. Indian Service, 1951); and "Chona: Her Land and Time," which is "Part One" in *Papago Woman* (1985).

39. Labeling Underhill's "editorial hand" as "heavy," David Brumble argues that *Papago Woman* represents very little of an Indian perspective. Brumble, 79.

40. For the fullest account of Underhill's transcription process, see the chapter "Maria Chona: An Independent Woman in Traditional Culture," in Bataille and Sands, 47–68. While Bataille and Sands discuss Underhill's misunderstandings of what Chona told her, their overall assessment of *Papago Woman* is quite favorable. For another positive interpretation of Underhill as transcriber, see Nancy Oestreich Lurie, "A Papago Woman and A Woman Anthropologist," *Reviews in Anthropology* 7 (Winter 1980): 119–29.

41. For a discussion of Papago oral tradition and song, see Underhill, *Singing for Power,* and Donald Bahr, *Pima and Papago Ritual Oratory: A Study of Three Texts* (San Francisco: Indian Historical Press, 1975).

42. For an alternate discussion of Chona's emerging identity, see Lawrence C. Watson and Maria-Barbara Watson-Franke, *Interpreting Life Histories: An Anthropological Inquiry* (New Brunswick, NJ: Rutgers University Press, 1985), 176–83.

43. Margaret Mead, *The Changing Culture of an Indian Tribe* (New York: AMS Press, 1969, repr. of 1932), 133.

44. James Clifford, *The Predicament of Culture: Twentieth-Century Ethnography, Literature, and Art* (Cambridge, MA: Harvard University Press, 1988), 80.

45. See David Thelen, "Memory and American History," *Journal of American History* 75 (March 1989): 1117–29.

46. David Brumble contends that Underhill is one of "the Absent Editors, those who edit in such a way as to create the fiction that the narrative is all the Indian's own." Brumble, 75.

Chapter 4

1. Howard W. Odum and Guy B. Johnson, *The Negro and His Songs: A Study of Typical Negro Songs in the South* (Chapel Hill: University of North Carolina Press, 1925), 3. For another discussion of the same incident, see Lawrence W. Levine, *Black Culture and Black Consciousness: Afro-American Folk Thought from Slavery to Freedom* (New York: Oxford University Press, 1977), 205.

2. The term "poetic sociology" comes from Alan Dundes, ed., *Mother Wit from the Laughing Barrel: Readings in the Interpretation of Afro-American Folklore* (New York: Garland, 1981), 182. Representative examples include DuBose Heyward, *Mamba's Daughters* (Garden City, NY: Doubleday, Doran, 1929); Howard W. Odum, *Rainbow Round My Shoulder: The Blue Trail of Black Ulysses* (Indianapolis, IN: Bobbs-Merrill, 1928); Roark Bradford, *Ol' Man Adam an' His Chillun* (New York: Harper & Brothers, 1928); and Julia Peterkin, *Black April* (Indianapolis, IN: Bobbs-Merrill, 1927). More scholarly efforts include Mary Allen Grissom, *The Negro Sings a New Heaven* (Chapel Hill: University of North Carolina Press, 1930); Martha Warren Beckwith, *Black Roadways: A Study of Jamaican Folk Life* (Chapel Hill: University of North Carolina Press, 1929); Newman I. White, *American Negro Folk-Songs* (Cambridge, MA: Harvard University Press, 1928); Newbell

Niles Puckett, *Folk Beliefs of the Southern Negro* (Chapel Hill: University of North Carolina Press, 1926); and Dorothy Scarborough, *On the Trail of Negro Folk-Songs* (Cambridge, MA: Harvard University Press, 1925). Many of these works by white authors about black speech owe a considerable debt to the writings of Joel Chandler Harris. See, e.g., *Nights with Uncle Remus: Myths and Legends of the Old Plantation* (Boston: J. R. Osgood, 1881), and *Uncle Remus, His Songs and His Sayings: The Folk-lore of the Old Plantation* (New York: D. Appleton, 1888). Also see the important chapter on Harris and Charles Chesnutt, "The Spoken in the Written Word: African-American Tales and the Middle Passage from *Uncle Remus: His Songs and Sayings* to *The Conjure Woman*," in John F. Callahan, *In the African-American Grain: Call-and-Response in Twentieth-Century Black Fiction* (Middletown, CT: Wesleyan University Press, 1989), 25–61.

3. Robert E. Hemenway, *Zora Neale Hurston: A Literary Biography* (Urbana: University of Illinois Press, 1977), 89.

4. In this search for a white audience, Hurston was hardly alone among her black contemporaries. Hazel V. Carby notes: "The desire of the Harlem intellectuals to establish and re-present African-American cultural authenticity to a predominantly white audience was a mark of change from, and confrontation with, what were seen by them to be externally imposed cultural representations of black people produced within, and supported by, a racialized social order." Hazel V. Carby, "The Politics of Fiction, Anthropology, and the Folk: Zora Neale Hurston," in Michael Awkward, ed., *New Essays on Their Eyes Were Watching God* (Cambridge University Press, 1990), 74. Yet Hurston's efforts received considerable scorn from other black authors and intellectuals, among them Langston Hughes, Arna Bontemps, Wallace Thurman, and Richard Wright. See, e.g., the comments of Hughes and Thurman quoted in Hemenway, 64.

5. See Carby; Deborah Gordon, "The Politics of Ethnographic Authority: Race and Writing in the Ethnography of Margaret Mead and Zora Neale Hurston," in Marc Manganaro, ed., *Modernist Anthropology: From Fieldwork to Text* (Princeton, NJ: Princeton University Press, 1990), 146–62; Priscilla Wald, "Becoming 'Colored': The Self-Authorized Language of Difference in Zora Neale Hurston," *American Literary History* 2 (Spring 1990): 79–100; John Dorst, "Rereading *Mules and Men*: Toward the Death of the Ethnographer," *Cultural Anthropology* 2 (August 1987): 305–18; and Barbara Johnson, "Thresholds of Difference: Structures of Address in Zora Neale Hurston," in Henry Louis Gates, Jr., ed., *"Race," Writing, and Difference* (Chicago: University of Chicago Press, 1986), 317–28.

6. For discussions of these rhetorical strategies, see Geneva Smitherman, *Talkin and Testifyin: The Language of Black America* (Boston: Houghton Mifflin, 1977), 118–28. The phrase "talking black" comes from Roger D. Abrahams, *Talking Black* (Rowley, MA: Newbury House, 1976).

7. Zora Neale Hurston, *Mules and Men: Negro Folktales and Voodoo Practices in the South* (New York: Harper & Row, 1990, repr. of 1935), 125. All further references are to this edition and will be documented parenthetically in the text. Hurston's book consists of two narratives, "Part I: Folk Tales" and

"Part II: Hoodoo." "Part II: Hoodoo" concerns fieldwork conducted in Louisiana and is a slight revision of an ethnographic essay that had been previously published as "Hoodoo in America," *Journal of American Folklore* 44 (1931): 317–417. I am dealing here exclusively with the Florida fieldwork documented in "Part I: Folk Tales."

8. John Edgar Wideman, "Charles Chesnutt and the WPA Narratives: The Oral and Literate Roots of Afro-American Literature," in Charles T. Davis and Henry Louis Gates, Jr., eds., *The Slave's Narrative* (New York: Oxford University Press, 1985), 60.

9. Quoted in D. K. Wilgus, "The Negro–White Spiritual," in Dundes, 73.

10. Howard W. Odum, *Social and Mental Traits of the Negro: Research into the Conditions of the Negro Race in Southern Towns* (New York: AMS Press, 1968, repr. of 1910), 167.

11. Guy B. Johnson, "St. Helena Songs and Stories," in T. J. Woofter, Jr., ed., *Black Yeomanry: Life on St. Helena Island* (New York: Henry Holt, 1930), 49.

12. Sylvia Wallace Holton, *Down Home and Uptown: The Representation of Black Speech in American Fiction* (Rutherford, NJ: Fairleigh Dickinson University Press, 1984), 21.

13. See Melville J. Herskovits, *The Myth of the Negro Past* (New York: Harper & Brothers, 1941). Also see Lorenzo Dow Turner, *Africanisms in the Gullah Dialect* (Ann Arbor: University of Michigan Press, 1949).

14. Franz Boas, "Fallacies of Racial Inferiority," *Current History* (February 1927): 679. For a fuller discussion of Hurston's relationship to Boas, see Hemenway, esp. 88–101 and 206–15.

15. Thomas Jackson Woofter, Jr., *The Basis of Racial Adjustment* (New York: Ginn, 1925), 171.

16. Cp. Stephen Jay Gould, *The Mismeasure of Man* (New York: Norton, 1981).

17. Barbara Jeanne Fields, "Slavery, Race and Ideology in the United States of America," *New Left Review* 181 (May–June 1990): 107.

18. See John F. Szwed, "An American Anthropological Dilemma: The Politics of Afro-American Culture," in Dell Hymes, ed., *Reinventing Anthropology* (New York: Vintage, 1974), 153–81.

19. Adrienne Lanier Seward, "The Legacy of Early Afro-American Folklore Scholarship," in Richard M. Dorson, ed., *Handbook of American Folklore* (Bloomington: Indiana University Press, 1983), 50.

20. Ibid. For one important exception to this general rule, see the exemplary nineteenth-century collection of black folklore documents in *Southern Workman*, reprinted and discussed in Donald J. Waters, ed., *Strange Ways and Sweet Dreams: Afro-American Folklore from the Hampton Institute* (Boston: Hall, 1983).

21. Harold Preece, "The Negro Folk Cult," *Crisis* 43 (December 1936): 364, reprinted in Dundes, 34–8.

22. See James Weldon Johnson, *The Book of American Negro Spirituals* (New York: Viking, 1933), and W. E. B. Du Bois, *The Souls of Black Folks* (New York: Bantam, 1989, repr. of 1903).

23. Arthur Huff Fauset, "American Negro Folk Literature," in Alain Locke,

ed., *The New Negro: An Interpretation* (New York: Albert & Charles Boni, 1925), 241. Fauset is the brother of novelist Jessie Fauset.

24. Ibid., 240–1.

25. In addition to writings by Hurston, Abrahams, and Smitherman (already cited), studies of signifying include John Dollard, "The Dozens: Dialectic of Insult," *American Imago* 1 (1939): 3–25, reprinted in Dundes, 277–94; H. Rap Brown, "Street Talk," in Thomas Kochman, ed., *Rappin' and Stylin' Out: Communications in Urban Black America* (Urbana: University of Illinois Press, 1972), 205–8; and Claudia Mitchell-Kernan, "Signifying, Loud-talking and Marking," in Kochman, 315–35. Also see the essays by Mitchell-Kernan ("Signifying") and Abrahams ("Playing the Dozens") reprinted in Dundes, 295–328. These studies make clear that there are at least two dozen forms signifying can take and perhaps almost as many different names it can go by.

26. See the following selections by Henry Louis Gates, Jr.: "The Blackness of Blackness: A Critique of the Sign and the Signifying Monkey," in Gates, ed. *Black Literature and Literary Theory* (New York: Methuen, 1984), 285–321; "The 'Blackness of Blackness': A Critique of the Sign and the Signifying Monkey," in Gates, *Figures in Black: Words, Signs, and the 'Racial' Self* (New York: Oxford University Press, 1987), 235–76; and the essays in *The Signifying Monkey: A Theory of African-American Literary Criticism* (New York: Oxford University Press, 1988). For other examples of how signification has been used to interpret Hurston and other black authors, see Paola Boi, "Moses, Man of Power, Man of Knowledge: A 'Signifying' Reading of Zora Neale Hurston (Between a Laugh and a Song)," in Maria Diedrich and Dorothea Fischer-Hornung, eds., *Women and War: The Changing Status of American Women from the 1930s to the 1950s* (New York: Berg, 1990), 107–25; Jane Caputi, " 'Specifying' Fannie Hurst: Langston Hughes's 'Limitations of Life,' Zora Neale Hurston's *Their Eyes Were Watching God* and Toni Morrison's *The Bluest Eye* as 'Answers' to Hurst's *Imitation of Life*," *Black American Literary Forum* 24 (Winter 1990): 697–716; Klaus Benesch, "Oral Narrative and Literary Text: Afro-American Folklore in *Their Eyes Were Watching God*," *Callaloo* 11 (Summer 1988): 627–35; and Susan Willis, *Specifying: Black Women Writing the American Experience* (Madison: University of Wisconsin Press, 1987).

27. Smitherman, 118.

28. Roger D. Abrahams, *Deep Down in the Jungle: Negro Narrative Folklore from the Streets of Philadelphia* (New York: Aldine, 1970), 264, 52.

29. Mitchell-Kernan, "Signifying, Loud-talking and Marking," 322–3.

30. Ibid., 317, 326.

31. Smitherman, 121.

32. Ibid.

33. Michael Awkward, *Inspiriting Influences: Tradition, Revision, and Afro-American Women's Novels* (New York: Columbia University Press, 1989), 4–6.

34. For discussions of the subjectivities involved in the ethnographic process, see Renato Rosaldo, *Culture and Truth: The Remaking of Social Analysis* (Boston: Beacon, 1989), and the essays in James Clifford and George E.

Marcus, eds., *Writing Culture: The Poetics and Politics of Ethnography* (Berkeley: University of California Press, 1986).

35. Du Bois, 3.
36. Mary Louise Pratt, "Fieldwork in Common Places," in Clifford and Marcus, 31–2.
37. Du Bois, 3.
38. See Levine, *Black Culture and Black Consciousness,* 146–7. Also see Daryl Cumber Dance, *Shuckin' and Jivin': Folklore from Contemporary Black Americans* (Bloomington: Indiana University Press, 1978), 77–100.
39. For some discussions of ritual insult games, see Dollard; Roger D. Abrahams, "Playing the Dozens," in Dundes, 295–309; and Marjorie Harness Goodwin, *He-Said-She-Said: Talk as Social Organization Among Black Children* (Bloomington: Indiana University Press, 1990), esp. 258–79.
40. Mitchell-Kernan, "Signifying, Loud-talking and Marking," 319.
41. James Clifford, *The Predicament of Culture: Twentieth-Century Ethnography, Literature, and Art* (Cambridge, MA: Harvard University Press, 1988), 40–1, 79.
42. See Mitchell-Kernan, "Signifying, Loud-talking and Marking," 329–32.
43. Ibid., 333.
44. Ibid., 334.
45. Abrahams, *Talking Black,* 91.
46. The legend dates its probable origins back to the 1870s and the miserable conditions suffered by black workers who built the Chesapeake and Ohio Railroad in West Virginia. Levine, *Black Culture and Black Consciousness,* 421.
47. Ibid., 422.
48. Ibid.
49. Ibid., 422–3. Also see Louis W. Chappell, *John Henry: A Folk-lore Study* (Jena: Frommannsche Verlag, 1933).
50. Zora Neale Hurston, *Dust Tracks on a Road: An Autobiography* (Urbana: University of Illinois Press, 1984, repr. of 1942), 183.
51. Ibid., 185.
52. Ibid.
53. Abrahams, *Deep Down in the Jungle,* 58–9.
54. Dorst, 312.
55. "The Signifying Monkey," in Langston Hughes and Arna Bontemps, eds., *The Book of Negro Folklore* (New York: Dodd, Mead, 1958), 363. Other versions of this toast can be found in Abrahams, *Deep Down in the Jungle,* 142–57; Roger D. Abrahams, ed., *Afro-American Folktales: Stories from Black Traditions in the New World* (New York: Pantheon, 1985), 101–5; Dance, 197–9; and Bruce Jackson, *"Get Your Ass in the Water and Swim Like Me": Narrative Poetry from Black Oral Tradition* (Cambridge, MA: Harvard University Press, 1974), 161–79. These versions are far more obscene than the variation reproduced here.
56. Hughes and Bontemps, 364.
57. Mitchell-Kernan, "Signifying," in Dundes, 323.
58. Gates, "The Blackness of Blackness," in *Black Literature and Literary Theory,* 289–90.

59. See Abrahams, *Deep Down in the Jungle,* 142–56. On American black "toasts" as oral epic poetry, see William Labov, Paul Cohen, Clarence Robins, and John Lewis, "Toasts," in Dundes, 329–47.
60. Hurston, *Dust Tracks on a Road,* 185–6.
61. See Hemenway, 220–22, and Carby, 74–80.

Chapter 5

1. Tillie Olsen speaking at Emerson College in Boston in 1974, quoted in Deborah Rosenfelt, "From the Thirties: Tillie Olsen and the Radical Tradition," *Feminist Studies* 7 (Fall 1981): 404. This important essay on Olsen is reprinted in Judith Newton and Deborah Rosenfelt, eds., *Feminist Criticism and Social Change* (New York: Methuen, 1985), 216–48.
2. The list of Olsen's prose writings from the thirties discussed in this chapter is more extensive than in any previous scholarship, though it too may prove to be incomplete. The list is "The Iron Throat," *Partisan Review* 1 (April–May 1934): 3–9; "The Strike," *Partisan Review* 1 (September–October 1934): 3–9; "Thousand-Dollar Vagrant," *New Republic* 80 (August 29, 1934): 67–9; "The Yes-Men of the Sacramento C.S. Frame-Up," *Western Worker* (November 22, 1934): 3; and "Why They're Trying Don," *Young Worker* (December 18, 1934): 8. In addition, Olsen published two poems: "I Want You Women Up North to Know," *Partisan* 1 (March 1934): 4; "There is a Lesson," *Partisan* 1 (April–May 1934): 4. Finally, also in 1934, according to Deborah Rosenfelt, Olsen assisted in putting out the *Waterfront Worker* (see Rosenfelt, 384), and during 1935–6 Olsen is listed as a contributing editor to *Pacific Weekly*.
3. Rosenfelt, 403.
4. Paula Rabinowitz, *Labor and Desire: Women's Revolutionary Fiction in Depression America* (Chapel Hill: University of North Carolina Press, 1991), 5.
5. Ibid., 41.
6. Constance Coiner, "Literature of Resistance: The Intersection of Feminism and the Communist Left in Meridel Le Sueur and Tillie Olsen," in Lennard J. Davis and M. Bella Mirabella, eds., *Left Politics and the Literary Profession* (New York: Columbia University Press, 1990), 173, 179.
7. Alan Wald, *The New York Intellectuals: The Rise and Decline of the Anti-Stalinist Left from the 1930s to the 1980s* (Chapel Hill: University of North Carolina Press, 1987), 96.
8. Coiner, 174.
9. See Michael E. Staub, "Labor Activism and the Post-War Politics of Motherhood: Tillie Olsen in the *People's World,*" in Kay Hoyle Nelson and Nancy Huse, eds., *The Critical Response to Tillie Olsen* (Westport, CT: Greenwood, 1994), 104–9. Olsen's career as a fiction writer recommenced in 1956 with "I Stand Here Ironing," the first story in her collection of short stories, *Tell Me a Riddle* (New York: Delacorte, 1961).
10. "The Voice of Women Workers" was on the masthead of *Working Woman,* which emerged out of the National Women's Department of the Communist Party (CP) in 1929. "The Voice of Militant Labor" was on the masthead

of the Trade Union Unity League's *Labor Unity,* also a Communist publication.

11. "Woman's Voice" was in *Working Woman;* "Voices of the Workers" was from *Labor Unity;* "Voices from Prison" and "Voices of Protest" were both from the *Labor Defender,* the organ of the International Labor Defense, a CP organization.

12. These captions appeared in the following issues of the *Labor Defender:* "A New and Militant Voice" (March 1935), "A Hero Speaks" (September 1935), "Answer this Voice" (February 1934), "An Inspiring Voice from Sacramento" (June 1935), "Help Us Answer Their Cry" (November 1935), and "A Voice from the Isle of Torture" (September 1935).

13. "Woman's Voice," *Working Woman* (July 1933): 12.

14. Compare with the contemporary sentiments of bell hooks: "To understand that finding a voice is an essential part of liberation struggle – for the oppressed, the exploited a necessary starting place – a move in the direction of freedom, is important for those who stand in solidarity with us." bell hooks, *Talking Back: Thinking Feminist, Thinking Black* (Boston: South End Press, 1989), 17–18.

15. "Woman's Voice," *Working Woman* (July 1933): 12.

16. "Boss Mobs Terrorize Montgomery Mill Strikers," *Labor Unity* (June 1933): 27.

17. "An Inspiring Voice from Sacramento," *Labor Defender* (June 1935): 37.

18. "Woman's Voice," *Working Woman* (March 1933): 14.

19. "Our Answer," *Working Woman* (July 1935): 8.

20. "Woman's Voice," *Working Woman* (June 1933): 13.

21. Fraser M. Ottanelli, *The Communist Party of the United States: From the Depression to World War II* (New Brunswick, NJ: Rutgers University Press, 1991), 21.

22. "Voices of the Workers," *Labor Unity* 9 (April 1934): 21.

23. Ibid., 8 (June 1933): 28.

24. For example, see "The First Story in the Short Story Contest," *Western Worker* (November 26, 1934): 4.

25. "Sez Pat to Andy," *Young Worker* (October 20, 1933): 5.

26. Ibid.

27. Ibid., (November 7, 1933): 5.

28. Ibid., (November 21, 1933): 5.

29. Ibid., (February 13, 1934): 5.

30. Ibid., (December 5, 1933): 5.

31. Elsa Dixler writes: "The equation of homosexuality with the decadence of capitalism, counterposed against an idealized proletariat, vigorous and sexually uncomplicated, came right out of Lenin, whose sexual prejudices were frequently cited by American Communists as justification for their own." Elsa Jane Dixler, "The Woman Question: Women and the American Communist Party, 1929–1941," Ph.D. diss., Yale University, 1974, 46. In addition, it is worth noting that the links "Sez Pat to Andy" makes between Mae West, fascism, capitalist decay, and homosexuality were not unique within the CP press. In a collection of Robert Forsythe's *New Masses* col-

umns, *Redder than the Rose* (New York: Covici, Friede, 1935), see "Mae West: A Treatise on Decay," 105–10.

32. Cp. Nancy S. Love, "Politics and Voice(s): An Empowerment/Knowledge Regime," *Differences* 3 (1991): 95.

33. "Manual for Field Writers," *Western Worker* (August 29, 1935): 4.

34. Ibid.

35. Ibid.

36. Ibid.

37. "Manual for Field Writers: About Conventions, Union Meetings," *Western Worker* (September 9, 1935): 4.

38. "Manual for Field Writers," *Western Worker* (August 29, 1935): 4.

39. "Manual for Field Writers: Reporting the Santa Rosa Affair," *Western Worker* (September 30, 1935): 4.

40. Ibid.

41. Ibid.

42. "The First Story in the Short Story Contest," *Western Worker* (November 26, 1934): 4.

43. "Writers!! Workers!!" *Western Worker* (March 5, 1934): 1.

44. *Western Worker* (April 2, 1934): 6.

45. "Why No Short Stories Appeared," *Western Worker* (May 7, 1934): 6.

46. Ibid.

47. "Western Worker Short Story Contest Extended to July 15th," *Western Worker* (June 25, 1934): 6.

48. A useful discussion of this transitional period in CP history appears in Ottanelli, 49–80. For the often contradictory consequences of this new party line on writers, see Daniel Aaron, *Writers on the Left* (New York: Oxford University Press, 1961), esp. 269–76, and Walter B. Rideout, *The Radical Novel in the United States, 1900–1954: Some Interrelations of Literature and Society* (Cambridge, MA: Harvard University Press, 1956), 225–54.

49. Ottanelli, 48.

50. For an excellent history of the events surrounding "Bloody Thursday," see Bruce Nelson, *Workers on the Waterfront: Seamen, Longshoremen, and Unionism in the 1930s* (Urbana: University of Illinois Press, 1988), esp. 127–55.

51. Tillie Lerner [Olsen], "The Strike," repr. in Jack Salzman with Barry Wallenstein, eds., *Years of Protest: A Collection of American Writings of the 1930s* (New York: Pegasus, 1967), 142. "The Strike" originally appeared in *Partisan Review* 1 (September–October 1934): 3–9, and in two parts as "General Strike" in *Young Worker* (September 25, 1934): 8, 10, and *Young Worker* (October 9, 1934): 8.

52. [Olsen], "The Strike," in Salzman and Wallenstein, 140.

53. [Olsen], "Thousand-Dollar Vagrant," 68.

54. Harvey Klehr, *The Heyday of American Communism: The Depression Decade* (New York: Basic, 1984), 151. On criminal syndicalism laws and efforts to repeal them in California, see Eldridge Foster Dowell, *A History of Criminal Syndicalism Legislation in the United States* (Baltimore: Johns Hopkins University Press, 1939), esp. 122–7.

55. [Olsen], "The Yes Men of the Sacramento C.S. Frame-Up," 3. C.S. stands for criminal syndicalism.

56. For critical inquiries into the politics of trial proceedings, see Alessandro Portelli, "The Oral Shape of the Law: The 'April 7 Case,' " in his *The Death of Luigi Trastulli and Other Stories: Form and Meaning in Oral History* (Albany: State University of New York Press, 1991), 241–69, and Joan W. Scott, "The Sears Case," in her *Gender and the Politics of History* (New York: Columbia University Press, 1988), 167–77.

57. All quotes in this paragraph are from [Olsen], "The Yes Men of the Sacramento C.S. Frame-Up," 3.

58. [Olsen], "Why They're Trying Don," 8.

59. Telephone interview with Tillie Olsen, March 20, 1986.

60. Tillie Olsen, *Yonnondio: From the Thirties* (New York: Delta/Seymour Lawrence, 1989, repr. of 1974), 19. All further references are to this edition and will be documented parenthetically in the text.

61. On the speedup system discussed in *Yonnondio,* see Carolyn Rhodes, " 'Beedo' in Olsen's *Yonnondio:* Charles E. Bedaux," *American Notes and Queries* 14 (September 1975): 23–5.

62. For further elaboration of this issue with a different analysis, see Michael E. Staub, "The Struggle for 'Selfness' Through Speech in Olsen's *Yonnondio: From the Thirties,*" *Studies in American Fiction* 16 (Autumn 1988): 131–9.

63. The classic articulation of this question is in Gayatri Chakravorty Spivak, "Can the Subaltern Speak?" in Cary Nelson and Lawrence Grossberg, eds., *Marxism and the Interpretation of Culture* (Urbana: University of Illinois Press, 1988), 271–313.

Bibliography

Aaron, Daniel. *Writers on the Left*. New York: Oxford University Press, 1961.

Abler, Thomas, ed. *Chainbreaker*. Lincoln: University of Nebraska Press, 1989.

Abrahams, Roger D. *Deep Down in the Jungle: Negro Narrative Folklore from the Streets of Philadelphia*. New York: Aldine, 1970.

Talking Black. Rowley, MA: Newbury House, 1976.

Abrahams, Roger D., ed. *Afro-American Folktales: Stories from Black Traditions in the New World*. New York: Pantheon, 1985.

Agee, James. "TVA I: Work in the Valley," *Fortune* 11 (May 1935): 93–8, 140–53. Repr. in Paul Ashdown, ed., *James Agee: Selected Journalism*, 63–96. Knoxville: University of Tennessee Press, 1985.

Agee, James, and Walker Evans. *Let Us Now Praise Famous Men*. Boston: Houghton Mifflin, 1980, repr. of 1941.

Allen, Paula Gunn. *The Sacred Hoop: Recovering the Feminine in American Indian Traditions*. Boston: Beacon, 1986.

Aly, Lucile F. *John G. Neihardt: A Critical Biography*. Amsterdam: Rodopi N.V., 1977.

Andrews, William L. *To Tell a Free Story: The First Century of Afro-American Autobiography, 1760–1865*. Urbana: University of Illinois Press, 1986.

Avrich, Paul. *Sacco and Vanzetti: The Anarchist Background*. Princeton, NJ: Princeton University Press, 1991.

Awkward, Michael. *Inspiriting Influences: Tradition, Revision, and Afro-American Women's Novels*. New York: Columbia University Press, 1989.

Bahr, Donald. *Pima and Papago Ritual Oratory: A Study of Three Texts*. San Francisco: Indian Historian Press, 1975.

Bailey, David Thomas. "A Divided Prism: Two Sources of Black Testimony on Slavery." *Journal of Southern History* 46 (August 1980): 381–404.

Bancroft, Frederic. *Slave-Trading in the Old South*. Baltimore: J. H. Furst, 1931.

Bataille, Gretchen M., and Kathleen M. Sands. *American Indian Women: Telling Their Lives*. Lincoln: University of Nebraska Press, 1984.

Beckwith, Martha Warren. *Black Roadways: A Study of Jamaican Folk Life*. Chapel Hill: University of North Carolina Press, 1929.

Benesch, Klaus. "Oral Narrative and Literary Text: Afro-American Folklore in *Their Eyes Were Watching God*." *Callaloo* 11 (Summer 1988): 627–35.

Benson, William Ralganal. "The Stone and Kelsey 'Massacre.'" In Donald McQuade et al., eds., *The Harper American Literature, Vol. 1*, 743–8. New York: Harper & Row, 1987.

"The Stone and Kelsey 'Massacre' on the Shores of Clear Lake in 1849 – The Indian Viewpoint." *California Historical Society Quarterly* 11 (September 1932): 266–73.

Bergreen, Lawrence. *James Agee: A Life*. New York: Dutton, 1984.

Berkhofer, Robert F., Jr. *The White Man's Indian: Images of the American Indian from Columbus to the Present*. New York: Vintage, 1979.

Black Elk Speaks: Being the Life Story of a Holy Man of the Oglala Sioux as Told Through John G. Neihardt. Lincoln: University of Nebraska Press, 1979, repr. of 1932.

Blassingame, John W. "Using the Testimony of Ex-Slaves: Approaches and Problems." *Journal of Southern History* 41 (November 1975): 473–92.

Boas, Franz. "Fallacies of Racial Inferiority." *Current History* (February 1927): 676–82.

Boi, Paola. "Moses, Man of Power, Man of Knowledge: A 'Signifying' Reading of Zora Neale Hurston (Between a Laugh and a Song)." In Maria Diedrich and Dorothea Fischer-Hornung, eds., *Women and War: The Changing Status of American Women from the 1930s to the 1950s*, 107–25. New York: Berg, 1990.

"Boss Mobs Terrorize Montgomery Mill Strikers." *Labor Unity* (June 1933): 27.

Botkin, B. A. "The Slave as His Own Interpreter." *Library of Congress Quarterly Journal of Current Acquisitions* 2 (November 1944): 37–63.

Botkin, B. A., ed. *Lay My Burden Down: A Folk History of Slavery*. Chicago: University of Chicago Press, 1945.

Bradford, Roark. *Ol' Man Adam an' His Chillun*. New York: Harper & Brothers, 1928.

Brumble, H. David, III. *American Indian Autobiography*. Berkeley: University of California Press, 1988.

Brumble, H. David, III, and Karl Kroeber. "Reasoning Together." *Canadian Review of American Studies* 12 (Fall 1981): 253–70.

Cade, John B. "Out of the Mouths of Ex-Slaves." *Journal of Negro History* 20 (July 1935): 294–337.

Caldwell, Erskine, and Margaret Bourke-White. *You Have Seen Their Faces*. New York: Viking, 1937.

Callahan, John F. *In the African-American Grain: Call-and-Response in Twentieth-Century Black Fiction*. Middletown, CT: Wesleyan University Press, 1989.

Caputi, Jane. "'Specifying' Fannie Hurst: Langston Hughes's 'Limitations of Life,' Zora Neale Hurston's *Their Eyes Were Watching God* and Toni Morrison's *The Bluest Eye* as 'Answers' to Hurst's *Imitation of Life*." *Black American Literary Forum* 24 (Winter 1990): 697–716.

Carby, Hazel V. "The Politics of Fiction, Anthropology, and the Folk: Zora Neale Hurston." In Michael Awkward, ed., *New Essays on Their Eyes Were Watching God*, 71–93. Cambridge University Press, 1990.

Castro, Michael. *Interpreting the Indian: Twentieth-Century Poets and the Native American*. Albuquerque: University of New Mexico Press, 1983.

Chappell, Louis W. *John Henry: A Folk-lore Study*. Jena: Frommannsche Verlag, 1933.

Clifford, James. *The Predicament of Culture: Twentieth-Century Ethnography, Literature, and Art*. Cambridge, MA: Harvard University Press, 1988.

Clifford, James, and George E. Marcus, eds. *Writing Culture: The Poetics and Politics of Ethnography*. Berkeley: University of California Press, 1986.

Coiner, Constance. "Literature of Resistance: The Intersection of Feminism and the Communist Left in Meridel Le Sueur and Tillie Olsen." In Lennard J. Davis and M. Bella Mirabella, eds., *Left Politics and the Literary Profession*, 162–85. New York: Columbia University Press, 1990.

Coltelli, Laura. *Winged Words: American Indian Writers Speak*. Lincoln: University of Nebraska Press, 1990.

Cordasco, Francesco, ed. *Jacob Riis Revisited: Poverty and the Slum in Another Era*. New York: Anchor, 1968.

Couser, G. Thomas. "*Black Elk Speaks* with Forked Tongue." In James Olney, ed., *Studies in Autobiography*, 73–88. New York: Oxford University Press, 1988.

Dance, Daryl Cumber. *Shuckin' and Jivin': Folklore from Contemporary Black Americans*. Bloomington: Indiana University Press, 1978.

Davis, Charles T., and Henry Louis Gates, Jr., eds. *The Slave's Narrative*. New York: Oxford University Press, 1985.

Davis, Natalie Zemon. "Toward Mixtures and Margins." *American Historical Review* 97 (December 1992): 1409–16.

de Angulo, Jaime, and William Benson. "The Creation Myth of the Pomo Indians." *Anthropos* 27 (April 1932): 261–74.

de Angulo, Jaime, and L. S. Freeland. "Miwok and Pomo Myths." *Journal of American Folklore* 41 (1928): 232–52.

de Certeau, Michel. *Heterologies: Discourses on the Other*. Trans. Brian Massumi. Minneapolis: University of Minnesota Press, 1986.

DeMallie, Raymond J., ed. *The Sixth Grandfather: Black Elk's Teachings Given to John G. Neihardt*. Lincoln: University of Nebraska Press, 1984.

Denning, Michael. "Towards a People's Theater: The Cultural Politics of the Mercury Theatre." *Persistence of Vision* 7 (1989): 24–38.

Densmore, Frances. *Teton Sioux Music*. Washington: United States Government Printing Office, 1918.

DiLeonardo, Micaela. "Malinowski's Nephews." *Nation* 248 (March 13, 1989): 350–2.

DiLeonardo, Micaela, ed. *Gender at the Crossroads of Knowledge: Feminist Anthropology in the Postmodern Era*. Berkeley: University of California Press, 1991.

The Disinherited Speak: Letters from Sharecroppers. New York: Workers Defense League for the Southern Tenant Farmers' Union, n.d.

Dixler, Elsa Jane. "The Woman Question: Women and the American Communist Party, 1929–1941." Ph.D. diss., Yale University, 1974.

Dollard, John. "The Dozens: Dialectic of Insult." *American Imago* 1 (1939): 3–25.

Dorst, John. "Rereading *Mules and Men*: Toward the Death of the Ethnographer." *Cultural Anthropology* 2 (August 1987): 305–18.

Dos Passos, John. *The Big Money*. New York: Harcourt, Brace, 1936.

Facing the Chair: Sacco and Vanzetti – The Story of the Americanization of Two Foreign Born Workmen. New York: Oriole Editions, n.d., repr. of 1927.

Dowell, Eldridge Foster. *A History of Criminal Syndicalism Legislation in the United States.* Baltimore: Johns Hopkins University Press, 1939.

Du Bois, W. E. B. *The Souls of Black Folks.* New York: Bantam, 1989, repr. of 1903.

Dundes, Alan, ed. *Mother Wit from the Laughing Barrel: Readings in the Interpretation of Afro-American Folklore.* New York: Garland, 1981.

Egypt, Ophelia Settle, J. Masuoka, and Charles S. Johnson, eds. *Unwritten History of Slavery: Autobiographical Account of Negro Ex-Slaves.* Nashville, TN: Social Science Institute, Fisk University, 1945.

Escott, Paul D. *Slavery Remembered: A Record of Twentieth-Century Slave Narratives.* Chapel Hill: University of North Carolina Press, 1979.

Fabian, Johannes. "Presence and Representation: The Other in Anthropological Writing." *Critical Inquiry* 16 (Summer 1990): 753–72.

Farm Tenancy: Report of the President's Committee. Washington: United States Government Printing Office, 1937.

Fauset, Arthur Huff. "American Negro Folk Literature." In Alain Locke, ed., *The New Negro: An Interpretation,* 238–44. New York: Albert & Charles Boni, 1925.

Fields, Barbara Jeanne. "Slavery, Race and Ideology in the United States of America." *New Left Review* 181 (May–June 1990): 95–118.

"The First Story in the Short Story Contest." *Western Worker* (November 26, 1934): 4.

Forsythe, Robert. *Redder than the Rose.* New York: Covici, Friede, 1935.

Frisch, Michael. *A Shared Authority: Essays on the Craft and Meaning of Oral and Public History.* Albany: State University of New York Press, 1990.

Gates, Henry Louis, Jr. "The Blackness of Blackness: A Critique of the Sign and the Signifying Monkey." In Gates, ed., *Black Literature and Literary Theory,* 285–321. New York: Methuen, 1984.

"The 'Blackness of Blackness': A Critique of the Sign and the Signifying Monkey." In Gates, *Figures in Black: Words, Signs, and the 'Racial' Self,* 235–76. New York: Oxford University Press, 1987.

The Signifying Monkey: A Theory of African-American Literary Criticism. New York: Oxford University Press, 1988.

Gates, Henry Louis, Jr., ed. *"Race," Writing, and Difference.* Chicago: University of Chicago Press, 1986.

Georgia Writers' Project. *Drums and Shadows: Survival Studies Among the Georgia Coastal Negroes.* Athens, GA: University of Georgia Press, 1940.

Goodson, Martia Graham. "The Significance of 'Race-of-Interviewer' in the Collection and Analysis of Twentieth Century Ex-Slave Narratives: Considering the Sources." *Western Journal of Black Studies* 9 (1985): 126–34.

Goodwin, Marjorie Harness. *He-Said-She-Said: Talk as Social Organization Among Black Children.* Bloomington: Indiana University Press, 1990.

Goody, Jack. *The Domestication of the Savage Mind.* Cambridge University Press, 1977.

Goody, Jack, and Ian Watt. "The Consequences of Literacy." In Jack Goody, ed., *Literacy in Traditional Societies,* 27–68. Cambridge University Press, 1968.

Gould, Stephen Jay. *The Mismeasure of Man.* New York: Norton, 1981.

Grele, Ronald. *Envelopes of Sound: Six Practitioners Discuss the Method, Theory, and Practice of Oral History and Oral Testimony.* Chicago: Precedent, 1975.

Grissom, Mary Allen. *The Negro Sings a New Heaven.* Chapel Hill: University of North Carolina Press, 1930.

Hall, Stuart. "The Determinations of News Photographs." *Working Papers in Cultural Studies* 3 (Autumn 1972): 53–87.

Hardy, Forsyth, ed. *Grierson on the Movies.* Boston: Faber & Faber, 1981.

Harris, Joel Chandler. *Nights with Uncle Remus: Myths and Legends of the Old Plantation.* Boston: J. R. Osgood, 1881.

   Uncle Remus, His Songs and His Sayings: The Folk-lore of the Old Plantation. New York: D. Appleton, 1888.

Hartman, Charles O. *Jazz Text: Voice and Improvisation in Poetry, Jazz, and Song.* Princeton, NJ: Princeton University Press, 1991.

Hegeman, Susan. "Native American 'Texts' and the Problem of Authenticity." *American Quarterly* 41 (June 1989): 265–83.

Hemenway, Robert E. *Zora Neale Hurston: A Literary Biography.* Urbana: University of Illinois Press, 1977.

Herskovits, Melville J. *The Myth of the Negro Past.* New York: Harper & Brothers, 1941.

Heyward, DuBose. *Mamba's Daughters.* Garden City, NY: Doubleday, Doran, 1929.

Hirsch, Jerrold M. "Portrait of America: The Federal Writers' Project in an Intellectual and Cultural Context." Ph.D. diss., University of North Carolina, Chapel Hill, 1984.

History of Napa and Lake Counties, California. San Francisco: Slocum, Bowen, 1881.

Holler, Clyde C. "Lakota Religion and Tragedy: The Theology of *Black Elk Speaks.*" *Journal of the American Academy of Religion* 52 (March 1984): 19–45.

Holton, Sylvia Wallace. *Down Home and Uptown: The Representation of Black Speech in American Fiction.* Rutherford, NJ: Fairleigh Dickinson University Press, 1984.

hooks, bell. *Talking Back: Thinking Feminist, Thinking Black.* Boston: South End Press, 1989.

Hurston, Zora Neale. *Dust Tracks on a Road: An Autobiography.* Urbana: University of Illinois Press, 1984, repr. of 1942.

   "Hoodoo in America." *Journal of American Folklore* 44 (1931): 317–417.

   Mules and Men: Negro Folktales and Voodoo Practices in the South. New York: Harper & Row, 1990, repr. of 1935.

Hymes, Dell. *"In Vain I Tried To Tell You": Essays in Native American Ethnopoetics.* Philadelphia: University of Pennsylvania Press, 1981.

"An Inspiring Voice from Sacramento." *Labor Defender* (June 1935): 37.

Jackson, Brian. *The Black Flag: A Look Back at the Strange Case of Nicola Sacco and Bartolomeo Vanzetti.* Boston: Routledge & Kegan Paul, 1981.

Jackson, Bruce. *"Get Your Ass in the Water and Swim Like Me": Narrative Poetry from Black Oral Tradition*. Cambridge, MA: Harvard University Press, 1974.

Jacobs, Donald M. "Twentieth-Century Slave Narratives as Source Materials: Slave Labor as Agricultural Labor." *Agricultural History* 57 (April 1983): 223–7.

Johnson, Guy B. "St. Helena Songs and Stories." In T. J. Woofter, Jr., ed., *Black Yeomanry: Life on St. Helena Island*, pp. 48–81. New York: Henry Holt, 1930.

Johnson, James Weldon. *The Book of American Negro Spirituals*. New York: Viking, 1933.

Kazin, Alfred. *On Native Grounds: An Interpretation of Modern American Literature*. New York: Doubleday, 1956, repr. of 1942.

Kelley, Robin D. G. "Notes on Deconstructing 'The Folk.' " *American Historical Review* 97 (December 1992): 1400–1408.

Klehr, Harvey. *The Heyday of American Communism: The Depression Decade*. New York: Basic, 1984.

Kochman, Thomas, ed. *Rappin' and Stylin' Out: Communications in Urban Black America*. Urbana: University of Illinois Press, 1972.

Kramer, Victor A. *James Agee*. Boston: Twayne, 1975.

Krupat, Arnold. *For Those Who Come After: A Study of Native American Autobiography*. Berkeley: University of California Press, 1985.

Levine, Lawrence W. "American Culture and the Great Depression." *Yale Review* 74 (January 1985): 196–223.

    Black Culture and Black Consciousness: Afro-American Folk Thought from Slavery to Freedom. New York: Oxford University Press, 1977.

    "The Folklore of Industrial Society: Popular Culture and Its Audiences." *American Historical Review* 97 (December 1992): 1369–99.

    "The Historian and the Icon: Photography and the History of the American People in the 1930s and 1940s." In Carl Fleischhauer and Beverly W. Brannan, eds., *Documenting America, 1935–1943*, 15–42. Berkeley: University of California Press, 1988.

Love, Nancy S. "Politics and Voice(s): An Empowerment/Knowledge Regime." *Differences* 3 (1991): 85–103.

Lurie, Nancy Oestreich. "A Papago Woman and A Woman Anthropologist." *Reviews in Anthropology* 7 (Winter 1980): 119–29.

Manganaro, Marc, ed. *Modernist Anthropology: From Fieldwork to Text*. Princeton, NJ: Princeton University Press, 1990.

Mangione, Jerre. *The Dream and the Deal: The Federal Writers' Project, 1935–1943*. Boston: Little, Brown, 1972.

"Manual For Field Writers." *Western Worker* (August 29, 1935): 4.

"Manual For Field Writers: About Conventions, Union Meetings." *Western Worker* (September 9, 1935): 4.

"Manual For Field Writers: Reporting the Santa Rosa Affair." *Western Worker* (September 30, 1935): 4.

Mascia-Lees, Frances E., Patricia Sharpe, and Colleen Ballerino Cohen. "The Postmodernist Turn in Anthropology: Cautions from a Feminist Perspective." *Signs* 15 (Autumn 1989): 7–33.

Mattina, Anthony. "North American Indian Mythography: Editing Texts for
the Printed Page." In Brian Swann and Arnold Krupat, eds., *Recovering the
Word: Essays on Native American Literature*, 129–48. Berkeley: University of
California Press, 1987.

Mattina, Anthony, ed. *The Golden Woman: The Colville Narrative of Peter J.
Seymour*. Tucson: University of Arizona Press, 1985.

McCluskey, Sally, "*Black Elk Speaks:* And So Does John Neihardt." *Western
American Literature 6* (Winter 1972): 231–42.

McDowell, Deborah E., and Arnold Rampersad, eds. *Slavery and the Literary
Imagination*. Baltimore: Johns Hopkins University Press, 1989.

Mead, Margaret. *The Changing Culture of an Indian Tribe*. New York: AMS
Press, 1969, repr. of 1932.

Mellon, James, ed. *Bullwhip Days: The Slaves Remember*. New York: Weidenfeld
& Nicolson, 1988.

Minh-ha, Trinh T. *Woman, Native, Other: Writing Postcoloniality and Feminism*.
Bloomington: Indiana University Press, 1989.

Mitchell, H. L. *Mean Things Happening in This Land*. Montclair, NJ: Allanheld,
Osmun, 1979.

Neihardt, John G. "Preface: The Book That Would Not Die." In *Black Elk
Speaks,* ix–xiii. New York: Pocket, 1972.

Nekola, Charlotte, and Paula Rabinowitz, eds. *Writing Red: An Anthology of
American Women Writers, 1930–1940*. New York: Feminist Press, 1987.

Nelson, Bruce. *Workers on the Waterfront: Seamen, Longshoremen, and Unionism in
the 1930s*. Urbana: University of Illinois Press, 1988.

Nichols, Bill. "The Voice of the Documentary." In Alan Rosenthal, ed., *New
Challenges for Documentary*, 48–63. Berkeley: University of California
Press, 1988.

Nichols, Charles H. *Many Thousands Gone: The Ex-Slaves' Account of Their
Bondage and Freedom*. Leiden: Brill, 1963.

Odum, Howard W. *Rainbow Round My Shoulder: The Blue Trail of Black Ulysses*.
Indianapolis, IN: Bobbs-Merrill, 1928.

    *Social and Mental Traits of the Negro: Research into the Conditions of the Negro
    Race in Southern Towns*. New York: AMS Press, 1968, repr. of 1910.

Odum, Howard W. and Guy B. Johnson. *The Negro and His Songs: A Study of
Typical Negro Songs in the South*. Chapel Hill: University of North Carolina
Press, 1925.

[Olsen], Tillie Lerner. "I Want You Women Up North to Know." *Partisan* 1
(March 1934): 4.

    "The Iron Throat." *Partisan Review* 1 (April–May 1934): 3–9.

    "The Strike." *Partisan Review* 1 (September–October 1934): 3–9. Repr. in
    Jack Salzman with Barry Wallenstein, eds., *Years of Protest: A Collection of
    American Writings of the 1930s*, 138–44. New York: Pegasus, 1967.

    "There is a Lesson." *Partisan* 1 (April–May 1934): 4.

    "Thousand-Dollar Vagrant." *New Republic* 80 (August 29, 1934): 67–9.

    "Why They're Trying Don." *Young Worker* (December 18, 1934): 8.

    "The Yes-Men of the Sacramento C.S. Frame-Up." *Western Worker* (Novem-
    ber 22, 1934): 3.

Olsen, Tillie. *Tell Me A Riddle*. New York: Delacorte, 1961.

    Yonnondio: From the Thirties. New York: Delta/Seymour Lawrence, 1989, repr. of 1974.

Olson, Paul A. "*Black Elk Speaks* as Epic and Ritual Attempt to Reverse History." In Virginia Faulkner with Frederick C. Luebke, eds., *Vision and Refuge: Essays on the Literature of the Great Plains*, 3–27. Lincoln: University of Nebraska Press, 1982.

Ong, Walter J. "Oral Remembering and Narrative Structure." In Deborah Tannen, ed., *Analyzing Discourse: Text and Talk*, 12–24. Washington: Georgetown University Press, 1982.

    Orality and Literacy. New York: Methuen, 1982.

Orvell, Miles. *The Real Thing: Imitation and Authenticity in American Culture, 1880–1940*. Chapel Hill: University of North Carolina Press, 1989.

Ottanelli, Fraser M. *The Communist Party of the United States: From the Depression to World War II*. New Brunswick, NJ: Rutgers University Press, 1991.

"Our Answer." *Working Woman* (July 1935): 8.

Pells, Richard H. *Radical Visions and American Dreams: Culture and Social Thought in the Depression Years*. New York: Harper & Row, 1973.

Perdue, Charles L., Jr., Thomas E. Barden, and Robert K. Phillips, eds. *Weevils in the Wheat: Interviews with Virginia Ex-Slaves*. Bloomington: Indiana University Press, 1980.

Peterkin, Julia. *Black April*. Indianapolis, IN: Bobbs-Merrill, 1927.

Phillips, Ulrich Bonnell. *Life and Labor in the Old South*. New York: Grosset & Dunlap, 1929.

Phillips, William, and Philip Rahv. "Literature in a Political Decade." In Horace Gregory, ed., *New Letters in America*, 170–80. New York: Norton, 1937.

Portelli, Alessandro. *The Death of Luigi Trastulli and Other Stories: Form and Meaning in Oral History*. Albany: State University of New York Press, 1991.

    "Oral Testimony, the Law and the Making of History: The 'April 7' Murder Trial." *History Workshop Journal* 20 (Autumn 1985): 5–35.

    "The Peculiarities of Oral History." *History Workshop Journal* 12 (Autumn 1981): 96–107.

Powers, William K. *Oglala Religion*. Lincoln: University of Nebraska Press, 1977.

Preece, Harold. "The Negro Folk Cult." *Crisis* 43 (December 1936): 364, 374.

Puckett, Newbell Niles. *Folk Beliefs of the Southern Negro*. Chapel Hill: University of North Carolina Press, 1926.

Rabinowitz, Paula. *Labor and Desire: Women's Revolutionary Fiction in Depression America*. Chapel Hill: University of North Carolina Press, 1991.

Radin, Max. "Introduction," to William Ralganal Benson, "The Stone and Kelsey 'Massacre' on the Shores of Clear Lake in 1849 – The Indian Viewpoint." *California Historical Society Quarterly* 11 (September 1932): 266–8.

Rawick, George P. *From Sundown to Sunup: The Making of the Black Community*. Westport, CT: Greenwood, 1972.

Rawick, George P., ed. *The American Slave: A Composite Autobiography*, Vol. 19. Westport, CT: Greenwood, 1972.

Reed, T. V. "Unimagined Existence and the Fiction of the Real: Postmodernist Realism in *Let Us Now Praise Famous Men.*" *Representations* 24 (Fall 1988): 156–76.

Rhodes, Carolyn. " 'Beedo' in Olsen's *Yonnondio:* Charles E. Bedaux." *American Notes and Queries* 14 (September 1975): 23–5.

Rideout, Walter B. *The Radical Novel in the United States, 1900–1954: Some Interrelations of Literature and Society.* Cambridge, MA: Harvard University Press, 1956.

Riis, Jacob A. *How the Other Half Lives: Studies Among the Tenements of New York.* New York: Dover, 1971, repr. of 1890.

Rosaldo, Renato. *Culture and Truth: The Remaking of Social Analysis.* Boston: Beacon, 1989.

Rosenfelt, Deborah. "From the Thirties: Tillie Olsen and the Radical Tradition." *Feminist Studies* 7 (Fall 1981): 371–406. Repr. in Judith Newton and Deborah Rosenfelt, eds., *Feminist Criticism and Social Change,* 216–48. New York: Methuen, 1985.

Said, Edward. "Representing the Colonized: Anthropology's Interlocutors." *Critical Inquiry* 15 (Winter 1989): 205–25.

Samuel, Raphael, and Paul Thompson, eds. *The Myths We Live By.* New York: Routledge, 1990.

Sayre, Robert F. "Vision and Experience in *Black Elk Speaks.*" *College English* 32 (February 1971): 509–35.

Scarborough, Dorothy. *On the Trail of Negro Folk-Songs.* Cambridge, MA: Harvard University Press, 1925.

Schudson, Michael. *Discovering the News: A Social History of American Newspapers.* New York: Basic, 1978.

Scott, Joan W. *Gender and the Politics of History.* New York: Columbia University Press, 1988.

Seward, Adrienne Lanier. "The Legacy of Early Afro-American Folklore Scholarship." In Richard M. Dorson, ed., *Handbook of American Folklore,* 48–56. Bloomington: Indiana University Press, 1983.

"Sez Pat to Andy." *Young Worker* (October 20, 1933): 5.

"Sez Pat to Andy." *Young Worker* (November 7, 1933): 5.

"Sez Pat to Andy." *Young Worker* (November 21, 1933): 5.

"Sez Pat to Andy." *Young Worker* (December 5, 1933): 5.

"Sez Pat to Andy." *Young Worker* (February 13, 1934): 5.

Shloss, Carol. *In Visible Light: Photography and the American Writer, 1840–1940.* New York: Oxford University Press, 1987.

"The Signifying Monkey." In Langston Hughes and Arna Bontemps, eds., *The Book of Negro Folklore,* 363–6. New York: Dodd, Mead, 1958.

Smitherman, Geneva. *Talkin and Testifyin: The Language of Black America.* Boston: Houghton Mifflin, 1977.

Spivak, Gayatri Chakravorty. "Can the Subaltern Speak?" In Cary Nelson and Lawrence Grossberg, eds., *Marxism and the Interpretation of Culture,* 271–313. Urbana: University of Illinois Press, 1988.

Staub, Michael E. "As Close as You Can Get: Torment, Speech, and Listening in *Let Us Now Praise Famous Men.*" *Mississippi Quarterly* 61 (Spring 1988): 147–60.

BIBLIOGRAPHY 169

"Labor Activism and the Post-War Politics of Motherhood: Tillie Olsen in the *People's World*." In Kay Hoyle Nelson and Nancy Huse, eds., *The Critical Response to Tillie Olsen*, 104–9. Westport, CT: Greenwood, 1994.

"The Struggle for 'Selfness' Through Speech in Olsen's *Yonnondio: From the Thirties*." *Studies in American Fiction* 16 (Autumn 1988): 131–9.

Stone, Albert E. *Autobiographical Occasions and Original Acts: Versions of American Identity from Henry Adams to Nate Shaw*. Philadelphia: University of Pennsylvania Press, 1982.

Stott, William. *Documentary Expression and Thirties America*. Chicago: University of Chicago Press, 1986, repr. of 1973.

Sullivan, Paul. *Unfinished Conversations: Mayans and Foreigners Between the Two Wars*. New York: Knopf, 1989.

Susman, Warren I. "The Culture of the Thirties." In Susman, *Culture as History: The Transformation of American Society in the Twentieth Century*, 150–83. New York: Pantheon, 1984.

Swann, Brian, ed. *Smoothing the Ground: Essays on Native American Oral Literature*. Berkeley: University of California Press, 1983.

Szwed, John F. "An American Anthropological Dilemma: The Politics of Afro-American Culture." In Dell Hymes, ed., *Reinventing Anthropology*, 153–81. New York: Vintage, 1974.

Tedlock, Dennis. *Finding the Center: Narrative Poetry of the Zuni Indians*. Lincoln: University of Nebraska Press, 1977.

The Spoken Word and the Work of Interpretation. Philadelphia: University of Pennsylvania Press, 1983.

Terrill, Tom E., and Jerrold Hirsch. *Such as Us: Southern Voices of the Thirties*. Chapel Hill: University of North Carolina Press, 1978.

Thelen, David. "Memory and American History." *Journal of American History* 75 (March 1989): 1117–29.

These Are Our Lives as Told by the People and Written by Members of the Federal Writers' Project of the Works Progress Administration in North Carolina, Tennessee, and Georgia. Chapel Hill: University of North Carolina Press, 1939.

Turner, Lorenzo Dow. *Africanisms in the Gullah Dialect*. Ann Arbor: University of Michigan Press, 1949.

Underhill, Ruth M. *The Autobiography of a Papago Woman*. Memoirs of the American Anthropological Association 46 (1936).

"Chona: Her Land and Time." In Underhill, *Papago Woman*, 3–27.

Hawks over Whirlpools. New York: Augustin, 1940.

Papago Indian Religion. New York: Columbia University Press, 1946.

Papago Woman. Prospect Heights, IL: Waveland, 1985.

People of the Crimson Evening. Washington: U.S. Indian Service, 1951.

Singing for Power: The Song Magic of the Papago Indians of Southern Arizona. Berkeley: University of California Press, 1938.

Social Organization of the Papago Indians. New York: Columbia University Press, 1939.

"Voices of the Workers." *Labor Unity* 8 (June 1933): 28.

"Voices of the Workers." *Labor Unity* 9 (April 1934): 21.

Wald, Alan. *The New York Intellectuals: The Rise and Decline of the Anti-Stalinist*

Left from the 1930s to the 1980s. Chapel Hill: University of North Carolina Press, 1987.

Wald, Priscilla. "Becoming 'Colored': The Self-Authorized Language of Difference in Zora Neale Hurston." *American Literary History* 2 (Spring 1990): 79–100.

Walker, James R. *Lakota Belief and Ritual*. Ed. Raymond J. DeMallie and Elaine A. Jahner. Lincoln: University of Nebraska Press, 1980.

Ward, Cynthia. "The Rising of the Bones: The Oral and the Written." *Modern Fiction Studies* 35 (Spring 1989): 121–35.

"What They Told Buchi Emecheta: Oral Subjectivity and the Joys of 'Otherhood.' " *PMLA* 105 (January 1990): 83–97.

Ward, J. A. *American Silences: The Realism of James Agee, Walker Evans, and Edward Hopper*. Baton Rouge: Louisiana State University Press, 1985.

Waters, Donald J., ed. *Strange Ways and Sweet Dreams: Afro-American Folklore from the Hampton Institute*. Boston: Hall, 1983.

Watson, Lawrence C., and Maria-Barbara Watson-Franke. "Chona: A Woman-Oriented Interpretation." In Lawrence C. Watson and Maria-Barbara Watson-Franke, *Interpreting Life Histories: An Anthropological Inquiry*, 176–83. New Brunswick, NJ: Rutgers University Press, 1985.

"Western Worker Short Story Contest Extended to July 15th." *Western Worker* (June 25, 1934): 6.

White, Newman I. *American Negro Folk-Songs*. Cambridge, MA: Harvard University Press, 1928.

"Why No Short Stories Appeared." *Western Worker* (May 7, 1934): 6.

"William Ralganal Benson." In Donald McQuade et al., eds., *The Harper American Literature, Vol. 1*, 742–3. New York: Harper & Row, 1987.

Willis, Susan. *Specifying: Black Women Writing the American Experience*. Madison: University of Wisconsin Press, 1987.

"Woman's Voice." *Working Woman* (March 1933): 14.

"Woman's Voice." *Working Woman* (June 1933): 13.

"Woman's Voice." *Working Woman* (July 1933): 12.

Wong, Hertha D. "Pictographs as Autobiography: Plains Indian Sketchbooks of the Late Nineteenth and Early Twentieth Centuries." *American Literary History* 1 (Summer 1989): 295–316.

"Pre-literate Native American Autobiography: Forms of Personal Narrative." *MELUS: The Journal of the Society for the Study of the Multi-Ethnic Literature of the United States* 14 (Spring 1987): 17–32.

Woofter, Thomas Jackson, Jr. *The Basis of Racial Adjustment*. New York: Ginn, 1925.

"Writers!! Workers!!" *Western Worker* (March 5, 1934): 1.

Yetman, Norman R. "The Background of the Slave Narrative Collection," *American Quarterly* 19 (Fall 1967): 534–53.

Young, William, and David E. Kaiser. *Postmortem: New Evidence in the Case of Sacco and Vanzetti*. Amherst: University of Massachusetts Press, 1985.

Index

Continued from the front of the book

For EU product safety concerns, contact us at Calle de José Abascal, 56–1°,
28003 Madrid, Spain or eugpsr@cambridge.org.

www.ingramcontent.com/pod-product-compliance
Ingram Content Group UK Ltd.
Pitfield, Milton Keynes, MK11 3LW, UK
UKHW010047140625
459647UK00012BB/1664